D0809700

Acknowledgements

No journey we make should ever be made on our own. We need others alongside us-to support, encourage, and provide counsel and companionship. My end of life journey with my mother was gifted with many individuals who did just that, and my gratitude overflows for their love and kindnesses.

For the doctors, nurses, and therapists who cared for my mother, a heartfelt thank you. You listened patiently, never rushed, and supported her in her decisions. You always had her best interests at heart.

To my friends and extended family, I love all of you. You always listened unconditionally, and your support was unwavering.

Michelle and Mike, you always kept the candle in the window. Our late-night stops were my time to empty my heart, knowing you always understood, and hurt with me. Michelle, thanks for reading each chapter so eagerly, and always asking if there was more. Your belief in my story kept me writing.

To Dan and Mary Claire, thanks for the friendship of a lifetime, (literally) and your faithfulness in prayer. Your home was, and is, my second home and refuge, and you were always there when I needed you. Thanks for the laughter, your loving encouragement and for the honest feedback you gave me on so many of the ideas I developed.

To my co-workers at Highbridge, Jeannie, Lynsey, and Liz, thanks for always asking, and for letting me tell you the stories. It meant the world. You took good care of me.

And to my childhood church at Good Shepherd, all my love. You are my roots, and I drew so much strength from being with you. The love and care you lavished on my mother are truly the hands and feet of Christ, and I carry each one of you with me in my heart.

To my precious Amy Holt, you typify what a friend is, and what a sister in Christ looks like. Your prayers gave me strength and the courage to keep going.

And to my cherished family, Mike, Callie, and Kerry, thank you for loving my mother as much as I did. You always knew what I needed, even when I didn't. You were my fall net. Mike, thank you for believing in this story before the first word was ever written. Your belief in me kept me writing and gave me wings. This book is my dream come true.

And to my brother Craig, you are my rock. I never could have done this without you, and in your quiet, organized way, you handled all the things I don't do well. We were, and still are, a formidable team. You were always there for Mom and me, and I relied heavily on your loyalty, level headedness, and heart. Thanks for supporting the idea of this book, reading it from beginning to end, and for offering sound advice on so many little changes that would only matter to you and me.

Sheila Fein, thanks for the joy you've given me in your beautiful book cover. I couldn't have captured the essence of the story any better.

Lastly, to my publisher, Cherry Hepburn, my gratitude for your willingness to read my unfinished manuscript and for seeing the worth in this story. It's been a blessing to work with you.

Take what you learn on your journey and share it with others on their way.

With a heart full of gratitude,

Jillian Calder

Foreword

It is true enough to say that some events in our lives shape us more powerfully than others. These experiences often carry the legacy of our past as well as the potential of scripting the future. The final three years of my mother's life were a touchstone for me in this respect, and that's the story I want to tell.

Adopted as an infant, I owe a huge debt of gratitude to both of my parents, and my words are a small way of thanking a humble, self-effacing woman who shone most brightly in her darkest hours. Many choices were made, on many fronts, by both my siblings and me over the course of those three years. My intent in recounting this story is not to judge anyone else's decisions or actions but portray this time as I remember it.

Of course, there will be subjectivism. I was my mother's only daughter, as well as the oldest sibling in our family, both of those factors contributing strongly to how and what I felt. Ultimately, that lens of perspective can't help but shape my sense of reality. At all points, I tried to allow grace to prevail. Where I stood, what I thought, feelings I had or didn't have, were not only based on who I am, but on what I felt was best for my mother. Above all, my desire was to honor her and the wishes she communicated to me. To the best of my ability, I feel that was accomplished. All names have been changed to protect both my family and my friends, as have all locations.

This is a reminder that life can be rich and full of blessings even during those times of deep uncertainty and pain. God always provides the strength and the courage necessary to move through them and providentially surrounds us with people willing to make the journey with us; some of whom may seem unlikely travel companions at the time. And while I might have wished for different outcomes, love triumphed-repeatedly. That is what has been carried forward in my heart, while the lesser things have diminished with the passing of time. The vivid memories of those final three years of Mom's life, begging to be given word and voice, are finally satisfied. This is Mom's story, but it's unmistakably mine, too, and that of my siblings.

Thank you, Mom, for allowing me to grow, 'not under your heart, but in it', as you always told me. The life you gave me is a blessing beyond words, and I cherish every memory I have of you. It was a gift to share those final three years with you…they were life changing, and you showed me what true courage looks like. You are my hero, now and always.

With deepest love,
Jillian Calder

Chapter One

SOUTHBOUND
(Memorial Day Weekend – Early June 2009)

I arrived to begin my new life with Bill and Joan Bradshaw when I was four days old; courtesy of my social worker. This was long before infant seats were the law and I suppose I was safe enough in a large basket, wrapped, swaddled, and padded into layers of protection. This visual of Baby Me can still make me smile. I was a big infant by 1957 standards, weighing in at eight and a half pounds and I picture myself bumping and bouncing my way to my new home from within my haven of basket. If there had been a speech bubble issuing from my mouth like in the comics, the word would have been, "Wheeeee!"

I picture the social worker hefting my basket out of her modest car and lugging me up to the door of Mom and Dad's small ranch, rapping smartly on the screen door. The heavy storm door would have already been opened and standing ajar, based on my parents' level of anticipation. No doubt they were already anxiously milling about their small living room, waiting for my arrival. I feel certain my parents saw her pull up and met her at the door.

"Here she is!" I can hear the social worker saying gaily, as my dad, ever the gentleman, holds the door open for her.

Dad was a slender, sandy haired 33, Mom a beautiful auburn haired 29 the day I became Elizabeth Jo Bradshaw. Seven years of marriage had provided them with many things, but up until now, children weren't one of them. The years had allowed my father to finish med school and his residency and to begin his small but growing family practice. My mother taught elementary school those seven years to finance my father's education. They had moved from a tiny apartment to their own home in a new suburb of Cincinnati. And now, here I was, ready to become the center of their lives. I know it happened this way, because Mom shared these details with me numerous times over the years.

To further confirm my arrival and the preparations leading up to it was a stack of letters Mom came across years later during one of her dresser drawer cleaning binges. They had been written to her old college suitemates: she referred to them as Round Robin letters. Apparently, they were quite the fad in the 1950's and functioned as a sort of written conference call. One friend would write a letter, mailing it to another friend. Once it reached Friend B, they would add their own newsy tidbits, now mailing both the letters from Friend A and themselves to yet another recipient, Friend C. This process continued in chain fashion until eventually all enclosed letters found their way back to the original writer. In this manner, everybody in the chain was updated on each person's news without everyone needing to write separate letters.

I was in my mid-40s when Mom re-discovered these letters, and we sat side by side on her bed reading them. This particular Round Robin sheaf chronicled my entire adoption process, starting with my parent's initial decision to adopt. There followed Mom's recounting of their home evaluation, and the anxious breath holding until they were told they'd passed it. Then their names went on a waiting list, and the nursery preparation began. Mom's portions of these letters brought tears to my eyes, both because her excitement jumped off the pages, and because I realized how badly she wanted a child. By then I was a parent with two daughters of my own, five years apart, and reading her words of hopeful waiting leveled me. In subsequent letters, her descriptions of my infant self once I had arrived were priceless.

Mom and Dad didn't stop with me. They went on to adopt my brother Donny in 1958, and Craig in 1960, each of us with different biological parents. Shortly after Craig arrived, Nature smiled, and Mom became pregnant with Rob. He was born in 1961. I often thought about the amazing fact that it took Mom and Dad 11 years to conceive a biological child. Mom's perspective was that God needed a home for Donny, Craig and I before He brought Rob into the picture, and that works for me. I don't think God makes mistakes.

I never thought of Mom and Dad as my "adoptive parents". That term gets tossed around a lot today and I understand the designation-I just didn't perceive them that way. They were my Mom and Dad; end of story. Nor can I adequately express the debt of gratitude I owe them. Without them, I wouldn't be who I am. They gave me a life, security, opportunities and an identity in a family and extended family. Each in their own way fostered my faith in God and loved me beyond measure.

From the time we were old enough to grasp the idea, my parents talked frankly to us about being adopted. They made it seem like the most natural thing in the world and it became part of our life's fabric. We were special and comfortable with this knowledge. As we grew and were able to formulate more questions based on our curiosity, Mom and Dad provided us with honest answers and more details. Their ease and openness with the entire situation translated into our own. Because Donny and I shared a very similar sense of humor, we'd inevitably speculate on our backgrounds as we got older, sometimes poking fun at them. As raunchy as we could be, it attested to a comfort level with our 'dual identities', because with it came an awareness of how differently we might have ended up.

I'm idly thinking about my family as I'm driving from Louisville, Kentucky to Cincinnati to pick up my mother this warm Memorial Day weekend. She's coming to stay with us for the week, which is a first. She's been to our home frequently through the years, but never to stay for this length of time. I'll be curious to see how this plays out.

My husband Mike and I have lived in Louisville for the past 25 years, having been transferred here in 1985. Our family has been up and down I-71 more times than I care to count, but I'm sure it figures well into the hundreds. First with our girls in car seats, then in booster seats, eventually graduating to seat belts, Callan and Kerry made trip after trip with us for every holiday, plenty of birthdays, and even some anniversaries for both sides of our family. Then the trips morphed into hospital visits, visitations, and funerals that outweighed other events. Now the drives I make are mostly solo, and instead of big family get-togethers, these solitary treks up north mostly just involve Mom. It's a new and different chapter for both of us, but we're embracing it.

My mom has lived with my youngest brother Rob and my sister-in-law Colette, since the spring of 2002, when both she and my dad moved into Rob's newly built home in Cincinnati. My father died in November of 2003, so Mom has been by herself there ever since. I'm thinking she could do with a change of scenery, and, in all fairness, Rob and Col could probably use a break, too. Truth be told, I'm looking forward to the time with Mom in my world. I don't get a lot of alone time with her. There will be plenty for us to do and she's pretty low maintenance.

My main concern is her being home alone in our place for several of the days she'll be with us and part of me feels guilty that I haven't taken those days off. We've talked about it, and she's hastened to assure me she'll be just fine. Logistically, Rob and Colette are gone for even longer periods of time with their jobs than I'll be at work, so it's not like I'm leaving her in a situation she hasn't been in before. According to her, she's 'gotten behind' on her church Bible study and she'll be using the time to catch up. I think she wants to be the perfect houseguest, so we'll invite her back again.

Mom has made several comments recently to me about feeling like she's in the way at Rob and Col's, and I hope this trip gives her a chance to spread her wings a bit. For having her living quarters directly downstairs from my brother and sister-in-law, I think she sees very little of them, and I'm beginning to wonder if this grand plan of her living with them has outkicked its coverage. I do my best not to think about it too much, because the whole situation is a huge source of frustration for me. Back in the late 1990's, my parents placed their name on a waiting list in their handpicked retirement village, called Beecher Springs. This community was a short 10-minute drive from where they lived at that point and many of their friends had already retired there. In moving, everything familiar would still be at their fingertips and within short driving distance.

During this same time, Rob had begun plans for his new home and had asked them if they would consider moving in with him and Colette. The plan was to build separate living quarters for them. The area they were building in was about 40 minutes from where Mom and Dad lived in Cincinnati in an area called Heritage Hills. Making this move would hopscotch them to a completely different side of the city, where all of Colette's family lived. Dad loved the idea of moving in with them; Mom hated it. She made no bones about expressing it to me, either. I think she could see the writing on the wall. With my father's poor cardiac history, she knew she'd outlive him, and her fear was that she'd be stuck there once he passed. Because Rob is a doctor and Colette a nurse, Dad was hugely comforted knowing that Mom would be surrounded by medical expertise should she need it, and that should an emergency arise, she'd receive the best of care. In his mind, that one factor overrode all else. To Mom, it was a minimal selling point at best.

In the time frame they were considering the move, I encouraged Mom countless times to talk to Dad about her feelings and let him know how she truly felt. If she did, she never mentioned it to me. She's never been one to deal with conflict head on and I don't think she wanted to be the 'heavy' in refusing my brother's offer. In the end, my father won out, if you can call it that, largely, I think, because Mom never shared her misgivings with him. When their name reached the top of the waiting list at Beecher Springs, which was in early 2002, dad declined the opportunity, and their name was removed from the list. I felt like it was a death sentence for my mom.

I'm thinking about all this today as I cruise up I-71, noting the lush greenery of the trees and the newly planted fields; so peaceful, so good for the soul after my work week. This landscape has changed little over the course of 24 years, and I appreciate that constancy when so many things are changing in my life. I grimace slightly as I turn up the air conditioner to offset a momentary hot flash. They're dwindling in both frequency and intensity at 52, but every now and then they can still roar into internal flame.

I want Mom to feel loved and special while she's staying with us…I want her to feel free to talk and know she's being listened to. She spends way too much time alone at Rob's. I've made no set plans for us; we'll figure it out as we go.

My relationship with Mom has redefined itself significantly since Dad died and I've seen a whole new side of her emerge, both to my surprise and delight. I've always loved my mom, even though we're very different. But since Dad's passing, she seems more authentic, somehow. She speaks what's on her mind more and expresses herself with less restraint. To balance that, she seems to listen and respond in a more unconditional way. She's become quite an encourager, which was something she didn't do a lot of in my childhood years. And, at this late stage, I feel like her sense of humor is developing to a degree I never thought possible.

Is it just her mellowing with age? Partly, I'm sure, but I also have another theory. She's no longer standing behind my dad. They came of age in the World War II era and I feel like Dad was always the dominant force in their relationship. Now that he's gone, she's come into her own more fully.

Truth be told, for Mom's era, she was an independent gal, especially in college. She and my dad met in the summer of 1948 working in Colorado at a state park. He was from Cincinnati; she hailed from Chicago and was between her junior and senior year at Carleton College. Their paths crossed when a group of them decided to climb Long's Peak. By the end of the summer, they had become quite an item and as Mom headed back to her senior year of college, Dad was driving to California to end a relationship. Bill and Joan had fallen in love. They were married a year later, in August of 1949, a scant six weeks after the death of Mom's father from a fatal heart attack. She moved to Cincinnati following their wedding and their entire married life was rooted there. Once our adoptions occurred, Mom left teaching to be home with my brothers and me full time.

Over the years, as Dad moved from a huge family practice into full time orthopedic surgery as his specialty, Mom virtually ran our family. She had to; Dad's hours were long and demanding, and even though he loved what he did, there were many nights he'd return to his office after dinner to see more patients.

Mom was one of the most organized, efficient people I knew, and she took running our household seriously. Appearances mattered, and the family name was of great importance to her, as she viewed it as a direct reflection on my father. Our manners and good behavior, especially in public, were a given expectation. And, most of the time, we were happy to oblige.

Based on her natural reserve, she had a tougher time with communicating and showing affection. Her love language was that of doing for others and she nurtured us through her acts of kindness even more than she did her words. To this day, she is one of the most thoughtful people I know. In watching her over the years, I learned a great deal about what caring for others looked like. Sincerity of intention and the joy of doing for others were modeled time after time and those visuals remain with me even now. Growing up, I remember walking into my bedroom countless times to find a big vase of flowers on my dresser, beautifully arranged from her garden.

There was also Mom's tradition of The Birthday Dress. Every year, it would arrive in the dark of the night preceding my birthday. It would be quietly smuggled into my room after I was asleep and surreptitiously hung on my closet door handle. When my eyes opened on February 11th, there it was in all its crisp new glory, begging to be worn. There was nothing better than anticipating that dress each year as I drifted off to sleep the night before my birthday. And, in different ways, I knew each of my brothers felt the same way about Mom's kindnesses. It was the simple act of doing that gave her the greatest pleasure, rather than any recognition of the act itself. She preferred there be no attention drawn to it.

Mom was a doer, a creator, the one who preferred to remain behind the scenes, while Dad was the social one. He interacted with people comfortably and reached out to others with his warmth and teasing. Mom was truly happiest in the kitchen, not having to make small talk or be social. Even though our house was constantly a hub of entertainment for both extended family and my parents' friends, we seldom saw Mom sit down to enjoy guests or to engage in prolonged conversation. Yet these prescribed roles seemed to work well for both of my parents. None of my brothers or I ever witnessed my parents in a heated discussion. Instead, Mom would just shut down, or, as my daughters refer to it, 'stonewall' my Dad, going mute, like a wall of stone. I can clearly recall Mom being in this mode periodically as we grew up and I'm sure to some degree it shaped how all four of us handle conflict in our adult lives.

Because I was, and still am, very in tune with other people's moods, when Mom would go silent, I would immediately blame myself for her decision to shut us out, racking my brain for some specific act of wrongdoing. Had I practiced the piano twice that day? Check. Had I made my bed that morning? Check. As I got older: had she heard me say something inappropriate to one of my friends on the phone? No…and check. What I couldn't understand was that in almost every case, Mom's silences had nothing to do with me whatsoever.

As my brothers and I got older and began developing our own communication with each other, we'd discuss these Mom Silences. Craig, three years younger than I, would take no prisoners. Nor does he to this day. Lolling in the doorway of his bedroom, his dark eyes would accost me as I came down the hallway to my own room.

"What'd you do to piss Mom off?" He'd ask me, sotto voce. It was imperative that Mom never hear any of our discussions.

"Nothing," I'd respond, in a tone of contrived detachment, because one could never be sure of that fact. Then I'd twist the knife. "One of your teachers probably called about you," I'd reply offhandedly, knowing there was always a possibility this could have happened.

Donny and Craig were more suspect in their academic performance than Rob or me and I knew how to make Craig sweat on this. Donny, hands down, was a challenge to our school system and to many of his teachers, beginning in elementary school and tracking right on through high school. There were academic issues, behavioral issues, phone calls from teachers, bad progress reports and ugly report cards and as his older sister, it broke my heart for him. It's my private belief that he probably had attention deficit hyperactivity disorder 30 years too early and that if he went back to school in this era, he'd be a completely different type of student.

Craig was more of a middle of the road student. He got by, sometimes better than others. The difference was, Craig cared about his grades to some degree, while Donny showed zero concern. Craig worshipped Dad and didn't want to let him down, so if there HAD been a teacher phone call, I knew I had him over a barrel. And, because I knew no teacher would call about me, I was safe on high ground.

Craig shakes his head firmly in denial. "None of my teachers this year would call. They all like me… Has to be Donny."

Sometimes, all four of us would have a pow-wow regarding Mom's Silences. We knew exactly when progress reports came out each semester at both our high school and middle school, and three or four of those from subjects Craig and Donny were jointly struggling with could undo Mom. I think it made her feel like SHE had somehow failed. Because Rob and Craig were almost exactly a year apart in age, they shared a bedroom, and we'd usually pile in there to have our MOM DISCUSSIONS. Donny and I would sit on the floor, because Craig never let us use his neatly made bed. Rob, the antithesis of Craig in terms of tidiness, usually had so much piled on his bed that there was no space to sit. We'd quietly close the doors to all our rooms, so that Mom would think each of us was in our own room, thus arousing no suspicion on her part.

Then the inevitable, "What is going on with Mom?" from one of us, and the discussion would begin.

First ruled out were progress reports and report cards, depending on the time of year for this Mom Silence. After ruling these causes out, it would grow more challenging. That was usually when the finger pointing began. Rob, being the youngest and by far the least confrontational, usually stayed in the background on this. Our theories would vary, and seldom was any consensus reached. I think we just liked the solidarity of knowing that Mom's silence confused all of us. It made me realize that all of us carried some subconscious amount of guilt, thinking we *might* be responsible for causing it, or we'd never be meeting to discuss it in the first place. For me, being the only girl in the family, this fact was oddly comforting.

Ironically, for as much turmoil as Donny could cause at school, and, subsequently, at home, he was usually the one to ferret out the exact cause of Mom's behavior and it usually had to do with my Dad. Donny thought outside the box in a way the rest of us hadn't yet learned to and he could make connections that never occurred to the rest of us.

"No, you guys, listen to me," I remember him saying to us during one of our bedroom meetings when Mom's Silence had spanned the better part of a week, with no current signs of abating. Donny and I were in high school at the time; Rob and Craig had just finished 7th and 8th grades. It was mid-June, and we'd ruled out progress reports and reports cards immediately, based on school already having ended. Everyone's year-end report card had been satisfactory, and we had even gone out to dinner at Ponderosa Steak House to celebrate. We were coming up empty handed.

"Oh, this'll be good," Craig comments acidly to the room at large. He and Donny don't see eye to eye on much. "Five dollars it has something to do with you."

Donny ignores Craig completely, which I give him credit for. Craig is not one to be dismissed easily in his cocky self-assurance.

"Think about it," Donny continues. "Remember Mom talking about wanting to go to her elementary school thing in Chicago? She said it's in August, right?"

"You mean her elementary school reunion?" I ask Donny, by way of clarification. I want to be sure we're on the same page here.

"Yeah, that," Donny confirms. "With people she hasn't seen for at least three decades." Why Donny felt he needed to add this, I'm not sure, but it has the dual effect of amusing both Rob and me.

Rob titters, and then contributes a pithy piece of

information in his clear, treble voice that hasn't changed yet. (It's earned him the nickname 'Chippy' from Donny.) "Yeah, I remember Mom telling Gram about that last Sunday when she was here for dinner. 'Member, guys?"

Gram is my Mom's mother and she always comes over to eat with us on Sundays. Craig says nothing, but Donny and I both nod in assent.

"Yes." I affirm. "She does want to go to it. So, what's your theory?" I ask Donny, playing the role of facilitator.

Donny leans in slightly and lowers his voice conspiratorially. "Think about this," he entreats us. "That reunion is the same weekend Dad wants to go to Michigan for the canoe trip with Uncle Henry and Scott and Stephen. And, we know who's going to win that contest."

We sit silently for a minute, processing this. I think Donny has something here. Dad has been talking about this canoe trip since early in the spring. Uncle Henry is my Dad's older brother and all of us love these junkets to Michigan.

"Wow." I'm the first to speak. How Donny had made this connection with the weekend dates is beyond me, but it seems more than plausible.

"You could be totally right about this. But why can't Dad just change weekends that we go to Michigan?" I quiz him.

"Betsy," Donny starts, looking at me like I have three heads, "Dad wouldn't be caught DEAD at that stupid reunion. He wants to be in Michigan THAT weekend."

"So, I wonder how many more days Mom won't talk?" Rob muses, wanting to cut to the bottom line of our collective misery. He's a lot like me and he hates it when people are upset. He's also very close to my mom.

Craig has been very quiet, but he speaks up now.

"I don't think that's it at all," he states, but he knows Donny has convinced Rob and me otherwise. No one responds to his comment.

"Well, meeting adjourned, I guess," I say. "Events to be determined."

And, in August, there is a canoe trip in Michigan. There is not an elementary school reunion in Chicago. None of us are ever sure how things are resolved. Since we are strongly inclined towards making the Michigan trip, none of us care to question how the decision is reached. We witness no arbitration, no mediation, and no reconciliation, other than Mom starting to speak again.

I suppose my parents' communication style also reflected their generation. Open dialogue wasn't rated at the premium it is today and I'm not sure how well my mom would have handled a higher level of emotional transparency. It's a skill I'm still working on in my own marriage, and it's taken a lot of trial and error to figure out. Mike and I do our best, but it's been a work in progress and sometimes I wish I could have seen it modeled now and then as I was growing up. And, had my parents' communication been better with one another, it easily could have impacted their decision to move in with Rob.

Traffic thickens as I junction onto 75 North and with it being Memorial Day Saturday, I know the bridge traffic will be heavy. Crossing the Brent Spence into downtown Cincinnati is my least favorite part of the drive and I breathe a sigh of relief once I'm over it. I emit another jubilant exhalation when I roll onto I-74 and traffic pares down. I'm home free now.

Mom is packed and ready when I arrive at Rob's and seems to be in a quasi-giddy mood, which is my confirmation that she's excited about the trip. I feel her frail shoulder blades as I wrap my arms around her in a big hug. At 5'5", I stoop to place my head alongside hers. I forget the difference three inches can make. She's barely 5'2" now, and I feel like she gets smaller every time I see her.

"You look good, Mom," I tell her, and I mean it.

She looks at me and winks. "It's my Clinique," she states,

referring to the hypoallergenic line of cosmetics she's used for years.

I walk down the stairs to her living area, Mom following more slowly behind me. I grab a Diet Coke out of her refrigerator, and popping the top, look around her place. It looks as tidy as it can for my Mom. She is a 'stacker' and a 'saver', and there is cheerful clutter everywhere, especially on the wide end of the kitchen counter. I'm struck again by how dark it is down here, even on sunny days, because her living space is the lower level of Rob and Colette's home. There are only windows along the outer side, and that cuts out 50 percent of the natural light.

She asks me if I want to rest before we head back, remarking that, "This is a lot of driving for you, especially after working this morning."

I'm touched that she is conscious of this. I've worked for a pediatric practice for about a year now, following my retirement from teaching, and they have Saturday morning hours. I left directly from work to drive up here. Assuring her that I'm good to drive back, I tease her about wanting to get her vacation started as soon as possible.

We load up my Jeep and as I'm backing down the driveway, I ask her where Rob and Colette are.

"I think at one of the boy's ball games," she replies, "but I could be wrong."

I smile to myself at this last statement. "They DO know you're leaving, don't they?" I ask her, half in jest, but half serious. I know she's been growing more forgetful, and I could imagine her thinking she'd told Rob and Colette about her trip to Louisville when she really hadn't.

"Oh, yes," she says dismissively, staring straight ahead. "They know. I'm sure they're glad to see the old lady go."

At this, I burst out laughing, mostly because of Mom's frankness. "Okay, so you all need a break from each other," I giggle, trying to find some middle ground. "Nothing wrong with that; your family in the south loves you, Joan Bradshaw."

Now it's Mom's turn to laugh, and I love hearing her. In the past six years, making her laugh has become one of my favorite things to do, and she seems to be doing more and more of it. Crossing the bridge into Covington, I grab her arm and exclaim, "Southbound! It's official! Welcome to Kentucky!"

Mom grins and shakes her head. "I'm honored, I guess," is her rejoinder.

Our drive home slips by. Mom is very talkative, and I love asking her about things. She needs this, I'm thinking. Good Shepherd, the church that all of us grew up in, is still a strong source of community for Mom and she has plenty to fill me in on. That includes her thoughts on their new minister of whom she is not fond. No surprise. Mom has never done change well and Pastor Stutts was at Good Shepherd for over 30 years before he retired. Pastor Morehouse, their new minister, is pushing for a much more contemporary format, especially in terms of music, and Mom doesn't want any part of that. In short, she feels like she's losing her church. This is hard for me, especially because I can see the issue both ways and enjoy attending a church in Louisville that is extremely contemporary. We discuss this, then move on to her updating me on her various friends.

Then we turn to catching up on my brothers. She hears the least from Donny these days, which is no surprise. Donny has always been willing to accept any generosity extended by my parents, which has been vast through the years, but rarely expresses any appreciation in return. Ironically, my parents probably did more for Donny than for any of us, based on the support he needed from them over the years. Married twice, his second failed marriage concluded with him getting custody of all three of his girls; no small feat for a father in the state of Ohio. From that point on, Donny raised them to the best of his ability and my parents were right there in the trenches with him. They took his girls to and from pre-school, babysat them after school, bought their clothes, shoes, school supplies and anything else they needed. When ends didn't quite meet financially, they were always willing to lend a hand.

Donny had his work cut out for him during those years and worked like a crazy man, even picking up a paper route that meant getting up at 3 AM every morning. Eventually, the lawn care business he started took off and things eased a bit, but life was never easy street for him. I'm sure that he appreciated all that my parents did for him on some level. He had to have, and they always had his back. Being able to express his appreciation probably didn't come easily to Donny and I'm sure deep down he wished he could have managed it on his own. But once things improved for him, he rarely contacted Mom for any reason. She'll call him now and leave occasional messages on his voice mail, checking in, but he never returns her calls. It's as if she's ceased to matter to him now that he no longer needs her assistance. I try my hardest not to be derogatory towards him when Mom and I talk, knowing it will only make her feel worse, but it hurts me for her.

"I hate it that he never calls you back," I tell her now as we drive.

We move on to Craig, Loire, and their girls. Loire, Craig's wife, is, like Colette, a great sister-in-law to have. Generous, loving and kind towards Mom, and a real asset to our family; she's a lot of fun to be around. By the time Mom catches me up on their girls, Vivie and Emmy, we're pulling into our driveway. Southbound trip complete. Mike is out cutting our front yard and looks up as we pull in, waving animatedly at Mom. He and my mom are good buddies and that bond has deepened since both of Mike's parents have passed. As she tries to get out of the Jeep, I can tell she's stiff and very unsure of herself.

"Wait for me, Mom," I instruct her, realizing that my Jeep sits much higher than her compact Honda. Once I get around to her, I support her right side as she slides slowly off the seat, hanging on to me. I can tell by her death grip she's having trouble figuring out how much farther down the ground is.

"A little bit farther," I prompt her. "My Jeep sits up higher than your Accord."

"I'll say it does," she remarks grimly. "I feel like I'm getting out of a semi."

"Complain if you must," I tease her, "but you'd better respect your ride, woman. After all, you're in Louisville now."

She smiles, an open, real smile and I can see traces of the girl she used to be even at 82. Her beautiful auburn hair has gone snow white but is every bit as thick as it was when I used to brush it as a little girl, pretending to style it for her. Her eyes are still a rich blue grey, and when she's amused, they twinkle with humor. I can look at younger pictures of her and immediately see why my Dad was so smitten with her.

She looks around the yard now, spotting Mike coming towards us with the mower roaring. As he approaches the driveway, he kills the motor and mops his face with an old golf towel. Walking directly over to Mom, he states, "I'm really sweaty, don't touch me," as he leans down to kiss her on the cheek.

Mom literally melts as he does this, and replies, "Don't you worry about me. A little sweat never hurt anyone. Your yard looks very good." I notice her straightening her posture and standing a little taller, as if to catch up to Mike's six foot four inch frame.

She and Mike gaze out at the yard together and he comments, "It's nice and green right now, because we've had lots of rain these past two weeks. I sure hope it'll stay this healthy. Once the summer heat kicks in, it can dry out in a hurry."

Mom nods sagely. "Our ongoing battles with Mother Nature," she replies.

Mike looks at me and grins in amusement. This is one of those 'New Sense of Humor Mom' comments that neither of us is accustomed to, and I can tell he finds it humorous.

"I'll take you both out to dinner if you give me awhile to finish up and shower," he offers.

We tell him to take his time. We're going to unpack Mom and then relax on the deck. Mike carries her suitcase in, and I follow with her book bag. She goes up the stairs ahead of me, giving me a chance to see how she manages them. This is my biggest concern about her being here alone; the possibility of her falling. In Rob and Col's home, her flight of stairs is carpeted, and not nearly as long. She manages well, though. There's a quirky hitch to her right knee, which was replaced three years ago, but her balance is fine. I notice she holds firmly to the railing all the way up. To welcome her, I've put a big vase of flowers on her bedroom table, along with a single white hydrangea in a slender vase in her adjoining bathroom. She takes note of these as she enters the room.

"Oh, these are pretty," she remarks. "Nothing like flowers to brighten a room!"

"Remember how you always used to put flowers in my room?" I ask, looking at her quizzically.

She purses her lips slightly in thought. "If I did, I've forgotten," she says, somewhat hesitantly, as if I might think less of her for not remembering. "But I guess I did if you remember it."

I've put plenty of spare hangers in her empty closet and she unpacks surprisingly quickly as I sit in the wicker chair, watching.

"Was it hard to get packed up?" I ask, wondering if it overwhelmed her.

"Not at all," she answers simply, shaking her head for emphasis. "I was looking forward to doing it." She takes her cosmetic bag into the bathroom, refreshes her lipstick in the mirror, and asks me, "Did this used to be Kerry's room?"

"Yeah, until Callie went to Western and then Kerry moved down to the basement and took her room," I reply, surprised that Mom remembers this.

"I guess Kerry liked having her own separate space down there," Mom remarks.

"Kind of like you at Rob's," I tease.

Mom shakes her head again. "The space no one visits," she says flatly. "I can go days without seeing Rob, or talking to him, and I don't see much of the boys anymore, either, now that they're getting older."

By 'the boys', she's referring to Rob and Colette's three sons, two of whom are twins. John is their oldest at 15, James and Jack both 13.

"Times are changing, aren't they, Mom?" I ask, but it's really more of a statement. "They're busy with all of their activities, and I know how Rob can be. That's tough."

Colette is the one Mom sees the most of and who is faithful about popping in to check on her daily, but it's still a bare minimum of interaction. I'm not quite ready to steer the conversation back to Rob, because I don't want to focus on his detachment from her. Instead, I divert the discussion to some interesting stories from work and we settle out on the deck to enjoy the sunset. Mike joins us about 40 minutes later and we sit talking companionably before we head out to eat.

We have a fun evening at the seafood restaurant we take Mom to. She's engaged in the conversation, following it readily, asking Mike appropriate questions about his job. As a general manager for a large supplier of pipe, valves and fittings, she's always been interested in what this entails, and with each piece of information Mike shares, she follows up with either another pertinent question about what has just been said, or a comment that shows she's digested the information he's provided. I'm encouraged to see this. Mike is very aware of my feelings regarding Mom's isolated living situation and he's good about asking her questions that help clarify what her day to day living is like without inserting any bias of his own.

"Do you still see a lot of your old friends from Good Shepherd?" he asks her now. He knows them all from our countless trips back to Cincinnati over the years.

"Not as much as I'd like," she answers, matter of fact. "I'm not crazy about driving I-74 and 275 anymore, and it's a lot to meet them anywhere in Southwoods. I'll go out to brunch with Nancy Rhodes sometimes after church, and now and then some of us go out to lunch after our Bible study on Wednesdays."

Southwoods is the area of Cincinnati we grew up in, and it's very close to the retirement community Mom and Dad had hoped to end up in prior to Rob's offer. His area of the city puts her quite a drive away from the hub of church and friends she'd been so close to before their move. This is the first mention I've heard of Mom not liking to drive on the interstates, and it concerns me. Up until now, she's been fearless in her driving back and forth to her old community. I've been wondering about this a lot lately, from the standpoint of her being almost 82. Her reaction time must be slowing down significantly, as well as her overall awareness. I wonder if she's had a close brush on the road and just doesn't want to tell any of us. Another thing niggles at me as well; is she starting to stay home from her weekly commitments at church because she no longer trusts her own driving? Could that be why she told me she's behind on her Bible study? I don't say anything, but store this away for future reflection.

After a leisurely meal, we head home and the three of us curl up on our couch and love seat and watch the 10:00 news. Mike and Mom are both nightly news watchers and I know this is a part of Mom's ritual at home as well. It has been ever since I was a little girl. She heads up to bed shortly after the news ends, and I follow suit. Kissing her goodnight at the top of the stairs, I tell her I'm glad she's here.

"I'm glad, too," she answers, patting my back as she returns my goodnight kiss. "Thank you for everything today."

* * * * *

The week goes well and more quickly than I want it to, boding well for future visits. Having Mom here makes me realize this is good for her and it's very doable for Mike and me. It also gives me some perspective on what Rob and Colette's living situation is like in terms of the constant presence of that 'other person' in your household. Even though Mom is a full floor below them, she's there constantly, probably more now than ever before, because she no longer drives at night. Just having Mom here for six days, I can feel the difference in my energy expenditure. It's significant and I've fallen asleep in five minutes flat every single night. Even as easy a houseguest as she is, there are adjustments you make to accommodate another person in your home.

Still, it's been a good change of scenery for Mom, and she's done well by herself on the days that I worked. I always leave notes on the counter for her, reminding her of what's in the refrigerator. Any dishes I think she might need, I leave out on the counter for easy access, so she won't have to search cabinets or reach up to try to get them down. Snacks I think she might enjoy stay out as well, along with a plate of chocolate chip cookies that we bake. Anything I can think of to streamline her daily routine, I do it and check in with her at least twice each day that I work. She seems to enjoy her days of me being gone as much as she does our time together, and I know she spends hours out on our deck, monitoring the progress of a gazebo that's being built by our neighbors a couple of houses down.

We play a lot of gin rummy sitting out on the deck, Mom beating me soundly two rounds out of three, which delights me. We drink our share of piña coladas, too, Mom never minding when I refill her glass with what's left in the blender. I always use the excuse that I need an adult beverage to wind down when I get home from work and Mom tells me 'she'll be happy to keep me company.' It does my heart good to see how content she seems.

Mike is a godsend as well, bending over backwards to make Mom feel welcome and a part of things; even on the nights when he doesn't arrive home until well after I do. We meet Kerry in Frankfort for dinner on Sunday night, since it's her night off from her golf course job in Lexington as a drink girl. Mom assures us she's up for making the drive, which I take as a good sign. She had really wanted to see Mom while she was staying with us and is wonderful with her. Asking Mom a million questions about her activities, she shares some funny stories about her recent move into the house that she'll be living in this coming year off campus.

Monday, Memorial Day, Mike and I take Mom to lunch at one of our favorite restaurants on the river, called The Bend. There's something hypnotic about sitting in the late spring sunshine watching the boat traffic and Mom seems to enjoy it immensely. Another night, Mike cooks for us, fixing sea bass and grilling veggies while Mom and I have our happy hour on the deck. She devours her meal.

The Wednesday I'm off, we go out to lunch and then browse around in a couple of local shops, ending up in a home interior center. Pilfering through various prints and paintings they stock, I end up buying a canvas print of some abstract flowers in a vase and Mom helps me pick out a funky beveled gold frame for it. Notoriously indecisive when it comes to selecting artwork, I never would have tackled this project on my own. Somehow, Mom being there made it seem not so insurmountable. And, as a sidebar, I decidedly enjoyed how vocal she was about her likes and dislikes of the various prints. The main reason I chose the one I did was because of her positive affirmation. Mom's tastes run to the well-appointed early American look, a la Ethan Allen furniture and accoutrements, while mine over the years have evolved into a much more contemporary preference. With this print being very modern, I'm surprised by her edict.

"It's the perfect style for your great room, Bet," she pronounces, using her decades old nickname for me. 'Elizabeth' became 'Betsy' in my infancy, and my family and closest friends have shortened it further over the years to just 'Bet'. "Warm, but not fussy."

What I also discover is how much I like coming home to Mom on the days I work. I look forward to her company at the end of them. I realize, too, as I look back over the course of the week, that I really didn't alter my routine as much as I just fit Mom into most of my regular evening activities by including her. In an odd way, it reminds me of how I involved Callie and Kerry when they were younger. If I cooked, I asked Mom to help me, and gave her tasks that she could assist with. I loved her working beside me in my own kitchen.

Having her here for this chunk of time has given me a detailed picture and I've taken lots of mental notes. My humble assessment: Mom could do with much more socialization on a consistent basis than what she's getting at Rob and Colette's. There's no blame here; it's not their fault in the least. It's just where Mom is in her life, especially with her decreased driving. I've also watched for overall signs of deterioration. Granted, I've not watched her in any form of extended task completion, like fixing her own dinner from start to finish, or driven with her in quite a while, but she seems like she's holding the line decently, at least for the time being. I do notice her perseverating on inconsequential details of life more and more, but I feel like that probably goes hand in hand with the shrinking boundaries of her life in general. At least she's continuing to notice the small details, right? So, as she and I drive to northern Kentucky on Friday evening, where we've agreed to meet Rob in Richwood, I'm truly sorry to see the week over.

"You're good company, Mom," I tell her. "Our house is going to seem empty without you."

"It was a nice break for me," Mom volunteers, "and I appreciate everything you and Mike did for me. You've got a keeper there, Bet. But it'll be good for you to get back to your regular routine without having to worry about me."

"But I'll miss you in my 'regular routine,'" I persist. "I never would have picked out my artwork without you here to help me."

"That was fun," she agrees. "I can't wait to see it up once it's framed."

Rob pulls into Chili Time a few minutes after we do, which we had decided was about halfway for each of us. Walking over to greet us, we put Mom's stuff in his SUV. Four years younger than me, his hair is swiftly tracking towards being snow white like Mom's and Gram's before her. He still has tinges of his previous grey blond, but the white is already much more prominent. I give him a hug and we go in to grab dinner.

Rob is a carbon copy of my father, in all ways except, perhaps, his personality. Dad, at his tallest, was about 5'10", while Rob is an even 6 feet and a slightly expanded grid of my Dad's build. Slender and lithe, very much a runner's build, his shoulders are broader. Same defined jaw line, so many of Dad's facial expressions, but with my Mom's slightly oversized, gently hooked nose and her blue grey eyes with their piercing gaze.

Almost always, Rob looks weary to me. There's a nebulous fatigue about him that I can't quite quantify; maybe just years of exhaustion that can't be erased. It's almost a look of being not quite healthy; it could just be aging. For each one of us, that's different. Rob's may show most prominently in his face and hair; Craig's in his increasing LACK of hair; me with my waning hot flashes and the more than occasional strand of 'platinum', (okay, grey) hair, that I do my best to keep covered in my natural brunette color.

Rob seems wound tightly tonight and I ask him how his day was.

He shrugs. "The usual," he answers without animation, and I don't pursue it.

Mom seems to shrink a little. He and I get Five-ways, Mom decides on a chilidog without onions. How I love my Chili Time! I search for another topic of conversation and decide Rob's boys are a safe one. Indeed. Rob warms to the topic. Largely due to Colette's upbringing and her roots in

Catholicism, all three of their boys are products of Catholic schools. John is finishing his sophomore year at St. Titus, one of Cincinnati's male Catholic high schools and the plan is for James and Jack to follow him there once they finish eighth grade. Currently, they're finishing seventh.

We discuss their academics, my younger nephews' plans for high school, and the sports all three of them are currently playing. His interest in whatever they do is obvious, yet at the same time there's a hint of…what is it? Expectation on his part? A certain mental agenda? Maybe that's not such a bad thing, I tell myself as I'm listening. It's probably different for a dad who has sons instead of daughters. Never having raised boys myself, I'm certainly in no position to judge Rob. I just know there's an intensity to what he's relaying to me that indicates a lot of significance attached to their performance.

I try to just listen without judging, believing in my heart that while as parents we can encourage, be present, and offer advice and encouragement, ultimately our children find their way, more often based on what we put in their hearts and minds early on, and the things in life they see are important to us. But, while those parenting years may be removed from me, they have also taught me that sometimes what we want is not what our children want. Imposing our expectations on them doesn't always mean we're doing the best thing for them.

Mom is soaking all this in, not saying a word. It dawns on me that this may be the most she's heard Rob speak in months. He digresses into the admittance criteria for St. Titus, what will be expected of James and Jack, and when they will apply for entrance. I realize I've completely lost interest in this discussion. Maybe Mom really is better off not talking to Rob frequently. He's so intense and serious. I don't think he's smiled once since we sat down, nor has he asked Mom how she is, or how her week went.

We finish dinner and I notice Mom's chili dog is still almost uneaten on her plate. Rob picks up the check and I thank him as we head out to the parking lot. Hugging them both goodbye as we stand outside his SUV, I feel my heart already starting to miss Mom.

"I'm so glad we had this week," I tell her. "Mike and I loved having you and you'll need to come back. Behave yourself at home." I hug her hard and hold her to me for several long seconds.

Mom seems…I can't quite put my finger on it. Worried? Distracted? It's like all her vibrancy has evaporated, and now she seems truly elderly, in the space of a scant hour. She returns my hug, but I can tell her mind is somewhere else. Is this Rob's impact on her? Or is she sad about leaving me but not wanting to say anything in front of him? My eyes tear up as I watch them pull out of Chili Time in front of me, veering left up the access ramp to I-75 North. I go the opposite direction. I miss her terribly already. It's like being five again and having to get on the school bus to go to kindergarten when all I want to do is stay home with her. No matter how old I get, that feeling remains whenever we separate.

I think a lot on the way home, my mind ricocheting from topic to topic. Much of it swirls around Rob. He was always the brother I was closest to growing up and the one I felt I was the most like. What's happened to him? He's truly become someone I don't even know anymore. There's an edge and an arrogance to him that never used to be there. I wonder if this is a recent development, or a slowly accumulating hubris of years. If that's the case, I sure haven't seen it coming. Does Colette experience this? There's an unspoken sense of him having the monopoly on insight… this brother who rarely spoke up as a child, who shunned conflict at all costs, and who cried so easily when his feelings were hurt. Is this the flip side of that shy, vulnerable little boy? Is his arrogance protection from the world, or just an inflated ego? Both? I just know I miss my old Rob, the one I could tell anything to as we grew up, knowing he'd listen and understand. Now, I feel like I'm not worth his time. I can see why Mom feels the way she does.

I know nothing about Rob's 'core' anymore; his spirit, his

heart, and that's part of the grayness I feel in him. It's like he's depleted, with no way of refueling. That might be the edge I sense. Could the overstated self-worth be a cover-up for someone living in internal chaos? Is there anything I can do to help him? I suppose it's possible Rob has reached a point where he doesn't enjoy practicing medicine anymore and is burnt out, but feels it's too late to do anything else, especially with his boys the ages they are and the standard of living they enjoy.

I've always wondered if, because Dad was a doctor, Rob felt that he needed to follow him into medicine. Neither Craig nor Donny felt that call, but Rob was pre-med from his freshman year on in college. He took a year after graduation to study for his MCAT's, going on to attend med-school in Columbus. Returning to Cincinnati to do his residency, he met Colette, who was a cardio ICU nurse, during his time at Holy Disciple Hospital.

I remember thinking they were Ken and Barbie; such a perfectly matched couple in their attractiveness. Colette petite and blond; Rob so all-American and blond, too. Callie, six when she first met Colette, idolized her, and Kerry, barely two, followed right in Cal's footsteps. Colette was so good to them, showering them with attention and affection. When Rob and Col married, Callie was their flower girl-a dream come true for a seven-year old. Real life set in for Rob and Col after that. They both worked full time, Rob's life becoming on-calls, middle of the night emergencies, surgeries, and malpractice insurance. John was born, they moved into their first house, and it was slowly becoming clear to me that Colette enjoyed a high standard of living. They were always doing something to their house, with The Next Big Project always in the pipeline.

Whether it was new cars, new curtains, or new cosmetics, there was always a need for more. At that point in time, I was home full time with Callie and Kerry, putting my music degree to great use by teaching private piano, which I loved doing. Still, I admit, there were times when I was a bit envious of their life. It all looked so good on the surface-the successful husband and wife, with their (after the twins) three darling boys, always dressed in their matching Health-Tex outfits. And now, after five granddaughters, there were finally three boys from their biological son to carry on the Bradshaw name. I know that pleased my parents greatly, especially Dad.

But slowly, I noticed things; small, subtle cues that flashed a yellow caution light. Mike and I had been in Louisville close to 10 years by this point, but there were plenty of holiday get-togethers and birthdays when we were all present, and the thing I noticed the most was the way Col and Rob spoke to each other. There always seemed to be a tinge of acidity in their exchanges and neither was shy about criticizing or correcting the other in front of family. I never saw any warmth or shared humor between them, and I found myself wondering if they were this caustic in front of other people, what it must be like when no one else was around. Mike and I certainly know how to push each other's buttons, but criticizing one another in mixed company has always been off the table for us. The longer I watched this dynamic play out between Rob and Col, the more it felt like they were competing on some weird level, although that struck me as ridiculous. There was a genuine feeling of dislike for one another that began to be evident, and that bothered me even more.

Mike and I had always felt that Rob's relationship with Col was a 'tit for tat'...you know, the kind where the husband says, 'Well, I'm going on this golf trip to Hilton Head', and in reply, the wife takes a trip to Florida with her girlfriends. Over the years we saw a pattern develop with this, too. Rob parked a '67 black GTO in the garage; Col redid their entire kitchen after only four years. Mom noticed Col's penchant for spending, but that seemed to be the tip of the iceberg to me. Their lack of emotional intimacy seemed the much bigger problem, and their inability to be content. Dad seemed oblivious to all of it, or maybe chose not to acknowledge it. Rob HAS changed, no doubt about it, but is that due to how unhappy he is in his marriage? Was he the one to start picking at Colette until she began to fire back? Or was Col the instigator of the derisive comments that have become so commonplace? It's hard to know, and I'm not even sure I want the answers.

Lately when Col and I talk on the phone, I've noticed her making very pointed references to Rob being just like my dad, which I haven't asked her to clarify. I'm assuming she means in terms of his personality traits, but I've never put Rob and my dad anywhere in the same camp as far as that goes. But then, in fairness to their screwed-up living situation, Colette may have seen quite a few things I didn't those last 18 months that Dad was with them.

I think about all of this as I blow past the exits for Owenton, Sparta, and Warsaw. It makes me sad…for all of us, but especially for Rob and his family. Life can happen so fast and furiously, especially during those child rearing years, and sometimes it's hard to slow down enough to evaluate the course you're on. More and more I get the feeling Rob and Colette have kicked their issues down the road, choosing to stay on the hamster wheel and tread frantically in place.

The whole situation is so fraught, and I go around and round with it in my head. Mom being there, even though she's not actively doing anything to add to the problem, is not beneficial for anyone, most of all her. Though I can't say how, I feel like this whole deal will be reaching critical mass soon. More than anything, I want Mom in a place where she feels happy and wanted; where there are people her own age to talk to and help shape her day to day reality. She needs that, and more importantly, she deserves it. Rob's home is no longer an optimum living situation for her.

Paradise lost, I'm thinking.

Chapter Two

SUMMER DAZE
(July 2009)

The summer has passed swiftly, leaving Father's Day, the Fourth of July, and our trip to Florida in its wake. Now it's Rob and Colette's turn to go on vacation, and for the first time ever, they've asked Craig and me to 'keep' Mom for the week. My instincts regarding Mom's living situation have served me well, and there's been much more undercurrent than usual in the seven weeks since she was here with us. I have a distinct feeling the wheels are starting to come off. Based on Rob and Col's request that she stay with either Craig or myself while they're gone, it's clear that they feel she's declined to a degree where they're not comfortable leaving her home alone. About a month ago, shortly after she returned home from staying with us, Mom had smelled something burning in their house, become alarmed, and went upstairs to ask whoever was home about it. Thank goodness at least someone WAS home, which often isn't the case, and this day it happened to be Rob. He came back downstairs with Mom to see if he could locate the source of the smell, and after looking around, walked over to Mom's stove. There, as big as life, was a kettle with eggs in it, boiled completely dry, still on high heat...hence the mystery odor. Mom, of course, was beside herself, and mortified to have been the source of the problem.

Colette had shared this with me the day she'd called to enlist my help. I readily agreed, telling her that either Mom could stay the whole week with us, or that Craig and I would work something out jointly. Deciding it was time to open the door on other potential living options for Mom, I made a bold comment in that direction. Even though they've engineered her current living situation, I want Col to know up front that we don't expect Rob and her to keep Mom there with them indefinitely. Something tells me they might have a difficult time admitting that they're in over their heads.

"Maybe Mom needs to start spending more routine time with each of us," I had commented, wondering if it was hard for Colette to come out and ask us to do that specifically.

"Sure," she'd replied. "Your Mom would probably enjoy that."

We also talk through the idea of framing up Mom's stay with us in more of a 'chance to visit' light, versus a 'Rob and Colette don't trust you alone' kind of thing. Mom may put two and two together anyway. Col asking for help with Mom is significant. I'll be curious to see how much decline I notice compared to her last visit. After talking with Craig, we agree to split the week. That way, Mom can see both of us, and will be able to spend time with my nieces, who are seven and five. Craig will drive down from Dayton to pick her up for the first weekend, and she'll stay with them until Tuesday. Then he'll bring Mom back to Cincinnati, and I'll drive up Tuesday evening to spend the night with her. We'll come back to Louisville on Wednesday until the following Saturday afternoon, when Rob and Colette will return home. Thus, my cruise up I-71 again on a sun-dappled summer evening, trying to get a handle on my irritation with my entire family, but especially Mom, before our time together.

Being Mom's only daughter puts me in the unique position of being told more than she tells my brothers. I'm not sure this is the case in all families, but it is in ours, and it's not always a good position to be in. So often I feel smack in the middle of everything, the one responsible for brokering healthy communication between all parties involved. And, because Mom shares more with me, I know far more about her worries, day to day life events, and her feelings in general. Generally, I'm a good holding receptacle for all these things, but lately I'm getting frustrated.

In the past month, she has begun to perseverate on failing the vision part of her driving test when she retakes it this August. Turning 82 then, she's worried to death about losing her license. This anxiety inducing topic comes up in every single phone conversation we have, and no matter what options I offer, it's met with complete negativity on Mom's part. Craig and I have found a lot of common ground on this issue and have talked about it extensively. One of his closest friends from high school, Mark Spencer, owns a car leasing service in Cincinnati, and as part of his business, provides personal drivers who are bonded and background checked for clients who can no longer drive themselves. He has made this service available to Craig, knowing Mom well, even offering to call her himself to ease her mind. Mom flat out refuses to even consider talking to Mark.

"I don't need to talk to Mark Spencer about being driven around Cincinnati by a stranger," is her arch response to Craig.

Both Craig and I are working on her to try out the service on a night where there's something going on at her church.

Mom's response: "Are you crazy? I'm not getting in a strange car with a man I've never met before! That's ridiculous!"

Craig and I have hastened to assure her that Mark has known and worked with these personal drivers for a long time; that they do this for numerous clients like Mom all over Cincinnati. I've even offered to hire one of these drivers while I'm up visiting Mom, so that she wouldn't be by herself-we'd be together.

"C'mon, Mom, it would be fun," I'll state. "We can do dinner and a movie and then the driver can bring us home."

Mom's response: "And what's he supposed to do while we're enjoying ourselves? I'd feel like I'm putting him out the whole time! There he sits twiddling his thumbs while he's waiting for us."

"Mom, really?" I finally explode in exasperation. "He probably goes home, or he grabs a bite to eat, or runs errands. Maybe he just sits in his car and reads! He's USED TO DOING THIS! At least give it a try!" And then, because I can't resist, "Because if you don't pass your vision test in August, you'll be making friends with him pretty fast, since he'll be taking you everywhere!" *Lord, please forgive me.*

This is the side of Mom I struggle with so much. She can be so negative, and so incredibly stubborn. No matter what positive options Craig and I present, Mom shoots them down. There's always a reason they won't work, some angle Craig and I haven't thought of. My gut feeling is that she truly doesn't WANT any of them to work. Twice in phone conversations over the past two weeks, I've simply had to end the conversation and make an excuse to hang up, rather than risking something coming out of my mouth that I'll regret.

Mom's summary assessment of what happens if she loses her ability to drive goes like this: "If I fail that vision test and am stuck over here alone, (meaning at Rob's place) I'll just die."

More than she knows, for as much as she can irritate me with her negativity, I feel her pain. And her statement speaks volumes to me. The terminology 'stuck over here' is a clear indication of how isolated and cut off Mom feels, and it's pretty telling. More than once in the past several months, she's made the comment that 'your dad thought this would be such a great idea, and now I'm stuck here for good', at which point I really need to be careful. To this day, Mom conveniently chooses to ignore the fact that she did have a say in the decision to move to Rob's, and she chose not to utilize it. All she had to do was stand her ground, tell Dad that she preferred to live in the retirement community of their choice, where she'd be surrounded by friends if he passed before she did. But, as I've mentioned before, that never happened. Sadly, there was no dialogue to be had between my parents when a decision that would affect all of us long-term had needed to be made.

As events always impact more than just one party, Mom and Dad's decision to live with Rob and Collette altered the dynamic of our entire family from that point forward. Given Dad's medical prognosis at that time, I know he was far more concerned that Mom not be alone than he was about how it would impact our relationships with one another, and I doubt that thought ever occurred to him. But I lost a piece of my parents once they moved in with Rob, because never again would I be able to go to visit JUST my parents, under their own roof. Every visit now would mean interaction not just with my parents, but also with my brother, sister- in-law, and nephews, on some level. I didn't mind it, per se…but I missed being able to experience Mom and Dad as a separate entity. Now they were just an extension of my brother's life. The idea that Mom pins this on Dad now, when he's dead and gone, instead of owning her total reticence to speak up back when it could have made a huge difference, is very difficult for me.

It also meant that I heard far more than I would have chosen to about the daily goings on in the lives of my brother and his family, because Mom and Dad were there to witness every bit of it. I love all three of my nephews dearly, and I have a good relationship with Rob and Colette, but sometimes it was hard to hear about all the daily interaction my parents had with my nephews when my own immediate family (Mike, Callie, Kerry and I) were two hours away. For the most part, I feel like I did a good job adjusting to these changes. I reminded myself that my daughters had been blessed to have grandparents who were considerably younger at the time than Mom and Dad were now, and they had reaped the benefits of that. Both of our girls had gone on numerous trips with my parents, going up to Cincinnati every summer to stay for week-long visits on their own. I had a wealth of memories to look back on when I got to feeling envious. Instead, I tried very hard to be thankful that my parents were both still here to enjoy my three nephews.

I have come to deeply appreciate our move to Louisville in 1985, though it was completely unexpected when it happened, and very difficult to leave my family and best friend, Mary Claire. It's given us the ability to become our own family entity in a way that we probably never would have if we'd remained in Cincinnati. There was a lot of freedom in being two hours away, and in having a certain amount of insulation from the pettiness of small family disagreements. I have no doubt, looking back, that part of God's plan in transferring us was to provide us with that healthy autonomy. It has remained a gift to Mike and me since that time, in ways we never could have predicted.

I've always wondered if, in hindsight, I should have gone to Dad with Mom's concerns and all her backchannel handwringing about moving to Rob's. If I had, I'm not sure how well anyone would have been served. Bottom line, it would not have been healthy for me, their 42-year old daughter, to run interference for my own mother, and I knew that then. Knowing my mom, she would have acted completely shocked if Dad had called her out on my having shared her lack of desire to move to Rob's. Her response to him probably would have been that I was exaggerating, rather than using it as a starting point for a discussion between them. It would also have placed me in the role of potentially clarifying for Rob something that only my parents should have owned.

So, I wisely (or so I thought at the time) refrained on all fronts. These living negotiations didn't involve me, nor did I want them to. Yet now, Mom can play the martyr so convincingly. Based on some of her comments, you'd think she was tied, bound, and forced to sign her name in blood for the move to occur, and this is where my normally vast reservoir of patience completely runs out. When she starts with these comments in our phone conversations, it takes every ounce of self-discipline I have not to verbally lambast her. I've perfected my verbal marksmanship over the years, and it would effectively seek and destroy its target. But I always stop short. Yes, I'd feel better momentarily for speaking my mind, but Mom is far from being an equal opponent. I can't bring myself to do it to her.

Craig and I talk off and on about wishing we could get Mom out of Rob's, and into a retirement community somewhere, and both of us, without the other knowing until we ran into each other, spent some time looking several years ago, but the cost of Beecher Springs had risen significantly at that point, and I'm not sure Mom would want to be anywhere else. Still, something's got to give soon. Craig seems less invested in his desire to pursue other living alternatives, possibly because he hears less about Mom's level of discontent. And maybe, somewhat like me, he feels that since he wasn't a part of the decision to make the move to Rob's in the first place, he's not going to own it now. In truth, it's not his or mine TO own.

I'm mentally revisiting each stepping-stone along the way that has placed our family on the path it's stumbling down now. It's hard for me to admit to myself the level of disillusionment I feel with the decisions my parents have made this last decade of their lives. My love for them, and for all they've given me, supersedes all else…always. The hard part for me is accepting that they made decisions I would not have, and I'm wrestling with this in my heart, and in prayer. Like that small stone tossed into the lake, the ripples continue to broaden, impacting each one of us in ways we never could have foreseen earlier. I'm struggling not to lose sight of the big picture of their lives, but there's been such a loss of respect in me towards Mom recently that

I'm in no man's land right now. Although I understand why I feel this way, there's a lot of guilt that comes with it.

In tandem with the guilt is significant ambivalence towards my siblings. I'm sick of always feeling like I'm the one in the middle. Mom talks to me. Rob and Col talk to me, but not to Craig. Craig talks to me, but not to Rob and Col. I'm the middle ground for everyone; listening, considering everyone's perspective and feelings, and I'm the one who pays the price for having to process all of it. I'm tired of being caught in Craig and Rob's crossfire; tired of Mom's stubbornness and negativity, tired of her dead-end living situation that I had no decision in yet hear about constantly. But, as much as I loathe functioning as that middle ground, it may be exactly the role God needs me to continue in for the time being. There can still be a level of detachment that will help me maintain my own personal equilibrium. I firmly believe God will show me a way to honor my mother as I move forward, which is critical to me. What she means to me far outweighs her current mindset, as is her feeling loved and valued.

Right now, my hands are tied in terms of being able to do much to change the situation. It begs for God's intervention and leading, and I know He'll move when He's ready. When that happens, His timing will be perfect. It always is. Even though I feel vague stirrings of things lining up to change, there's a strong confirmation of the need to simply wait. More important is staying the course and being faithful to what is right in front of me, which is taking care of Mom this week. Creating more conflict in my family than already exists serves no purpose. Things have grown so complicated, and I wonder if we are just the sum-total of each family member's dysfunction. Those glossy 10 x 14 portraits of our smiling family in earlier years seem to have splintered into shards of sharp-edged glass. The subtext reads, in jagged black letters, 'WHAT HAPPENED TO THIS FAMILY?'

I often wonder if it would have been any different if we had all been biological siblings. Would there be a stronger denominator of common traits between us, and a more resilient bond? Of course, there's no way to quantify this thought, and, if Rob is any valid indicator at present, we might all be on Dr. Phil. There always were, and still are, differences in temperament, personality, and our senses of humor, but that would hold true in any family, biological or otherwise. Our family runs the gambit. Cases in point: growing up, Craig and I were very neat and organized, Craig to the point of bordering on obsessive compulsive. Donny and Rob, on the other hand, were complete slobs. I was the only avid reader in the bunch, devouring anything and everything I could get my hands on. Donny, at the opposite end of the spectrum, has probably read five books in his entire life. We joked that his book report every year of elementary school was the same book, titled 'Rifles For Wattie', that he would fluff up for the current year's effort.

In terms of my brothers, Donny and Rob were much more athletic than Craig, but Craig could tell you the make and year of every car on the road by the time he was five, with an emphasis on luxury cars. (Or, for that matter, anything that connotated wealth.) Craig and I were the two most apt to notice when Mom or Dad needed help with something and to step up; Donny and Rob stuck strictly to their allowance chores, even those completed begrudgingly.

Our developing senses of humor were a force to be reckoned with as well, and I realized somewhere between the end of middle school and my early years of high school that mine was of a completely different genre than my parents. Sarcasm came easily to me, and it became a delightful resource with multiple uses. I could have my friends rolling on the floor or protect myself with it as sharp-edged weaponry. Unfortunately, Mom was often on the other end of my verbal experimentation, and I quickly realized it gave me the upper hand with her. Measuring my words was not my strong suit in high school, and I could be coldly unmerciful about unleashing them. Both of my parents were very middle of the road when it came to their own senses of humor, leaning towards the more serious side, and they didn't particularly appreciate mine. It was too extreme; too 'out there', and I really felt like I had to keep it under wraps around them. Luckily, I had Donny, and his dry, tongue in cheek responses matched my own. It almost felt like speaking a foreign language that only he and I appreciated. But as different as we all were, I loved the variety of attributes and personality in each of my brothers. It was a rich, multi-faceted environment to grow up in, and I reveled in who all of us were, both similarities and differences.

Even more compelling was the idea that because I was adopted, I possessed the equivalent of a second, mysterious identity. I knew who I was, yet I didn't know ALL of who I was. This gave me great license to imagine all kinds of back stories to my hidden birth identity, and with my overactive imagination, I came up with some doozies. In the back of my mind, I always wondered about my birth mother-what she looked like, how old she'd been when she had me, and what she had gone on to do with her life. This was strictly from a standpoint of my own curiosity, rather than from any void in parenting on Mom's part. As I graduated from college and moved home while I applied for teaching jobs for the next school year, that spark of interest in finding my birth mother grew. I had also begun to wonder about possible biological siblings. I think my own personal growth in independence during my college years had a strong influence on my desire to begin this search. I'd had five years to discover who I was outside the walls of my family, even as I retained that identity. I had gained strength, maturity, and confidence in who I was, and the amalgamation of these factors led me to begin my search in the spring of 1980.

Ironically, (or maybe not so ironically, knowing Mom) during the nine months I lived at home before finding my first apartment, Mom asked me if I'd be interested in having a copy of my original birth certificate. From the standpoint that I had been contemplating this search and had talked at great length to my best friend Mary Claire, about it, it seemed almost too coincidental. In hindsight, I think Mom felt like I was mature enough to handle the situation, and since I was home in that time period, felt it might be helpful to me. We did a day trip up to Columbus to get the birth certificate, and while we were there, obtained copies of Donny's and Craig's as well, should they want them. Neither of my brothers has ever expressed any desire to find their birth mothers. Perhaps the motivation to search is higher in a female child than a male.

Yet another huge act of unconditional love on the part of my parents was made clear to me that day as I was informed by the state clerk that my adoption files had remained 'Open'. This involved a deliberate choice on the part of my parents when they signed our adoption papers in our infancy, and it allowed us to have access to all information within our files should we desire it as legal adults. Up until 1964, when the law swung to the side of protecting the biological parent, and ALL files were legally closed, an adoptive parent had the choice of leaving a file open for their child or legally closing it to deny them access at the time of their adoption. My parents could just as easily have closed our files and never given us that option, but agreed to leave them open, thinking that one day we might want that information. Talk about selfless. Again, that debt of gratitude wells up. Who knew what we'd find if we started looking into things? For me, that piece of paper was my ticket forward, because it provided me with the name of my birth mother, (Sandra Ulrich) her age at my birth, (21) and, amazingly, her address at the time of my birth. I never could have begun my search without that information, and it served me well. Because my birth father chose not to marry my mother, he was not legally required to place his name on my birth certificate. To this day, I have no idea who he is.

After going to Columbus, Mom also suggested visiting the adoption agency they had worked through in Cincinnati. This would allow us to talk to a case worker about my biological family background and flesh out some of my background details. Of course, I was all too happy to take this next step, and we went for our consultation about a month after we'd gone to Columbus. No names were given, out of protection for my biological parents, but information on their physical traits, ages, education, and what they had been doing when they met were all provided. I learned that my birth father had been 25, working for the Army Core of Engineers. Better, the case worker shared detailed facts about my birth mother's siblings. Mom sat patiently through this appointment, seemingly as enthused as I was. I can't imagine what that felt like to her. Did she feel like this would be enough information to satisfy me? Or, and I lean more towards this thought, because she knew me so well, did she guess that I'd continue seeking answers beyond today's appointment, and just wanted to help me get started? This made me want to know the whole story, and I had the foundation I needed.

The rest of my search was done 'underground', and Mom knew nothing about it. Mary Claire and eventually Mike, who I had begun dating in this same time period, were my co-detectives. Part of me felt horribly guilty about not telling Mom, but I couldn't be sure of her reaction to my contacting my birth mother and family. I had a feeling she'd think I was taking it way too far and would make her very uncomfortable. What she didn't know couldn't hurt her. Part of it, too, was out of pure protection for her feelings. She'd been generous enough to suggest these first two big steps in gaining background info, and I didn't want her to feel like my interest in pursuing things was because she 'wasn't enough' as a parent. The hunt was a story in and of itself, and included were a wealth of phone calls, assumed identities on my part to protect all involved, research, letters, and lies to get the answers I grew obsessed with finding. It took an entire year for me to connect the dots and contact my birth family, but every step of my search was worth it.

I learned that my birth mother, Sandra, had died of colon cancer a scant year before I started my search. Instead of meeting Sandra, I was able to form a lasting relationship with her younger sister, Bobbie, and was blessed to be able to meet my biological grandparents and Bobbie's family when I was 23. Meeting your own DNA is powerful, and I'm thankful I initiated the process when I did. Looking back, I know God's Hand was in that timing as well, because with their family having lost Sandra just two years prior, I believe there was a special comfort for them in discovering this missing piece of her that had been at large for 23 years. I am the spitting image of my biological mother, and the first time I met Bobbie, her reaction was emotional. My aunt and I got together for lunch several times after our initial meeting, and she set up a dinner at her home so that I could meet my grandparents. The night of our meeting, my grandmother gave me a beautiful scrapbook of my birth mother, with pictures from her infancy through adulthood. What a treasure, and our resemblance to one another in our baby pictures is undeniable. Being together that evening clearly revealed the origins of my sense of humor. As we sat around Bobbie's dinner table talking, that dry, sarcastic repartee was the currency of exchange.

There was also the revelation that I had two younger siblings-both sisters. Sandra had married two years after she put me up for adoption. At that point in time, because her death was so recent, and because of a promise Bobbie had made to Sandra's husband who was still living, my aunt asked me not to contact either of my sisters, who were 21 and 19 at the time. I kept that promise well into my 40's, when I finally did reach out to them once Sandra's husband had passed. They hadn't known I existed, and I was able to meet Leah, the younger of the two. Over the years, I have remained in contact with both my aunt and sister, which has been a gift.

After getting together with my biological family, I knew it was time to let Mom know I had met them. I owed her that. I was already very concerned about her feeling threatened by it, and by the frequency of my visits with my aunt. Sharing the photo album my grandparents had put together was probably the most insensitive thing I could have done, but I wanted to come clean. If I could do it over again, I probably wouldn't share the album with her. That was probably taking it one step too far. Mom, scrutinizing the pictures, commented, "You look nothing like her," which tugged at my heart. I realized she probably didn't want to see a resemblance, even if it was there right in front of her. But what a great sport she was, poring carefully over every picture instead of racing through the album. It had to be very painful for her. Again, her selflessness. She listened to me recount the whole story, told me how sorry she was that Sandra had died before I could find her, and never once made me feel guilty for my search.

"I'm glad you have the answers you need," was her quiet comment as we sat on the couch with the photo album open between us on our laps.

My search provided closure, and it answered a lot of questions. But the thing I realized over time as I moved away from those initial heady experiences is that my birth family, wonderful as they were, and sharing my DNA, are still not the ones who will ever know me best. They didn't raise me, grow up with me, or influence me year after year. And there was no way they could be a part of the every-day details of my life…the packed lunch boxes, the clean stacks of laundry neatly folded on my dresser, the birthday dinners when Mom made whatever we asked for, or the up-all-night illnesses. In the end, it was all the little, seemingly insignificant things, the broad sweep of time, that carried the true history of me. Woven into that tapestry was the trips to the orthodontist, the carpools, the Christmases together, and the cozy childhood winter evenings of early darkness and homework. Mom and Dad were present in every thread of that fabric. They are to this day.

My mind has gone a lot of places on this trip to Cincinnati, and as I pass Carrolton, it turns to Craig and Rob's current relationship. This is another prong of our family's existing state that is becoming more and more of an emotional minefield. I refuse to be in the middle of it, but that's often easier said than done. I know Mom feels the weight of it, too, because she's verbalized it to me. As the two youngest, Craig and Rob were extremely close, being almost exactly a year apart. They were a pair growing up-Craig dark haired, dark eyed, and serious; Rob tow-headed, fair skinned like Mom but minus her freckles, with an eager little smile. He was a butterball when he was a baby and toddler, and I was old enough by then to play the role of 'second mom'. There was a downright sweetness to him as a little boy that I loved.

Sharing a bedroom all the years they lived at home, Craig and Rob knew everything about each other, or at least I assumed they did. Their bedroom was next to mine, with a common wall between our rooms, and I can recall hearing them in their beds at night talking endlessly, laughing uproariously over some shared joke, or jumping back and forth between beds, using the walls to rebound. This would drive me crazy as I was trying to fall asleep, and often, in a fit of rage, I would fly out of bed and stalk down the hallway to our family room where Mom and Dad would be watching TV.

"Make them be quiet!" I'd implore my parents. "They're soooo loud!"

One of them, usually Dad, would get up from the couch and head to their room, opening their bedroom door without any warning. Often this meant catching them in midair, sailing from one bed to the other. This was never good for business.

"What have I told you both?" Dad would roar. "Now knock it off! Your sister is trying to sleep!"

No one questioned Dad except Donny, and that never ended well. We knew Dad's tone of voice that meant business. At that point, Craig and Rob would stop, but for the next half hour there would be muffled squeals of laughter erupting through the wall anyway. The two of them continued to be close through middle and high school, and I always thought of them as one solid unit of our family. Donny and I were the other older unit. We were always buddies, relating well to each other, and there is an ease between us that remains to this day. That said, I can acknowledge the grief he put my parents through, because he never considered consequences to his actions, and his impulsivity racked up a litany of bad decisions. I always wondered if Donny felt left out because Craig and Rob were so close, but it was never anything he verbalized to me. I truly don't think he cared one way or the other. He always did his own thing.

Rob's strong academic trajectory started early, as did his athleticism. There wasn't much Rob DIDN'T excel at, and whatever he did seemed to come naturally, even his artwork. (Dad was very artistic.) Craig never seemed to feel like he needed to compete with Rob-he was secure in himself. Craig's skills were social, and he possessed them in spades. In many ways, he paved the way for Rob in school by knowing everyone. None of the other three of us had Craig's confidence or self-assuredness at that time in our lives. It was as if he knew he was someone special. It wasn't in a cocky, stuck-up way, but more of a 'you want to know me' manner. He knew everyone's names, and undaunted by a three-year age difference, knew some of the people in my senior class better than I did when he was a freshman. Cliques didn't seem to exist for him-he either ignored them or they melted away in his ability to navigate them.

He also possessed a knack for talking to adults that I greatly envied. Whether it was his teachers, our older married cousins, my aunts and uncles, even our minister; he could carry a conversation better than many people twice his age. And whether it was cars, clothes, rock bands, or aftershave, he exhibited an innate sense of what was in vogue, popular, or state of the art at any given time. In short, he was a maven of knowledge and information. And, based on how different I was from Craig growing up, he was the sibling I was the least close to. He was serious, materialistic, and interested in things that didn't matter to me. With much less common ground between us, Craig was like having an adult for a brother even when he was still in middle school and I was in high school. He made me feel slightly off kilter, somehow, probably because of my less than polished social skills. I tolerated him but gave him a wide berth emotionally.

None of us attended the same college following high school, but Craig and Rob continued to remain close. Even after Craig had graduated and started his first job, when Rob was in med school, they stayed connected. And as Rob's graduation present from med school, Craig took Rob on a two-week trip of the South Pacific. Looking back, I can't pinpoint when the unravelling of their relationship started. I don't know if a single event triggered it, or if it was more of a compilation of small things adding up over time. Mike and I were already in Louisville by then, and in the thick of it with Callie and Kerry, so we weren't seeing a lot of Craig or Rob except on holidays, which was always in the context of larger family gatherings. By then, Craig had been with Merridan, an industrial conveyor belt company, for eight years, and was climbing the corporate ladder quickly. Life was moving fast for all of us at this point, and one evening when all of us were in Cincinnati over Thanksgiving, Rob brought Colette to Mom and Dad's to meet us. Poor Col... Nothing like being overwhelmed. I had felt sorry for her.

The evening hadn't gone well. Mom and Dad were unusually quiet, and Craig drilled Colette like she was on a talk show, asking her pointed questions about her nursing position at Holy Disciple, what her long-range career plan was...things that should have come out naturally in a conversational context much later. It made me very uncomfortable, and I had referenced it shortly afterwards, making a comment to him along the lines of "Remind me to grill the next girl you bring home the way you did Colette." His response was dismissive.

"I needed to know that she was in this for the right reasons, and not just a gold digger," was his reply, as if that justified everything.

Later, and I don't remember if it was the same visit, or if some time had passed, (possibly that Christmas) Rob had let my parents know that he was furious about how Craig had 'cross examined' Colette. According to Rob, my parents had kind of blown it off, stating that Craig had told them he just wanted to be sure she'd 'be a good fit in our family'. I'm not sure whether my parents were defending Craig, or if they were trying to smooth things over by passing along what his intended motives were, hoping to appease Rob. Whatever their reasoning, they failed miserably in their attempt. Craig may have had the best of intentions, but it wasn't his place to grill Colette, and he would have been livid if one of us had exhibited the same type of behavior to someone he brought home. None the less, my parents never addressed it with him. I think their rationale was to ignore it and hope the situation diffused itself over time. I remember apologizing to Rob that Colette had had to endure that and made it clear to him that Mike and I liked her very much. Putting myself in Rob's shoes, I couldn't imagine how alienating that would be, when all Rob had wanted was our family's acceptance in their relationship.

I suppose it's entirely possible that Craig's hardball interview of Colette shaped her view of him from the start and put her on the defensive. It probably had a negative impact on Rob's relationship with him as well. To this day, I wish that Rob would have confronted Craig, one on one, right after it had happened, but Rob is a carbon copy of my mom, shunning confrontation at all cost. Nothing was ever said between them about what happened. I think all of us weighed the cost of any confrontation with Craig during this time in our lives. I didn't do conflict well, either, but was slowly learning to speak up when it mattered. Sadly, though, in any situation involving Craig, I always felt like my parents would own his perspective, and that it wouldn't be worth the emotional energy I would expend justifying another viewpoint.

As these dynamics were playing out, Dad was also getting their affairs in order following a second and nearly fatal heart attack. All of us were adults by this time, and he appointed Craig to be the executor of their will, assigning Rob medical power of attorney. Craig had accrued a great deal of business acumen by then, and Rob could certainly weigh in on any medical issues that would arise. Dad felt that each of them was well suited to their designated responsibility. As controlling as Craig could be about many things, I know he never viewed this role as power, or the means to manipulate. Based on his deep love and loyalty to my father, he wanted to be sure he carried out exactly what my Dad's wishes were, and that meant taking the best possible care of Mom financially once Dad had passed. Once that happened, Craig and Rob would then became co-executors of Mom's trust.

But, even given that co-executor partnership once Dad died, it's been Craig that's taken the lead in going to meetings with Tom Peers, my parents' financial planner. Rob has always been invited to these same meetings, but has expressed zero interest in attending them, or knowing anything about Mom's finances. Yet somehow, over the years, he and Colette have found it appropriate to make any number of disparaging remarks about Craig's handling of Mom's finances. It's almost to the point of them suggesting he has helped himself to some of it, and/or mismanaged it, both of which couldn't be farther from the truth. Colette seems to be far more strident about it even than Rob, and it's really begun to bother me. One of Col's standard lines lately, (in addition to the one about Rob being like Dad) is "What has your mom done with all of her money?" This is nervy, in my opinion, and it's none of Colette's business. It also seems extremely hypocritical, because Rob could avail himself of these facts any time he chooses to and has been given so many opportunities to be involved yet has consciously chosen not to be. I usually shut that discussion down cold by suggesting that Rob go with Craig the next time he meets with Tom Peers, or that Rob schedule a joint meeting at his convenience. Colette changes the subject at that point.

So, the kettle of family animosity continues to simmer, and it seems like the heat is being turned up monthly. It's a continued stew of questioned motives, second guessing, and lines being drawn. Add in Mom's dysfunctional living situation, Rob's emotional detachment and stress level, the friction between Craig and him, and it doesn't look like a happy ending…for any of us. Is Rob overwhelmed with Mom's situation and resentful of Craig's autonomy? Deep down, I wonder how much of a factor Colette has been in turning Rob away from Craig. And, I remind myself that by being a sister instead of a brother, perhaps I have more built in insulation.

Being a sole sex sibling in a family is probably different than having other siblings of the same sex. Maybe as my brothers have reached adulthood, based on the trajectory of achievement Craig and Rob are both on, there is some form of very subconscious, insidious competition between them, now that they've experienced the standard of living that they have. Life's become a wedge between them, and it doesn't seem like either of them cares enough to reach back to restore their relationship and pull it into the present. Ultimately, they'll have to decide how much they want to fix things between themselves. Other than remaining open and loving to each of them, which is difficult right now, I can't change this situation. Nor can my mother.

It's a beautiful evening as I drive up 71, and then it's both hands on the wheel from the time I merge onto I-75 North until I exit I-74. I pull up in Rob and Col's driveway in the summer dusk, breathe in a deep breath, and exhale slowly.

* * * * *

It's a good four days with Mom, and I'm glad to be back with her. I spend Tuesday night at her place, so she can keep her weekly hair appointment the next day. The house is silent with Rob's family gone, and it's borderline strange not to hear them moving around upstairs. I'm thankful Mom doesn't have to be here by herself. If it were me here alone, it would give me the creeps. I linger in the kitchen, acting like I'm getting a drink, but really checking to make sure all of Mom's burners are shut off. Then I call Craig to let him know I made it safely and that Mom's fine as well.

"Yeah, well, keep a close eye on her, Betsy," he warns me. "She almost fell on our stairs twice while she was here. She doesn't lift her leg up high enough to clear the next step."

Great. Just the warning I need, especially working Thursday and Friday, with Mom home by herself.

Mom and I decide to go to a steakhouse nearby for dinner, and she relays tidbits about her stay at Craig's as we leisurely sip our drinks. She's gone outside the box and ordered a daquiri to keep my margarita company. I can tell it's done her good to spend time with Viv and Emmy. Because Craig and Loire married later, their girls are her youngest grandchildren, and they're sweet, funny girls. Back home, we watch the news in bed, and I sleep like a rock until 8:30 Wednesday morning. A few cups of coffee in me, which Mom prides herself on having ready for me when I get up, and we're off to her beauty shop. In a cold, nonstop rain, we drive back to Louisville after her hair appointment.

"I've got a surprise for you," I tell her on the way home.

"What is it? Do I get to move?" she asks me drolly, cutting her eyes sideways at me from the passenger side of my Jeep.

"Wow, Mom," I respond, wondering where this came from, "we'll revisit that later. But no, it's nothing that big. This involves meeting someone you've never met before."

"Let me think," she tells me, concentrating silently for a few minutes. "Oh…is it Callie's boyfriend Andy? Didn't you tell me they might come to Louisville this weekend?"

I'm shocked she remembers his name. "Good guess, Mom! You'll be the first person in the Bradshaw family to meet him."

Mom smiles happily to herself and reaches up to touch her freshly styled do. "Well, it's a good thing I got my hair done today," she remarks.

It will also be the first time that Mike and I have met

Andy, and I'm excited to see this man I've heard so much about over the past nine months. Callie really likes him. They'll be driving up from Nashville after work on Friday, and since it'll be late when they arrive, we're going to throw hamburgers on the grill and keep it relaxed. There's a part of me that wishes it could be just Mike, Callie, Andy and I for this first of meetings, but the bigger part of me is happy that Mom gets to be a part of this before anyone else in the family, even Kerry. It gives her some much-needed hand.

We stop in LaGrange for lunch on the way home, and it's still pouring. The little restaurant we eat at faces the railroad tracks that run the length of Main Street, and we sit facing a window looking directly out at them. Again, I'm struck by Mom's fascination with the fact that she might see a train go by. Sure enough, 25 minutes into our soup and sandwiches, the distant rumbling of a locomotive starts jiggling silverware and water glasses, and the blinking red railroad crossing lights kick on at the intersection. The gate arms descend to stop oncoming traffic, and I hear Mom say to no one in particular, "Here it comes…oh, my, look at this," and crane her head to peer farther down the track. It's a long train, and I don't realize she's counting the cars until I say something to her, several minutes in, and she responds loudly, without taking her eyes off the train cars, "Thirty-seven, thirty-eight, thirty-nine," and then I get it. Without realizing it, I start laughing.

"Nothing funny," Mom states, still staring straight out the window at the constant passage of the train cars. "Forty-four, forty-five, forty-six," and I know I need to be silent until the train has passed, and a total car count has been obtained. This is serious business. When Mom is in the 80's, our waitress comes over to ask us if we need drink refills, and Mom completely ignores her.

"I think we're good," I answer her, motioning to Mom and making a counting motion on my fingers. The waitress nods in understanding, and grins.

As the caboose passes, Mom sighs, and turns back to

the table. "That was one long train," she says importantly. "One hundred and fourteen cars, counting the caboose. It's amazing that it comes so close to this building."

We bum around several of the shops in LaGrange for a while, then go to pick up my finished print that she helped me select. The frame looks great on it, and Mom is generous with her compliments. We experiment with its placement on various walls when we get home, finally settling on a bare corner wall to the side of our front window.

One thing that does surface over the course of the week is Mom's desire to start looking for alternative living situations, driven in equal parts by her anxiety over her driving test, and her decreasing comfort on the interstate. I'm encouraged by her proactiveness on this front and tell her so.

"And along with that, Bet, I just really feel like I'm in the way over there," she tells me plaintively as we're sitting outside at The Bend on the river towards the end of the week. Mike is having dinner with customers, and it's just the two of us. "I don't want to step on Rob and Colette's toes after being there all these years, and I don't want them to think I'm not grateful, but they have their own lives, too," she tells me. "I'm ready to be on my own, and hopefully get back a little closer to Southwoods."

She's framed it up well, I'm thinking, and her perspective is legitimate. She's unsure about her finances covering it, but I assure her we'll find something, and mention talking to Craig about it as a starting point.

"Bet, let's just keep this between you and me for the time being," she suggests. "I just don't want Rob or Craig trying to give me advice or telling me what they think. I know you understand."

I assure her I'm a vault, and that I'll start making phone calls and getting information. Once we have more to go on, we can talk figures with Craig then. "We'll get you back to your world of Southwoods one way or another," I tell her.

"And once we get a feel for what's out there, I can come up on a day off, or over a weekend, and we can visit some of these places."

I've been waiting for this opportunity for a long time, and finally I have her personal go-ahead.

"I like that idea, Bet, as long as no one else knows we're doing it," she tells me. "If I'm going to move, I want everything decided and ready to go before I say anything to Rob and Colette."

I know the driving issues have pushed Mom to this point of readiness, and probably missing her friends as well, but I wonder if there's more to it. Does she see herself slipping? Are there other things she's noticed in herself that she's chosen not to communicate with me? I know the incident with the eggs boiling dry on the stove really rattled her, especially because Rob was the one that discovered it, and there was no hiding it from him. In being at Mom's, I noticed a couple of good-sized dings on the driver's side of her Accord and wonder about the origin of those. I'm just happy she's the one suggesting alternatives.

Eating on the river must put Mom in a wonderful place, because not only is it the evening she talks about her reasoning for her move, but it's also the night she reminisces at great length about how she and my dad met when they were working at Estes Park in Colorado. I've heard the story before, but never heard Mom tell it with so much detail or animation. She can forget that kettle of eggs yet recreate this story as if it happened yesterday. I listen, spellbound, as the sun slides into the river, and the white party lights lining the outdoor decks blink on. It really is a romantic story-two college kids from random states crossing paths during their summer jobs, ending up marrying one another. It was meant to be.

Mom is telling me how handsome Dad was, saying, "I hadn't even considered dating him that summer, because the word was, he had a steady girlfriend out in California. All of us thought he was such a gentleman. But then, after that group of us climbed Long's Peak, and I got to know him, I really wanted to see him again, and spend time with him. There was just something so special about him."

I'm sitting, chin in hand, leaning in and living this with her. There's a big lump in my throat as she talks. She misses my dad so much-still. That void has been there ever since his death, though she's never complained about missing him or being lonely. It's been so much harder for her than she'd ever acknowledge, even though she has quietly soldiered on without him. It's been almost six years since he died, and for this moment in time, she has him back. Slowly, it's as if God is erasing all the irritation I've felt towards her over the past six weeks. In its place is the realization that she has done the best she can in a challenging situation. My understanding of her is suddenly given a much broader context, and I'm so thankful we've had this evening, just the two of us. Never one to talk at length, having her open her heart up like this touches me deeply, and I feel honored she felt comfortable sharing this with me. Maybe I needed this even more than she did. I hate to see the night end. Reaching over, I squeeze her hand.

"Thanks for a wonderful story," I say. "And, selfishly, I'm so glad your paths crossed when they did. Look what I got out if it."

* * * * *

Friday afternoon my co-workers make me leave first. They know Mom has been staying with us this week, and they want me to get home to her. She's managed the week well, and there've been no mishaps. Callie and Andy aren't due in until 8:30 or 9:00 tonight, so I'm in no rush. Mom keeps me company while I devil the eggs I hardboiled last night and make some broccoli slaw. Once I finish those, I grab some mint from my back-garden bed and mix up some blender mohitos for us. With everything ready, we can enjoy our last evening together out on the deck. We talk for the next full hour until we hear a car pull into the driveway, followed by car doors slamming.

"Back on the deck!" I yell, and Mom struggles to her feet in greeting. Andy and Callie come down the deck walkway to where it widens off the back of our house, and they're both smiling broadly, completely at ease. I sense a very positive energy field between them, and it delights me that Andy hugs Mom right off the starting block. Mom seems perfectly comfortable with it. As a mother, I've always had a mental visual of the type of man Callie would be attracted to. Andy couldn't be farther from my visual, which means nothing, except that he isn't tall and lanky, nor is he light brown or sandy haired. And his voice! Callie is tall for a woman, about 5'11", and Andy is close to that height, with a slight, but solid, build. He moves easily and energetically, and has a big, ready grin. It's borderline impish, like a little kid's. Very dark haired, almost the darkest shade of brown before it passes for black; he wears a Titans baseball cap snugged over it. Big brown eyes, and a deep, resonant bass voice that seems oddly incongruous with the rest of him, it's the voice of a sportscaster or a Shakespearean actor.

Mike emerges from the kitchen with the plate of hamburgers, and there are hugs and handshakes all around. They unpack and rejoin us on the deck, and the conversation starts in earnest. Callie asks Mom about her week, wanting to know about her time at Craig's, and how his girls are. Mom jumps right in. I notice immediately that Andy is very attentive to Mom, even if he's just listening, and I appreciate that.

Callie has a sweet way of sharing tidbits about Mom with Andy, at which point Andy will step up and ask Mom something based on Cal's information-sort of a conversational tag team. This will be Mom's night, I decide. Mike and I will have other time with Andy, but I want her to be front and center tonight. She seems to be enjoying herself immensely. Asking Andy if his grandparents are still living, he tells Mom that his grandfather used to be the police chief for the city of Nashville, launching into some stories about him.

In the meantime, Mike finishes up the burgers, Callie and I bring the food out, and we lay into our late dinner. The night is clear and cool, and I find myself so grateful for this opportunity to all be here. It's rare for all three generations of my family to be together at the same time, and I wish Kerry was with us to share this. Talk continues as we eat, and well beyond, all of us catching up and bouncing from topic to topic. Andy works for Mac, trouble shooting and selling maintenance contracts on their business software and seems to enjoy the position and the people he works with. We ask him about his parents, and he talks about his younger sister, Sydney. Gabbing until close to midnight, I pack it in at this point, especially because I work tomorrow morning. I'll be driving Mom back to Cincinnati in the afternoon. Everybody takes this as their bedtime cue, and we head inside. Mom must be exhausted but seems energized instead. Good night hugs for everyone, and I remind Mom that I'm working tomorrow morning, and won't be here when she gets up.

"But we will, Gramma," Callie assures her. "And I'll fix you whatever you want for breakfast."

I know between Mike, Callie, and Andy, Mom will be in good hands. I fall into bed and am asleep instantly.

* * * * *

The house feels empty when I get home from Highbridge around 1 PM on Saturday. I'm wondering if Mom is out with Mike somewhere.

"Anybody home?" I bellow, because Callie's car is gone, too.

"Bet, is that you?" I hear Mom's voice drift downstairs,

and I can tell she's up in the guestroom. I walk to the stairs, look up, and she's peering down at me over the bannister.

"Well, hey!" I greet her. "You the only one here?"

She nods. "Right now, yes. Callie and Andy slept in and went out for breakfast a little while ago. Mike told me to tell you he had some errands to run…he offered to take me with him, but I thought you'd be wanting to leave for Cincinnati as soon as you got home from work. Isn't that what you told me?" she asks tentatively, obviously worried she might not have understood me correctly.

"Yeah, that's fine, Mom," I reassure her. "We can get on the road whenever you're ready."

Partly, I want to knock out this return stint to Cincy as soon as possible, because it's going to be a five-hour round trip of driving for me, since I'm coming back here tonight. I walk up the rest of the stairs, and uncharacteristically, as I get to the top, Mom reaches out and grabs my arm in *stop-I have to tell you something* gesture.

"What do you think of Andy?" she asks me, dropping her voice to a whisper. I realize she's forgotten that Callie and Andy aren't home right now.

"I like him a lot," I answer, amused by Mom's question. "He seems really comfortable in his own skin."

Mom nods, digesting this. "He's just not at all who I pictured Callie with," she says, but without judgment, and she's smiling. "I do like him, though. He's very talkative and outgoing." She pauses, as if she's debating verbalizing what will follow. "Bet, do you think he ever takes that baseball cap off? He had it on until we all went to bed last night, and then he's had it on ever since I laid eyes on him this morning."

Another short pause. "You don't think he's bald on top, do you?"

Leave it to Mom. She can boil a pan of eggs dry, but she still notices things I don't. I hadn't even thought about the ball cap, but she has a point.

"I don't know, Mom," I muse. "I don't think he's bald… at least Callie hasn't said anything about it, and she would've told me. But good call on the hat situation. I'll check on it when I get home from Cincinnati tonight. I mean, at some point it HAS to come off, right?"

We both start laughing. "I'd hope so," Mom replies. "Maybe you should offer to wash it. But Callie sure seems happy, and that's the most important thing of all," she finishes, almost as if she's afraid she's offended me.

"She does, and I guess time will tell," I answer. I change and pop a couple of ibuprofen…my lower back has really been bothering me lately. I'm not sure if it's how I'm sitting at work, or maybe how I'm sleeping, but it's a relentless throbbing. It feels like sore muscles, but way deep. Sitting in the car and driving for five hours probably isn't going to help, and I hope I can take the edge off before we start driving.

I load Mom's stuff in my Jeep and fix us each a sandwich and grapes. We leave after eating. I hope Rob and Colette aren't too far off their ETA of 6 PM, because I hate leaving Mom by herself any longer than an hour before they get home. I make up my mind to stay with her for at least 30-45 minutes if it's earlier than 4:30 when we get up there. Maybe I can take her to Kroger and help her get some groceries, so she doesn't have to worry about doing it later.

Our ride up is uneventful. She stays awake the whole time, and we talk easily. I find myself wondering if it's hard for her to go from an environment where she has had extensive conversation every day back to a setting where she may go for a long stretch of time having minimal interaction with anyone. I hope the boys and Colette will at least come down and sit with her for a while, so she gets to hear about their vacation. I can't imagine them arriving home and just resuming the normal pattern of their lives without at least checking in. Hopefully, too, they'll ask her about her week away. I wonder if Colette is noticing Mom's increasing isolation from Southwoods, her friends, and life in general.

I'm just not sure how to bring it up with her without it sounding accusatory, unless I focus on Mom's driving issues. Eventually, I'll figure out a way. When we reach Cincinnati, it's a little before 4:00, and I ask Mom if she'd like to run to Kroger to pick up any odds and ends she might need.

"Let's do it now while I'm with you," I suggest. "It'll take half the time with me there to help you."

Surprisingly, there's no argument from her, and we get milk, orange juice, bread, eggs, and Spaghettio's. She's a sucker for those. *Yikes, they involve burners, unless she microwaves them.* By the time we get back to Rob's and unload the groceries and her luggage, it's past 5:00, and I feel like I'm in the safe zone of time to be able to leave Mom on her own. I think she'll be fine until they get home. Giving her a big hug, I tear up a little.

"I'm going to miss you, Happy Hour companion," I say. "I'm so glad you got to be with us, and especially to see Callie and meet Andy. It was a special week for me." I hug her a second time. "I love you."

"And I love you, Bet," she hugs me back. "Tell Callie and Andy how good it was to see them and to meet Andy," she replies. "Last night was such a fun evening. Let me know if the hat comes off."

I ask her to call me once Rob and Colette get home, under the guise of my wanting to know they made it safely home from vacation. (My real agenda is knowing Mom isn't alone.) She commits with, "I will if I remember."

Now, the return segment of my journey. My heart is grateful that in the past two months, Mom has been able to see both of my daughters and meet the man in Callie's life. I can tell how comfortable she is in being with my family, and I hope we are a refuge of love and appreciation for her. Now begins my search for a new life for Joan Bradshaw. I'm going to call it *Joan On Her Own*.

Chapter Three

GETTING CLEARANCE
(August 2009)

I hate the month of August. Always have. The reasons for my loathing are several; the first involving heat and humidity. I'm always over summer by this point, and I long for the brittle cold of January. I should be grateful for the cooler than usual July we've had-our median temperature was only 79 degrees, which is very acceptable, with not one crack into the 90's, but right now, heat is heat. Labor Day beckons with its segue into September, but each day between is a sweaty cesspool of eternity.

Secondly, it's the month where I traditionally relinquish Cal and Kerry "back into the world" after having them home with me all summer. Granted, over the course of 23 years there have been summer camps, trips with friends, choir tours, and numerous summer jobs ranging from babysitting to Kroger's checkout, but the onset of school, which seemed to come earlier and earlier in August with each passing year, always reminded me that the train was pulling out of the station for real. It meant that each of my girls was officially a 'grade' older, with the physical, emotional, and social growth that came with it. I always felt like I lost something at the end of each summer, never to be re-found. To me, summer was less accountability and a time to just lay back and catch my breath.

Then there was always my professional preparation for the coming school year-the in-service days, the planning, getting my room ready, and all the kick-off events that went with the year's beginning. These included 'Meet the Parents' night, open houses, and it meant I was completely "on" again after being relatively detached for two months. School supplies, new clothes for the girls, the cutting edge-of-technology math calculator, and course books all ran together with dance team fees, PTA memberships, and the deluge of forms that needed completion. I viewed all this as reluctant compliance.

Now that I've left the field of education, there's been a radical change in my mental calendar of the year. As both a teacher and parent, my 'real' year's calendar ran from August to July, with each new year beginning not in January, but in August. This August is the first ever that hasn't felt that way to me, both because this is the first summer Kerry hasn't come home, but opted to stay in Lexington to work there, and because at Eastbridge, my pediatric practice, there is no real delineation to the year. It's pretty much business as usual no matter what. No more stops and starts of the school year to divide it into neat segments. Regardless, my dislike of August remains. Unfair, I know. People talk about being depressed in the winter? I struggle more with it in August than in any other month of the year.

This first day of August, (which happens to be a Saturday) I am trying my best to stay the course by being grounded and productive. I've spent the morning on our back deck, admiring my zinnias in full bloom along the deck walkway, and reading David Halberstam's 'The Best And The Brightest'-some of the best historical writing I've read to date. His narrative is well-developed and rich with detail, and I can't put it down. I'm eternally grateful to the stranger who, spotting me perusing the American History section at Barnes and Noble, was bold enough to ask me what I liked to read. At the time, I had answered honestly that I was an eclectic reader who would read just about anything, provided it was well-written. At that point, sensing I'd be open to his suggestion, he had pulled the Halberstam book on the Vietnam War.

Having been only five when JFK began sending troops over, and a junior in high school when Nixon drastically de-escalated the war prior to his impeachment, my growing up years closely paralleled the years of U.S. military involvement, but I remember very little about the true character of the war. At the time, it was something going on far away that didn't involve me. Both Mom and Dad were avid news watchers and newspaper readers, so I had plenty of exposure to the situational jargon of the war-the various battles and the geographic locations were familiar to me, as were the names of the key military and political figures-McNamara, Westmoreland, Bradley, and of course LBJ…but it was the analysis I lacked, and the political cause/effect that had shaped our involvement as a country.

Dad, having fought in World War II as a 20-year old, saw serving in Vietnam as a non-negotiable issue of patriotism, and had had very little tolerance for the draft dodgers and the anti-Vietnam protests of the 1960's. And, I'm sure the Cold War influenced his feelings as well-after all, he had fought to secure the freedom of democracy, and Vietnam was a fight over the expansion of communism…but that's about where my understanding tapped out. Halberstam, this hot August morning, is taking me places I haven't been before. So intense is my concentration that I am actually using a highlighter to underline main ideas and key facts. Pretty impressive, this nerdiness of mine. This is history at its best, and I wish I could have had a history teacher like David Halberstam. I read until I cannot process another detail and realize two hours has slipped by. I've covered close to 100 pages. Not bad.

Shifting gears, I journal for a while-these two activities are usually my go-to's on a deck morning, and if I can do both, I feel much better about life. This will be a different weekend format, since I was solo last night and will be all today, with Mike up in Cleveland at the Indians game. He, Eric Day (Mike's sales manager) and two of their customers were lucky enough to score tickets, so they flew up last night for the game, and won't be back until this evening. I've immersed myself in solitude since I got home from work last night, due in large part to the fact that it's the first weekend I've had in well over a month where I have no plans. I love it when my time is my own. We're going to the Moody Blues concert at the end of August, and there's a retirement party for one of our longtime nurse practitioners at Highbridge coming up, but that should be about the extent of my social calendar for the month.

What I really want to do, per my talk with Mom in July when she was here, is to start looking into some type of senior living for her that could put her closer to home-somewhere that will give her more and easier access to 'her world' and freeing up Rob and Colette. This is long overdue. I'm just not sure how far Mom's finances will carry her. Craig isn't sure about her having enough to place her in one of the nicer living options Beecher offers, but I'm not sure of the exact figures on that front. I know I need to look 'on the downlow', and to keep it strictly between Mom, Mike and me for the time being.

I sweat through a five mile walk in the early afternoon and have just taken a bath and dressed when the phone rings. It's Colette. *Perfect time for her to call*, I'm thinking. I have no plans, there's nothing to rush me, and I'm eager to catch up. I sit down cross-legged on our bedroom floor and scootch up to lean against the bed. Col and I don't have a lot of phone conversations, but I always enjoy talking to her. I know she's in the thick of it with my nephews, given all of their activities.

"Well, hey!" I greet her. "Are you counting it down to

school yet?"

Colette laughs, her quiet, throaty chuckle. "There's still too many days left-I'm ready for them to be back in now. Having them home while I'm working is more stressful than I signed up for."

We talk awhile, comparing notes on our summers, and how our vacations were, especially since they just got back from Myrtle Beach a week ago, and then Col says, "Betsy, my real reason for calling is that I wanted to talk to you about your Mom," and pauses.

I think I already know where this is heading, and I'm prepared-and, I have to admit, oddly excited, because if this is about what I think it is, it will pave the way for Mom to make her move with zero conflict. This races through my mind as I say, "Sure-what's going on?"

"Your mom is really slipping recently," she begins. "You probably noticed it too, based on your time with her this summer."

"I have noticed it, Col," I affirm, "but I guarantee you see it more frequently because you're exposed to it daily."

"Definitely," she concurs. "But I think she's reached a point where she needs much closer supervision, and I worry about her being here alone while Rob and I are at work. She seems like she's depressed, Betsy. She doesn't go out much anymore, and I feel like she's stopped getting together with her friends. I think she needs more socialization and mental stimulation than we give her...she's alone so much of the time. I feel like she needs to be around people her own age, and to be involved in activities to keep her mind challenged."

I literally want to throw the phone up in the air for joy-here, finally, is my answer to prayer after all these years of thinking that we're out of options. In tandem, another part of me wants to scream, 'Really? You think? You're just now noticing this? We should have had this conversation five years ago!'

How sad, I think, that it's taken Col and Rob this long

to even consider the fact that Mom living in the lower level of their house, 40 minutes of interstate driving from the heart of her social sphere, isn't "quite" working out. It makes me angry, is what it does. But I need to put my emotions back in the box for now, and let this situation work for all of us. Col needs an ally, I can already sense, and I will be one formidable ally.

"I couldn't agree more," I answer without hesitation. "Her driving is becoming more and more of an issue, too, Col, and I think she's getting skittish about being on the interstate-she doesn't trust her vision, and so she's not making the effort to connect with her friends anymore."

I don't know how I could make it any plainer. I'd be depressed, too, if I was afraid to drive, and knew I wasn't able to spend time with people I enjoyed being with. This conversation will also be the opportunity I've longed for to take the gloves off and air some of my concerns-both to bolster the case of Mom moving to a retirement community, but also because I'm Mom's advocate in this, and I want to make sure Col knows exactly how I feel, and what my perspective on her deterioration is.

"And," I continue, "plain and simple, Col, you and Rob need your lives back."

There. I've said it. I've never verbalized this before, mainly because I never thought their cutting Mom loose was something they would consider, and I didn't want to put them on the defensive. But, with the door opened, I'm running through it at warp speed. I'm grateful to Rob and Col, no doubt about it. Mom and Dad had moved in with them in the late spring of 2002; dad died roughly 18 months later in November of 2003, and Mom's been there ever since-roughly eight years. That's a long time to have one, or both, of your parents living with you, especially as you are raising your own family and working full time.

Granted, Rob and Col had built-in babysitters in Mom and Dad-they never had to worry about daycare or after-school care; all my parents did was walk upstairs. They drove them to school if Rob and Col had to be at work early, waited in carpool lines, got my nephews off the school bus, and even drove James and Jack on their paper routes in middle school. Mom and Dad loved being a part of their lives, and it was a win/win all the way around.

But, over time, as the boys grew, and after Dad passed, it was no longer the perfect fit it had seemed to be at the beginning. Mom saw less and less of the boys as their schedules became more and more social, and now she was completely alone for long stretches of time with the boys in school and Rob and Col working full time. I know Col truly does the best she can, and she's been very good to my mom. Over the years she's included her in family gatherings with her own family; inviting Mom up for dinner when they were all home on Sundays and bringing her down leftovers so Mom wouldn't have to cook herself. But, on practically every front, the plan has outlived its usefulness.

Dad's original premise of Mom always being 'surrounded by quality medical care' didn't quite pan out the way he'd envisioned it, partly because Mom was in the lower level of Rob and Col's home for eight to ten hours of every day, 40 minutes from any social contact. Add into the equation that Mom is one of the least socially outgoing people I know, so the odds of her establishing friendships on that side of town were 'Slim to none, and Slim left town', one of Craig's favorite sayings.

Another sad factor is that, as time has gone on, Rob very seldom comes downstairs to talk to Mom when he's at home-it's as if she doesn't even live there. When I'm there visiting, and Rob comes down to talk to me, Mom's comment is, "I only see him when you're here-I can go weeks without laying eyes on him."

I know she's not exaggerating, and this is unfathomable to me. I'm not talking hours of dialogue on Rob's part, but just running downstairs for a brief five to 10-minute chat to check in or taking a beer down and hanging out while you drink the beer and catch up, or even just poking your head down the stairs with a simple "Hi, Mom! Need anything?" But if anyone does that, it's Col, not Rob, and he seems to have grown increasingly detached and remote. Does he resent Mom being there? Probably a little, I'm thinking. Or, does he think, *Well, this is great, we're stuck with her now until she dies?* But again, all Rob needed to do was pick up the phone and talk to Craig or me about it… did he feel like he couldn't do that because it had been his idea in the first place to have my parents move in with him?

I can't possibly know any of his thought processes, and because Col and he had made the initial decision to have Mom and Dad move in without consulting any of us, I didn't feel like it was my place to ask leading questions about whether they were feeling like Mom had 'overstayed her visit.' And then, too, since Mom and Dad had paid a significant sum to Rob and Col to have their lower level living quarters finished, maybe Rob felt that there was no way he could suggest to Mom that she needed to give that up. (That payment to Rob had been Dad's idea-he couldn't bear the thought of them 'freeloading'. He actually tape-recorded the conversation with Rob agreeing to it should there be any future discussion-Craig had filled me in on this after it had taken place. Oh, the secrecy.)

I just know that the whole situation has become a tangled web for Mom, and, undoubtedly, for Rob and Col, too. It was a great idea for a minute that no one had considered the long-term ramifications to, and it turned out to be the worst possible living option for Mom. Of course, this is my take on it, but I think deep down Craig shares many of those feelings with me, though perhaps not to the degree that I do. The sooner we can get Mom out of here, the better. She may have a chance at a whole new beginning, and I want to make that happen.

"You've been so good to her, Col, for so many years," I tell her, and I mean every word of it. "You'll never know how much that means to me. But yes, I'm in complete agreement on the increased supervision and the socialization needs." I pause. "How does Rob feel about it?"

"I haven't mentioned any of this to him yet," Col confesses. "You know how he is."

This momentarily stuns me. Is Col worried that he'll disagree with her? Or, is this idea really coming just from her, because SHE wants Mom gone, while Rob's oblivious to Mom's deterioration? Nothing would surprise me, based on their total lack of communication. Maybe Col just needs me to spearhead it with Rob so it doesn't look like it's solely her idea? Whatever is driving her motives, I'm all in, and I'm thinking quickly.

"Why don't I bring it up to Rob?" I suggest. "I can call him, and I'll base my discussion on the amount of deterioration I've noticed between when she was with us Memorial Day weekend and the days at the end of July when you were on vacay. Then, it's a more objective observation, and maybe he'll feel freer to talk about it with me."

"I like that idea, Betsy, and I'd rather him hear it from you than me," is her reply.

For as outspoken as Colette usually is, this whole situation is surprising to me, but I'm willing to make it as easy as I can on her. Plus, as I dwell on it, this is Rob's mother and MY mother, not hers, and maybe that's part of her thought process. If Col doesn't want to look like the bad daughter-in-law, I'm happy to be the agent of change. We talk for a while longer, Col citing some specific examples of things she's noticed with mom that reinforce her feelings on Mom's cognitive deterioration. One is particularly chilling and involves a recent early morning when Colette heard their security alarm going off. They had purchased a security system back when the boys were babies, because Rob spent so many nights on call at the hospital, and Col was by herself with the kids. The beeping woke her, and she went racing down the stairs in her PJ's to find Mom on the landing, fully dressed, purse on her arm, randomly punching in numbers to try to get the alarm to shut off.

"Bet, when she turned to look at me, it was like she didn't even know who I was. She just had this wild look in her eyes, and I said, as calmly as I could, 'Joan, where are you going?' It's only 5:30 in the morning.' "

I realize I'm holding my breath.

Col continues, "She told me she had a doctor's appointment, and she was going to be late if she didn't get going. I tried reasoning with her and told her that maybe she just looked at her clock wrong-that it was way too early for any doctor to schedule an appointment. I told her I'd come down and check her calendar to see if we could figure out what time it really was."

"Was there even a legitimate appointment?" I feel compelled to ask. This is something far beyond what I've witnessed as just general forgetfulness-this sounds more like dementia.

"Not that I could find on her calendar," Col reports, "or on any appointment cards she had."

"Wow," I breathe. "Did she have a specific doctor's name?" I pursue, wondering about that angle of it.

"She said it was for a mammogram, but that was about it," Col tells me. "But Bet, I was really concerned about leaving her by herself after that-she was so agitated. The thing that saved us was her not being able to remember the security code. If she had walked out of here without us knowing, I'm not sure what would have happened."

This does ascribe a much higher level of urgency to our mission, and I also find myself thinking that for this one event Col happened to witness (Rob had been on call at Holy Disciple that night, so he failed to see it firsthand), there have probably been plenty of others that have occurred without anyone being the wiser, simply because they occurred when Mom was alone. Between her boiling the eggs dry, and this disturbing faux appointment, I can connect the dots on why Col feels it's time.

"Tell you what-I'll try to call Rob sometime this coming

week, or definitely next weekend, and we'll start moving on this. Do you honestly see him putting up a fight?" I ask, speculatively.

She hesitates. "Honestly, Bet, as little time as he spends with your Mom, I can't imagine why he would care," she answers, with an edge to her voice. "He pretty much ignores her, and I don't understand it. She's not going to be around forever, and I constantly tell him to go down and talk to her, or at least check on her. I thought maybe once your dad was gone, it might reinforce to your brother how important that remaining time is with her, but I don't think it's had any impact on him at all."

"I wouldn't have expected that either," I respond slowly, "but I'm not so sure I know Rob very well anymore."

We hang up after discussing a few more things relating to Mom, and I hope Col feels like a burden has been lifted. I want this accomplished as quickly and expediently as possible. Craig will also need to be brought into the loop, but I'm already feeling like that part of it will need to come from Colette…he needs to hear it directly 'from the horse's mouth.' I don't want to be in the middle on this. I've spent my entire life living in the middle, and I'm really trying to step away from that role in my family. Col and Craig are both adults, and I don't need to be the go-between. At some point, all of us will need to sit down together to work this through, but for starters, we need clearance from Rob, and if that's a battle Col needs help with, I'm happy to step up. I've been waiting for this opportunity for the past six years.

I pray a silent prayer asking God to bless our path forward, and for all of us to be able to reach a consensus.

* * * * *

Two weeks following my conversation with Col, my godmother, Aunt Frances, dies in Chicago. She and Uncle

Philip, my mom's younger brother by four years, were my favorite aunt and uncle growing up, and even though we didn't see a lot of them, my bond with them was strong. They were a couple that enjoyed one another immensely and were a lot of fun to be around. Aunt Frances was funny, easy going, and a great listener, and someone I wanted to emulate when I grew up.

We stayed in close touch over the years, well into my adulthood, and when I was in my late 30's she had been diagnosed with breast cancer. She was one of the fortunate ones who experienced a long remission of about a decade before it crept back, and she put up a good fight for five years, doing both chemo and radiation. Finally, she spiraled down into a brief period with Hospice, at which point Craig, Mom and I had been in touch with both of her boys, Randal and Peter, keeping us updated. After four days in Hospice care, Randal called to let us know she had died. My heart goes out to them at 38 and 40 with both of their parents gone. This will also be a heavy hit for Mom. Aunt Frances was the only remaining person she had on her side of a much smaller family than my dad's.

Immediately I start thinking about trying to make it up to Chicago for her funeral. I really want to be there, out of love and respect for both her and my cousins. Mom and Craig will be going up-Craig is returning from a business trip through Cincinnati, and he'll pick up Mom and they'll fly from there. Rob and Col are planning on going as well but driving instead of flying...probably leaving around 3 AM and driving straight through to Chicago for the Tuesday morning service, bringing Mom back home with them. There's my ride as well.

We make our plans, and after working Monday, I head on up to Cincy, gear in my Jeep. Marcy and LaDonna are nice enough to let me leave very early, so I beat most of the rush hour traffic over the bridge, and by 6 PM, I'm in Col's kitchen helping her get dinner ready. Rob's at the hospital, so it's just Col, the boys, and myself. It's very different to be at their place without Mom there too. Usually I feel like I'm dividing my time between Mom and Col when I visit, and this is oddly freeing to be with just Colette. We revisit our discussion about Mom-I've tried calling Rob twice and leaving voice messages, but he hasn't returned either of my calls. ("I'm not surprised," is Col's comment), so we decide that our road trip will be the perfect time for face to face dialogue with him about Mom's future.

We do the dishes together, sit and have a glass of wine, and then it's to bed-we're planning on pulling out around 3 AM to make Chicago by 8 AM. I curl up downstairs in Mom's bed-it's dark, quiet, and oddly disconcerting not to have my bunk buddy there beside me. I get up around 2 AM, groggy and disoriented, and shower, then dry my hair. I can hear someone moving around upstairs, and the heavier footfalls sound like Rob. I guess he got home after I fell asleep. Throwing what I'll need for the funeral service itself in a smaller tote bag, I head upstairs to Rob coming in from the garage, loading up the van.

"Have you had any sleep?" I ask, giving him a hug.

He looks wan and exhausted. "I napped for a few hours," he answers, somewhat tersely.

Col comes downstairs with her stuff, we load up, and are on our way. Col's mom Albi is on her way over to spend the rest of the night and get the boys up and to school. I climb into the middle seat of the van with my pillow and blanket from Mom's couch, noting that it's 3:03 per the clock in their van. I'm dying to go back to sleep.

"It would have saved time if you had done this earlier," I hear Rob say to Col in the darkness of the front seat, pulling into a Gas N' Go and getting out at the pump. I've not witnessed enough recent interaction between them to know where this will go, but I'm totally unprepared for Col's retort.

"I do it all the time, asshole. You can plan ahead for once in your life."

Ouch. Very awkward. I say nothing from my cocoon in the back seat, thankful for the dark.

Neither does Rob. He begins filling the tank, and when he finishes, walks toward the Gas N' Go building.

"Wouldn't you think he'd ask us if we needed anything if he's going in to get himself something?" Col spits out, as if she can't contain herself any longer.

I'm feeling some real bona fide anger smoldering here, and I have the distinct feeling this is not a recent development. To avoid furthering a situation that, in my opinion, has already gone far enough south, I say to Col, "What do we want? I'll go in and get us something."

All I really want to do is to flop my head back down on my pillow and sleep for the next five hours until we pull up in front of the church, but I guess Col's anger needs to be diffused first.

"I'll come in with you," she replies, and hops out of the passenger's side, slamming the van door hard. As I slide out of the back, she looks at me and says, "Damn him. I am SO tired of him thinking only about himself. For once, could he think about someone else? How much does it take for him to ask if you or I need anything while he's going in?"

At this point, Rob is coming out the door of the Gas N' Go with a drink in his hand and a bag of pretzels. He spots us, and as we draw parallel to him, Col says acidly, "Don't bother to ask us if we need anything."

I can barely even look at Rob; more out of choosing not to see the expression on his face than any embarrassment on my part. When I do see it, out of the corner of my eye, it's a look of almost zero affect, as if Col's comment evaporated as soon as it came out of her mouth, and Rob never even processed it. We grab waters and a bag of cheese popcorn, return to the van, and the trip gets under way without any further harsh words. After a few swigs of water, I nestle down again, double the pillow, pull the blanket over me, and am asleep in minutes. I doze through the night, shifting uncomfortably when my lower back and knees get stiff, but grateful I'm laying down. Col must at least be resting, because she's silent as well.

Gradually the darkness turns to the charcoal of pre-dawn, the grey thinning and the sound of traffic thickening as we pass through Gary, Indiana and hit the outskirts of the Chicago burbs. I sit up and stretch around 7:10, thinking I'd better be on deck and awake from here on out.

"Are we there yet, Dad?" I ask, in a high pitched, whiny voice, and I see a slight smile pull Rob's tightly drawn mouth in the rearview mirror. That's a rare sight these days, and it brings me a disproportionate surge of delight.

"Closing in," Rob answers me. "This is where traffic starts getting crazy."

We continue to crawl through suburban rush hour traffic for the next 30 minutes, then Col and I start discussing the necessity of breakfast.

"Let me get closer to the church, and we'll find somewhere to eat," Rob directs, and about 20 minutes later, in the general area of where we need to be, we find an IHOP. I scramble out of the car like a happy six-year old. We made it through the dark night; we're in Chicago, and hopefully Rob and Col will be nicer to each other for the rest of the trip; or at least now that it's a new day.

A strung-out looking hostess seats us, we order coffee all around for starters, and Rob slides out of the booth to use the restroom. I look across the table to Col.

"This will probably be our best chance to talk to Rob," I tell her. "Especially because Mom will be with us when we're driving back. Whaddya think?"

"Go for it, Bet," Col says in blessing, and smiles wryly.

We order our meals, and my blueberry pancakes are delightful. Intentionally waiting until Rob has about half of his meal consumed, I ease my way into my mission by way of a "Hey, I need to pick your brain."

Hopefully Rob feels non-threatened by this innocuity.

"Col and I have had a number of conversations recently about how much we feel like Mom's slipping. She told me about the morning Mom was up and fully dressed at 5:30, trying to remember what the security code on your alarm was so she could go to her imaginary medical appointment..."

I pause and look at Rob. He's just staring blankly into space, either processing or just waiting for me to finish, so I go on, steeling myself not to feel like an ad exec making a pitch.

"I know she's more and more reluctant to drive," I remark, determined to share things Mom has shared with me that Rob probably isn't aware of, "because she doesn't trust her peripheral vision anymore, and I think she's much less apt to make plans with any of her Southwoods friends for that reason. She's spending a lot more time alone, and Col and I have been thinking it may be time to get her into an environment where there's more supervision and structure...somewhere where there's more of an opportunity for her to be with people her own age, and to have more socialization." I pause, then continue, "You guys have done so much for her over the years, but I think she may need more than you can provide her with now. Your family deserves your time back, and Mom needs an environment to provide tighter boundaries and more stimulation. Col and I feel like it's time to start looking for a retirement community where she'd have access to all of that, with a potential for assisted living down the road."

The last part about the 'potential for assisted living' isn't something Col and I have remotely discussed, but I throw it in because I know Beecher has this option, and, common sense prevailing, Mom is probably going to need it at some point. "What are your thoughts about this?"

Rob shifts slightly in the booth, and I read it as discomfort. His eyes flick up at me and hold mine for a brief second, then he shrugs, passes his hand over the lower half of his face, and says, void of any emotion, "Whatever's best for Mom."

'Way to have an opinion', I think to myself, and this total non-response irritates me.

"Do you feel like she'd benefit from an environment like that?" I ask, deliberately narrowing the range of possible answers. I feel like I'm making this easier for a child.

"It's probably time," he asserts, which, for Rob, appears to be an emphatic 'Absolutely.' If this is what Col is dealing with 24/7, I can see why she's angry with him so much of the time.

"Well, we can start looking," I hear myself say, "and I think there will be a lot of options." I can't resist throwing in, "I'd love to see her get back a little closer to Southwoods," and leave it hanging.

Col looks relieved; Rob looks emotionless, and I am inwardly jubilant. CLEARANCE GRANTED.

Aunt Frances' church has that timeless patina of close dimness, otherworldliness, and the aroma of incense that causes you to lower your voice as soon as you enter its vaulted narthex. I don't think I was ever in this sanctuary growing up, but this was Uncle Philip and Aunt Frances' parish church. As part of their parochial education, it was also the church Randal and Peter had chapel in each week. I wonder if my cousins still worship here on a regular basis. Something in me doubts it. Dust motes dance in the sunlight streaming through several of the stained-glass windows towards the front of the sanctuary, and there's a palpable sense of neglect, as if the building itself knows its parishioners have turned their backs on it and moved on to other denominations where God can be found without Latin intercession. Yet, this was where Aunt Frances found her strength to keep on fighting, and it makes me sad that others haven't been able to find that. Being here evokes a deep nostalgia in me, and a longing for what was that I can never have back-that bygone era of childhood, and to be surrounded by Uncle Philip, Aunt Frances, and my Gram-to feel blanketed with the richness and love of family, instead of having to relinquish yet another loved one back to God.

Craig and Mom are already here, sitting in one of the back pews of the sanctuary, and they crane their necks as we enter. Craig helps Mom up, and they make their way out into the narthex to greet us. Mom looks game, but somewhat dazed, although she has on a nice pantsuit and her hair is freshly done. This will be hard for her, I think. Craig looks serious, but he reaches out to all of us, going first to Rob to shake his hand, which is a true act of generosity, based on the treatment Rob usually gives him. In turn he greets Col and gives me a hug. I find myself very thankful that Mom was able to fly up with him, versus enduring the van ride, Col and Rob's verbal exchanges notwithstanding.

Colette and I find a teeny bathroom off the narthex, where we take turns changing. I throw on some eyeliner and mascara, banging my left elbow hard on the ceramic tile of the wall because the room isn't wide enough to accommodate my arm span. Once in our church garb, we step outside to try to catch some air-it's sweltering inside the building, and I can feel a sheen of sweat breaking out on my face, arms, and snaking down my chest into my bra. We move under a couple of old cottonwood trees, helping Mom over the uneven ground, and find a slight cooling breeze. We're standing there savoring it, when we see Rob making his way up the street towards us with a bottle of water in his hand. (In spite of myself, I note that he got water only for himself.)

"Where've you been?" I ask, since no one else speaks.

"I took a drive, to see if I could find Uncle Philip and Aunt Frances' old building-it's just three blocks from here, so I walked back to it just to look around. Nothing has changed," he remarks.

I'm frankly surprised that Rob would do this on his own, or even have the desire to do it, but, oddly, this is one of those rare moments when I see glimmers of the Rob I used to know. There's light in his eyes, and I can tell that making this sojourn to see Aunt Frances' building was important to him. Over the years, I've tended to forget how sensitive Rob was as a little boy. Small objects were of great importance to him; he thought deeply about things and cried easily, in a way that none of the other three of us did. In many respects, Rob and I were more alike as children than either Craig or Donny, and I always knew we 'felt' things the same way. I realize that being here for this funeral is important to Rob for many of the same reasons I needed to be here-because we loved my Mom's family so much, and to have that last chance to say goodbye.

I look at Rob and smile. "Lots of good memories," I say.

To our right, another group of people are coming down the sidewalk, having parked farther down the street, and Craig says quietly, "That's Peter."

We move out from under the cottonwoods and Craig steps onto the sidewalk to acknowledge him, shaking his hand and putting his arm around Pete's shoulder. Peter slowly looks around, and his eyes pool with tears as he realizes that not just Craig is here, but Mom, Rob, Col, and me. He openly starts to weep and steps over to hug Mom, who immediately starts to cry as well.

"I can't believe you're all here," he chokes out, and Mom embraces him, patting him gingerly on his broad back.

"Of course, we're all here," she says comfortingly. We surround him, there are hugs all around, and he introduces us to his wife and three children, whom we've never met.

"Randal should be here any time," he tells us, looking up the street as if to spot him coming.

As we talk, the hearse pulls up, and Peter excuses himself to help direct them into the church. It saddens me to see him leading them up the steps with Aunt Frances' casket, and I hope Randal gets here soon so he's not all alone. We linger outside a few more minutes, then venture back into the church. People are starting to arrive now, and I'm looking for any of Aunt Frances' three brothers. We fall into the line filing by her casket to pay our respects. I haven't seen her for a long time, and the ravages of the cancer are wickedly apparent. Still, that face is beautiful to me, and so are my memories.

I witness a priceless moment when Mom, in front of me in line, gently leans down and kisses Aunt Frances on the forehead, and then, placing her hands on the top of Aunt Frances' folded hands, says quietly, as if there is no one else around, "Oh, my dear, dear Frances. We had so many good years together. You've struggled for such a long time, and now you're at peace with Philip and Bill. I'm going to miss you."

That's a lot for Mom, who is usually very self-restrained, and I know she means every word of it. We move quietly toward the front of the church, filing into a long pew where all of us sit, and we wait for the service to begin. Peter makes his way down the center aisle to us, leaning in towards me.

"Aunt Betsy," he asks hesitantly, "can I ask you to do something for our family? Would you be willing to offer the final prayer for my mom after all the other prayer concerns have been named? It doesn't have to be anything fancy… she would just like it if she knew you were the one doing it."

I tell Peter I'm happy to do it, and quietly begin composing a simple prayer that reflects the influence she has had on my life, and the joy she radiated. Randal has arrived; more hugs and emotion, but he's alone. His six-year old son Benson isn't with him, nor is his ex-wife, who apparently has chosen not to attend the service. Bad choice, I'm thinking. Randal doesn't look good. He's pale, gaunt, and his teeth, which used to be beautiful, are a sickly yellowish color. I wonder if this is in part the toll of having taken care of Aunt Frances round the clock.

By now the sweat is pouring freely down our faces, and it's obvious there is to be no air-conditioning turned on. Craig stands up and brushes by me in the pew, muttering, "I'm going to go get some water for all of us, since Rob couldn't be bothered…Mom's going to pass out in this damn heat."

He's back about 10 minutes later with a six pack of water, passing it down the pew. It does help. The lay person assisting with the service comes over and walks me through when to head up to the lectern to deliver my prayer, and a few minutes later, the service begins without much pomp. There are maybe 60 people in the entire sanctuary, and we are swallowed up in its vastness. It's a very rote, clinical service, and neither Randal nor Peter speaks, which bothers me, although I know it's not everyone's forte. The priest talks about Aunt Frances, but I find myself wondering if he even knew her personally, or if this is just secondhand information.

Then it's time for the prayers. I rise, and quietly make my way to the podium, stepping up to it and adjusting the microphone to my height. I offer the prayer from my heart, in what Cal and Kerry call my 'public speaking voice', thanking God for the joy Aunt Frances brought me as her niece, as well as to our entire family. I reference the gifts she had of making those around her feel special and treasured; for her interest in my life that mirrors Christ's interest in our lives, and for the blessing of having a role model who loved and listened the way she had. It flows out, as it always does when it's from my heart, and I lift Randal and Peter up for comfort in the loss of their mother, and someone who means so much to us. I conclude simply, thanking God for the example of her life, and for the strength of her faith. As I return to the pew to sit, Craig reaches over and puts his arm around my shoulder, leaning into me and whispering, "That was beautiful, Bet."

The service ends, the casket is carried back down the aisle by Randal, Peter, Aunt Frances' three brothers, and another man I don't know, and returned to the hearse to be taken to the cemetery. The meager procession there is arranged, and we join the line of flagged vehicles, planning to leave there directly to drive back to Cincinnati. At the cemetery, I seek out Randal and stand next to him. He seems so alienated from everyone else; even Peter. I had so much fun with him growing up, especially one summer when my

Gram and I had come to Chicago for a week-long visit when Randal was three and I was 15. He was so intelligent-so bright and animated as a little kid, and like Aunt Frances, so full of life…I had loved watching him grow up. Sadly, I don't see any of that little boy today; only a 40-year-old man who seems beaten down, older than his years, and, who, when I clasp his hand for the final graveside prayers, is noticeably shaking. I write this off to nerves and grief, yet deep down wonder if there is more to it than that. We leave shortly after that, hugging Randal and Peter goodbye, and exchanging farewells with Peter's wife and children. I wonder if we'll ever see these men again now that Aunt Frances isn't here to perpetuate that connection.

Craig carries Mom's luggage over to Rob and Col's van, and I help Mom get settled and seat-belted, hug Craig goodbye, and he leans in to give Mom a parting kiss. Few words are exchanged between Craig and Rob, but I do see them shake hands, and I wonder which one of them initiated it. My money's on Craig. Immediately out of the gate of the cemetery the tone for the ride is set when Rob turns left onto the main route, and Col reprimands him, "You should have let that car pass before you pulled out-that was way too close."

Mom and I had been talking about the service, and neither of us had noticed, but our conversation stops abruptly when we hear Rob respond, "If you make one more damn comment about my driving, I swear to you I will pull this van over and you will drive the whole goddamn way back to Cincinnati!"

Mom looks like she's been electrocuted-there's no doubt she heard this. Her expression freezes, almost in fear, and I wince inwardly. Without even thinking, my kneejerk reaction to divert the attention from the anger/profanity is, "Hey, do you want a backseat driver, too?"

I'm not sure why this even came out, or what my intent was, but Rob looks back at me in the rearview mirror and, miraculously, instead of blowing up, says, as if garnering support, "I get so sick of this. She does this all the time, and she thinks I'm not paying attention to the other drivers."

"Usually you're not," Colette states acidly.

I attempt lightheartedness, hoping that, like many other things, Mom will immediately forget this exchange happened.

"Sounds familiar," I assent. "That's Mike and me when we ride together," even as I'm in total disbelief that Rob would talk this way...both to Col, and with Mom in the car.

The entire ride home is tense-all five hours of it. Rob and Col continue to go back and forth, with Col criticizing him for tailgating the semis too closely, passing vehicles when it wasn't necessary, ("There's the truck you passed 10 minutes ago passing you now") and overall sloppy driving, him responding in irritation and with occasional profanity. I try to keep Mom as occupied with conversation as I can, and she dozes off for more than an hour, during which time I pretend to be asleep too. I just don't possess the energy to make conversation or try to diffuse this.

Our arrival at Rob and Col's is incredibly welcome-at least now Mom and I can escape downstairs to her abode. Not having witnessed the two of them interacting for any extended periods of time, this has been more than an eye-opener for me. The saddest part of all is that if they do this in front of Mom without a second thought, I wonder what their boys are witnessing.

I get Mom settled downstairs, Col leaves to pick up the boys at her parent's, and I decide to go up to Treadwell's to get hot fudge sundaes for all of us. My intent is to enjoy the boys for a while, and that way Mom can soak them up as well. I fully acknowledge my psychological motives here-it's an attempt to smooth everything over, especially for Mom. I run into Rob as I'm heading out to my Jeep, and tell him, "I'm pulling a Dad-going to Treadwell's for hot fudge sundaes for us," and, again, catch that momentary flicker of...what is it? Happiness? A glimpse of 10-year-old Rob?

And then it's gone, as quickly as it appeared. When we were kids, Dad used to bring us home hot fudge sundaes from Treadwell's occasionally after he wrapped up his evening hours at his office. There was nothing better than devouring one of those in my PJ's, all of us parked around the kitchen table, and then schlepping off to bed.

"Do you need money?" he asks, which touches me, but also makes me laugh. "I think I've got this," I assure him, and as I'm walking to my Jeep, the boys pull up with Albi, Col's mom. Jack comes sauntering over to my Jeep with a shy smile on his face.

"You're not leaving, are you?" he asks me. "I thought my mom said you were staying with Gramma tonight."

"I am," I tell him. "And, then leaving for work in the morning. I'm running up to Treadwell's to get us hot fudge sundaes."

"I'm coming, too," he answers, and slides in on my passenger side.

"Let John know you're with me," I tell him, because none of the boys have been inside yet to see Rob or Col, and I can see Albi heading in with John and James. Jack rolls down the window and yells, "Hey, Ginger!" to red-headed John. "Treadwell's with Aunt Bet!" and settles back into his seat.

John flips him the bird, and Jack laughs. "He's such a nerd," he says, looking at me in amusement.

We get seven sundaes home safely, and pull up around Rob and Col's kitchen table, mom included. Everyone's mood seems improved. The boys, normally quiet, are talking about school and a group science project Jack and James have, and they are quite humorous describing how they have delegated various tasks. I can tell even Rob is amused, and I'm glad to see that his boys possess the ability to make him laugh. Once we finish, I tell them goodbye, since I'll be leaving before they're up in the morning, and they head up to bed.

"Well, bunk buddy, are you ready to hit the sack?" I ask

Mom. She has got to be exhausted, because I can't wait to sleep myself.

Mom smiles. "I am, and we need to get you to bed. You'll have to be up at the crack of dawn tomorrow. What time do you want to leave?"

"Probably six, to be on the safe side," I answer. We head downstairs, and on the pretext of needing to ask Col something I forgot, I sneak back upstairs, hoping she's still in the kitchen so I don't have to go hunting for her. She is... starting on the boy's lunches for tomorrow. I tap her lightly on the shoulder even though I'm sure she heard me coming up the stairs.

"So, we have Rob's blessing on Mom," I say quietly.

She turns to look at me and nods. "Yeah, one of his typical enthusiastic reactions," she says wryly, shaking her head. "So much consideration expressed for your mom."

"There was a definite conservation of energy there, wasn't there?" I affirm, not wanting to discuss this in any more depth than necessary. "But the good news is, we have what we need to move forward with. Next step-call Craig and lay it out for him. Let him know exactly how you feel, I'll mention it to him, too, and we'll get to work on this. But DO call him-he definitely needs to hear this from you and to get your perspective on it."

"I will," Col replies. "Hopefully this week."

Mom and I are in bed 15 minutes later. It feels wonderful to lie down and stretch out. I make the executive decision not to shower in the morning. It will simply be a 'scrubs and eyeliner' kind of day so I can sleep in a little later. Mom and I talk for a few minutes, then I tell her I love her and we're both asleep in seconds. It's been an interesting 24 hours, and there are going to be some big changes in the months ahead. I don't want to say anything definitive to Mom until we have more to move forward on. One thing I'm certain of-I never, ever want Mom to know this moving idea was Col's. It would break her heart to think she has become a burden to Rob's family when she has tried so hard over the years to be anything BUT. I'll let it break my heart instead. The good news is, clearance granted.

Chapter Four

COMMITMENTS
(Fall-December 2009)

It takes Colette a lot longer to talk to Craig than I thought it would. I wonder if she had to work up the nerve. Once she and I had spoken with Rob in Chicago, I had pretty much 'checked the box' in my mind, feeling like now the ball was in her court. I'm perfectly willing to advocate, but Col needs to own this, too. For whatever reason, it's mid-November before she reaches out to Craig. He lit me up about the conversation shortly after it took place. The evening he called, I was tired, and not in the mood for histrionics, but I also realized that he was a huge step behind me in Mom's 'relocation process', because I had said nothing to him about my conversations with either Colette or Rob. I felt like whatever he heard from Col needed to be firsthand, whenever that conversation took place. I did my best to listen patiently and to give him the chance to process his exchange with her.

According to Craig, Colette began their conversation

with something along the lines of, 'I've got two problems, and I can't do anything about one until I deal with the other. The first one is your mom, the second one is your brother'.

Having witnessed their relationship firsthand in Chicago, that remark is easy enough to analyze, but I'm surprised she'd be that blunt with Craig, although it will certainly help the cause, I guess.

Then Col had talked to Craig about Mom's needs for more supervision and socialization. Craig is very aware of Mom's financial parameters, and had left it with Col that all of us would start looking into various living options for Mom. Again, I'm a huge step ahead of him in this process as well, having done some homework on it for Mom already. Once we have a better feel for cost and what's out there, we'll meet and make some decisions. In the meantime, I've assured Mom that I'm looking (which I am) and getting information sent to me from several other retirement communities in Cincinnati.

Shortly after Colette and Craig spoke, Col came across an ad in the Sunday 'Interlocutor' (Cincinnati's biggest newspaper) that Beecher Springs was running a special one-time signing deal that offered a significant amount off the deposit if the residency application is received before December 31st of 2009. She had called Craig immediately to let him know. This discount, based on the sluggish economy and slowing number of incoming residents, couldn't have come at a more perfect time.

I truly doubt it matters to Col where Mom goes, especially based on a comment she had made to Craig during their conversation stating, "I don't care where your mom goes, but she can't stay here." To date, Rob has expressed zero interest in where we're looking either, so I know Craig has moved quickly on the idea of Beecher, versus anywhere else in Cincinnati, since this was Mom's dream a decade ago. If we could pull this off it would be a dream come true for her. It's 10 minutes from where we grew up, everything she'd need would be within a 10 to 15-minute radius, and many of her friends through the years live there now.

And so, it is this cold first Saturday in December that Craig, Colette, Rob and I are meeting in Covington to discuss our findings and put together a game plan forward. Col located a little coffee shop in their main business district so I don't have to come all the way to Cincinnati. As I'm rolling along I-71 soaking up the barren hills and naked trees lining them, the three of them are touring two different resident cottages at Beecher, and meeting with the financial admittance department there to crunch Mom's numbers. I've brought all my material from several other retirement facilities in Cincy, but I think Beecher Springs is a foregone conclusion.

Hard to believe it'll be Christmas in 20 days, I'm thinking as I drive. This fall has flown, in a flurry of both work and things going on at home. I find myself looking forward to the time off I'll have later this month. I've taken off three days the second full week of December, and then two more days following Christmas, when Callie and Kerry will both be home. Add in my standard days off during the week for the Saturdays I'll work, and the month doesn't seem so demanding. There's something about knowing those days await me that give me additional momentum to power through right now.

I let my mind wander as I drive, vaporizing my recent five hours of work. Our trip to Chicago for Aunt Frances' funeral seems like light years ago, and it's been the last time I've seen either Col, Rob, or Craig. I took some time off in early October to go to Nashville for a long weekend with Callie, which had been a great time, both in terms of a break from work, and just the one on one with her. It also gave me an opportunity to spend time with Andy, which I had thoroughly enjoyed. Cal and I do so well together-we don't have to have hard and fast plans, and we enjoy all of the same things, so there were lazy coffee mornings on her couch, long walks on the miles of greenway that wind through the area near her condo, and some sightseeing and shopping down off Broadway and in Bellevue; all of it relaxing.

This fall also allowed me to complete my first home improvement project ever to the almost complete exclusion of Mike. He has never had a very developed palette for color; as the girls and I say, he's pretty 'vanilla'. While he can design a deck from start to finish, and build it himself, color is not his schtick. This project required virtually no emotional expenditure on his part whatsoever; and was done in his absence while he was on a fishing trip with a customer. There was no dismantling or reassembly required on his part at all, and I insured total completion when he returned home five days later. My project? The complete repainting of our kitchen and dining room.

After being in our home for eight years, I was tired of the neutral, peachy beige of every room on our first floor, the exception being our great room, which is a warm taupe. I was craving more depth and warmth of color, especially since the cabinetry in our kitchen is white. This face lift would add character and a strong 'through line' to the entire first floor if I could find two coordinating colors to pair with the taupe. Based on the huge windows we have in both the front and back of our home, and the generous amount of light exposure, I knew I could go fairly deep and bold in terms of color, and I started my search with that in mind. Through the years, I have learned to pretty much trust my instincts when it comes to color and décor. I know what I like, and I possess a pretty good feel for how to pull it all together. To me, painting alone is one of the best, and least expensive, face lifts for a room that exists.

After multiple visits to Home Depot, Lowe's, and Benjamin Moore, I had a stack of paint chips that equaled a deck of cards, and I kept returning to a beautiful, deep terra cotta for the kitchen, paired with an equally rich golden gingerbread color (pertly called 'Golden Retriever') for the dining room. These two colors seem made for each other, and they will still allow our dark jade countertops to be a good accent. Mike was aware that I was moving ahead with these plans yet was extremely reluctant to see this happen… all this color being far too risky of an equation for him. I had made it clear from the outset that I would be doing this with or without his blessing; inviting him to come to look at paint colors with me (he obliged once) and letting him know what my timeline was. But, as his trip drew closer, he begged me to wait until he got back, "and then we'll think about it". I'm pretty flexible about most things…this was one of the few times I decided I would stand my ground and operate on MY time frame. I love Mike more than life itself, but I'm also well acquainted with his stalling tactics when he's not signed on to something, but also wants to avoid a direct confrontation. I think he thought it would just "go away" if we put it off. But I wasn't having any of that this time around. I wanted this badly enough that I forged ahead regardless, and figured I'd deal with potential fallout after the fact.

Mike left on a Wednesday, and that Friday night I dismantled the kitchen and dining room to ready it for the painters the next day. Bright and early that grey October Saturday, they arrived-three men from a wonderful family owned business that I had researched and fallen in love with. I knew I had hit a home run when the painters enthusiastically called me downstairs to show me how good the first wall looked in the kitchen. "Look how it makes your cabinetry pop," one of them pointed out. "This is beautiful!"

The final result was stunning and everything I had hoped. Worth every bit of planning and organizing, it transformed both rooms with warmth and color. It was even more striking on Sunday, when the sun came out, and infused the colors with an additional dimension of body. I spent all of Sunday afternoon cleaning and re-arranging all the objects up on my cabinet tops with Mannheim Steamroller Christmas CD's blaring, happy as a clam.

Mike was not a happy clam when he arrived home that same evening to find that I was as good as my word, and that his kitchen and dining room were rich hues of autumn, but, three weeks later, having been encouraged by one of his male friends who does have a true eye for color that, "Bet did a great job picking these out," he surprised me with new countertops that he selected on his own. They were a beautiful compliment to the new wall color, flecked with sandstone, onyx, terra cotta, and caramel. Every night I got home from Highbridge, it was like re-opening a present.

Kerry was soldiering through her junior year at UK, doing a lot of soul searching about the rightness of being there, and questioning her decision to major in business. In our conversations, I could tell the stress was weighing on her. She was heavily debating finishing the semester and then taking a break, or possibly transferring, and I did what I was best at-listening. Whatever Kerry decided I would be behind her. I just knew she needed to heed her own inner voices. Having experienced a lot of that same indecision and self-doubt during my own college years, I was reminded again of what a fraught time that can be in life. Transferring myself at the end of my junior year of college, Kerry's peace of mind was worth far more than me telling her what I thought was right for her. I counselled her to just keep doing what was in front of her until the semester was over, and to pray and seek guidance, but also let her know that Mike and I would support her whatever she felt led to do. Knowing her level of motivation and perseverance, I knew she would find a way to finish her degree, whether at UK, at home, or somewhere else.

In November, all of us, including Callie and Andy, had gone to Lexington for Family Weekend, and I could sense Kerry was in a much better place with everything by then. She shares a big old house on Transylvania Avenue with four other girls, and we've enjoyed getting to know their families over the course of our visits there. It was a crisp, golden day, perfect for football and grilling out, a day that's frozen in my memory for its warmth, laughter, and the joy of our family being all together.

And then there was work, with its insidious pace. Well into my second year now, there were days that were effortless for me as I had learned the basic processes and was now refining my knowledge base. That said, there were still days that were demanding and long, especially as we were moving into our sick season and scheduling later into the evenings. In addition, we were deluged with patients coming in for flu vaccines, and it could often become the perfect storm.

Interestingly, I was finding that now that I was no longer a rookie, I was working circles around both Marcy and LaDonna. I had slowly developed my own sense of flow, efficiency, and overall productivity that, to me, was both streamlined and proactive. A lot depended on which window I worked on-whether it was the sick or well side (we had separate rooms and a separate sign-in window for each), but I could tell I was relaxing into the position and truly enjoying it, especially the relationships I was beginning to build with our patients and their families. Fewer and fewer situations stressed me, as I developed the ability to solve problems and anticipate them, and that was a good feeling.

I was also realizing how different my mindset was from Marcy's and LaDonna's. Both were only a year older than myself, but I often felt that I was working with two women who were well into their 70's. They hated to move quickly, got rattled easily, and struggled with multi-tasking. When this happened, Marcy would make mistakes; LaDonna would get very irritated with our patients, as if they were forcing her to move at a momentum that she couldn't control. In watching more closely over time, I came to realize that anything LaDonna couldn't control made her angry, because it was all about her dictating the pace of the transaction. She could be notoriously short and curt with our patients, and when she got busy, her level of irritation rose exponentially. LaDonna was one of those individuals who was truly incapable of self-monitoring. I would listen to the way she spoke to our patients and be flabbergasted at her rudeness, as would Lynsey, the youngest member of our team. It amazed me that no one ever called her out on it.

Marcy, on the other hand, just plain did not like to move fast, nor did she think quickly on her feet. The more I learned, the more I was able to trouble shoot my own work management style, and the easier the routine became. I noticed that both Marcy and LaDonna asked me for help now and treated me as much more of an equal. I had had my first yearly review, receiving a significant raise along with wonderful feedback from Linda, our business manager, especially in terms of how much the patients liked me, and Linda's appreciation for the way I interacted with them. I knew that these were traits that neither Marcy or LaDonna possessed to the degree that I did, and with them having been there longer than myself, I consciously made the decision to draw as little attention to it as possible.

They both felt there was only one way to do things (their way), and I could tell they struggled with any kind of change in their routine, especially when it came to what time they ate lunch. It was always easier for them to tell you why something was NOT a good idea rather than thinking about a better way to implement a procedure. Luckily, at least Lynsey thought more like I did–I was grateful for her younger, more proactive demeanor, and for her quick sense of humor. The things LaDonna and Marcy found humorous I found ridiculous.

One thing I had discovered, to my perverse pleasure, was that, on days when we were short-staffed, which happened on a fairly regular basis, (especially if someone called in), it became a Catch-22 for Marcy and LaDonna. When this happened, it generally meant that one of us that worked at the front desk would need to cover the responsibility of pulling and filing all the charts for that day's appointments. I had begun to volunteer for this task, because I loved being away from the front desk and their toxic, rigid attitudes, especially if Lynsey was working downstairs in billing, as she had started doing three days a week. Filing and pulling meant that I could move freely on my own away from Marcy and LaDonna and work my own 'system' in the back channels. It was a way to be productive and hugely helpful to them, yet not have to deal directly WITH them, and for me, it was truly like a day off. The catch for Marcy and LaDonna was that, with me NOT up front, it put far more pressure on them to step up, forcing them to move more quickly than they normally did. By the end of the day they'd both be grumpy and irritable, complaining about how busy they'd been, yet neither of them ever volunteered to pull or file, because they knew it meant being on their feet all day, and hauling themselves up and down our stairs. (Many of our charts were stored in the basement of our building.) As a rule, they both avoided the stairs at all costs, unless it involved Marcy's smoke breaks, in which case she couldn't get downstairs fast enough. I also noticed that she was sneaking out more and more frequently, which highly irritated LaDonna.

LaDonna was far and above the one I struggled with the most, both because of her critical spirit, and her obsession with small, anal details that, in the grand scheme of things, meant nothing to anyone else except her. Things like her desk supplies and where she kept personal belongings took on significance of outlandish proportion, to the extent that I almost felt sorry for her. I did my best to be both kind and professional, but I looked forward to her days off immensely, as well as to the Saturdays we weren't scheduled to work together. Our work environment was so different when she wasn't there, and even Marcy seemed more interactive. In an environment where we all worked in such close quarters, one person's behavior makes a huge difference. I always tried to be aware of that in the timbre of my interactions with others.

Over the 18 months I'd been there, I had also been able to get a good read on team dynamics, which was telling. While Lynsey, and even Marcy, to a lesser degree, were team players, I'd noticed that LaDonna only wanted to do those things that would bring her direct personal affirmation, or that could be visibly seen by others, and it drove her crazy when Marcy didn't do what LaDonna perceived as 'her share'. It was almost as if LaDonna's entire identity came from how she defined herself in comparison to those around her. I would periodically catch her studying me when she thought

I didn't notice, and it both amused (I always contemplated picking my nose) and irritated me.

Time reveals all, I think, and I have quietly set my own standards of interaction with each of my co-workers with the intention of building our team. This is such a different environment to work in than in education, and so much more riddled with pettiness and adults who never grew up. Who would have dreamed that it would be my co-workers, rather than the job description, that would be my biggest challenge? I can't wait for my time off this month. It will be a welcome re-charge.

I exit off I-75 into Covington, right before the bridge, and find our designated coffee house. Once inside, I realize I'm the first to arrive, and I get us a table for four. Ordering a cup of Chai tea, I idly leaf through the retirement community material. Colette arrives about 10 minutes later, followed by Craig, who is worried about where he parked his BMW.

"How'd it go?" I ask as we settle in at the table, ignoring Craig's concerns about the 'type of neighborhood' the Beemer is parked in. This can be vintage Craig, and I have no patience for it. Today is about Mom, not his vehicle. "Is Rob behind you guys?" I ask, assuming he's just driving separately.

Craig looks to Colette. "No, he's not coming," she answers, but there's a slight air of…guardedness? Defensiveness? "He ended up being on call-he traded days with another on-call doc," she responds.

"So, he didn't go with you to Beecher, either?" I ask, thinking that maybe he had, and then had gone on to Holy Disciple.

"No, he wasn't with us at all today," Craig answers.

I nod, not too surprised. "Well, fill me in on everything," I invite, leaning forward across the table. I'm anxious to hear their feedback, and to begin to form a mental picture of Mom's future.

"They showed us two different cottages, both of which

are vacant," Craig begins, "back in a section of Beecher called 'The Knolls'. They were each identical, except in terms of their location. One's a little farther back, at the end of a row of three…the second one, which is the one Col and I liked better, is in the middle of a row, with a porch and a decent sized green area out behind it because it backs up to Breck, their assisted living facility."

"Talk floor plan to me," I prompt, wanting more specifics, and Col takes over here.

"There's a huge vaulted ceiling in the center of the cottage with three windows across the top that let in tons of light," she recounts, which I already love, because Mom's living quarters at Rob's are so dark. "You come in off a front porch and walk directly into the living area…it's long and wide, with an eating area at the back of it, then you have a galley kitchen to the right of the living area, with a little hallway that runs along the back and accesses both bedrooms. Each bedroom has its own bath…you'd like it, Bet."

"What about a garage?" I ask, and Craig pulls out a floor plan from a glossy Beecher Springs folder to show me the layout. He indicates the garage, opening right off the kitchen, big enough for one car.

"This looks great," I comment. "Are they both available right now?" Craig answers that the cottage they preferred won't be available until February, because each time a resident vacates a cottage, it's automatically repainted and re-carpeted so it's virtually brand new for the next resident. He goes on to tell me that part of the entry fee covers a once a week housekeeper that comes to the cottage to clean, dust, and vacuum, so Mom would never have to worry about doing it; and mentions plenty of additional parking space in the lot in front of the cottage. All of it sounds too good to be true, and I can feel my spirits starting to soar. Since Colette and Craig were the two who did the legwork today, I lay back and let them control the pace of the discussion.

"So," Craig begins, "I think after seeing it, Col and I both feel like this is somewhere Mom would thrive." He looks at

Col as if waiting for her joint acknowledgment of this, and she nods.

"It's very nice," is her statement of affirmation.

"And," Craig continues, "we sat down afterwards with June Hettinger, the director, to review the financial qualifications, and the cost has risen significantly."

We go on to talk in more depth about the financial portion of it. Craig expresses concerns regarding their calculations, because even with the discount, costs for residents have risen significantly since Mom and Dad looked at Beecher. I trust him on this completely. I don't know a lot of the particulars when it comes to Mom's 'numbers', but Craig has always been on top of her finances, and if he's voicing concerns, I know they're valid.

"We'll just need to wait until they've run all their final figures," he states to Col and me now. Going on to explain to me that, using actuarial scales, and a series of metrics including overall health, current age, chronic medical issues, etc., Beecher requires that a document of financial responsibility be co-signed by family members stating that they will be financially responsible should the resident outlive their financial means based on the actuarial prediction. Given their metrics, they have Mom living till 89 years of age. She's 82 currently.

"So," says Craig, leaning back in his chair and pausing, then raking his hand across his face and leaning in towards Colette and me, "I think we need to be in complete agreement on one thing, because if we're not, this could tear things apart later on, nor do we ever want Mom to know that we cosigned this document of financial responsibility. We're all in agreement that she needs more structure, and more opportunity to be with people her own age, rather than at your place alone for a lot of the time," (he looks pointedly at Col) "so her NOT moving isn't any option anymore. We need to understand that we will be required to cosign for her protection in the unlikely event that Mom outlives her money. Again, this is based on Beecher's actuarial numbers, and their estimate of Mom's longevity matched to her financial portfolio. This is a non-negotiable requirement for all residents due to the recent financial crisis. Obviously, Donny isn't in the position to commit to this financially, and I wouldn't expect him to… that's okay. But our three families…we're all fortunate enough to be in a position to do this. The way I look at it, she's done plenty for us, and this is the least we can do for her."

There's silence following his words. He couldn't have put it any better. "Agreed," I say. "You're right, this isn't an option. And I know from talking to Mom that she'd rather be at Beecher Springs than anywhere else. We're in." (Meaning Mike and me.)

"Col?" Craig asks, looking directly at her.

"Count us in," she answers quietly.

Decision made. The three of our families will cosign their document of financial responsibility, and Mom will never know. If she were to find out, she would never agree to moving there. We talk about a few more details. June will be getting back to Craig early next week with final figures and payment time frames, and we'll go from there. The entry fee will secure the cottage, and the three of us agree on the one that Craig and Col liked more.

We all get back on the road by 2:00, and I am elated for what lies ahead. Merry Christmas, Mom! What a great gift this will be for her! We've agreed not to tell her until we have all the details nailed down, which will put us closer to the holidays. Popping a Christmas CD in my player, I zone out on the drive back to Louisville, feeling both peace and gratitude as I watch the sun sinking lower on the horizon.

A thought rises lazily to my consciousness…did Rob know that Colette did all this today? I don't know why this suddenly occurs to me, but I have a funny feeling about it, especially knowing how little they communicate. I hadn't thought to ask her when we were together, presuming he'd be coming with her, and would have wanted to see the cottage.

Could it be possible he doesn't know anything about this? Then an even darker thought occurs to me. Is it possible that Col doesn't want him to know any of this took place until it's a done deal? But surely…then I start thinking about her agreeing to sign the document of financial responsibility. Did she feel pressured to commit since Craig and I both did? *If Rob doesn't know any of this is taking place, they'll be having a lot of discussion about it this weekend*, I'm thinking. But despite that niggling thought, I am so happy for Mom. This is a prayer answered that I've prayed for a long time, and I thank God for His faithfulness.

* * * * *

It smells like December, I think as I get in the Jeep to drive home from work that following Thursday. The air has that sharp, bite-y scent that smells like frozen ground, snow, and the faintest hint of pine. I'm moving closer and closer to my time off, and it puts me in a wonderful mood, even after this long day. The week has gone quickly; I work Saturday, next Monday and Tuesday…then my glorious stretch of five days of vacation begins. I get home, walk into my Happy Kitchen, and breathe a deep sigh of contentment. Mike flew out yesterday for a power show that their industry holds every year-this year in Las Vegas, and I'm on my own until he gets back on Saturday. Three hours to do whatever I choose before my bed calls, and that feels divine. I plug in our Christmas tree, loving the soft glow of the white lights. We put it up last Sunday, and I've worked on it through the week until all the ornaments are hung. After I light a few candles, I sit down to go through the mail, setting aside two of the season's first Christmas cards to read. I'll miss getting Aunt Frances's card this year.

The phone rings, and it's Craig. I'm surprised I haven't heard from him earlier this week.

"Hey, Bet," he greets me, and he sounds exhausted.

June Hettinger had called him on Tuesday to inform him that she has the financial responsibility document to sign. The clock is ticking, because for them to hold the cottage, they need the document in hand. Craig had called Colette to let her know, and to make sure they were still on board, at which point Col had bluntly told him that they had decided not to co-sign. After she talked to Rob about it, they felt they had done enough for Mom already. (This is Craig's wording of the discussion.)

I'm surprised, but it also makes me revisit my thoughts from Saturday. I truly wonder if Rob had any idea this was taking place until Colette shared it with him after we met in Covington. Granted, even if she had mentioned it to him before our meeting took place, there would have been no discussion about co-signing the document of financial responsibility, because that wasn't anything that had been brought up until Saturday when they were at Beecher. I still just have a funny feeling Rob knew nothing about this-not Craig and Col going to look at the cottages, or our family meeting, until after the fact. This obviously was Rob's verdict following our time in Covington, as relayed to him by Colette. I can tell Craig is smoldering, and I'm not going to say anything about my thinking that Rob was completely in the dark until last weekend…that will keep.

Apparently, things got very heated between he and Col on the phone, and again, I'm wondering why she was the disseminator of information. Sadly, this lends credibility to my theory about Rob being in the dark on everything until after the fact. I could totally see him telling Col that she'd have to be the one to communicate with Craig since she had made the commitment without consulting him in the first place. Or, it could just be Rob's passive aggressive behavior, and his not wanting to deal with Craig himself.

In the heat of the discussion, Craig had really 'gone there', making a comment to Colette about their reluctance to share the responsibility being a fine way of showing gratitude to Mom after she and my dad had put Rob through med school loan free. Below the belt? Definitely. True? Yes, to that, too. Would I have said the same thing if I'd been having the conversation with Rob? Probably not…because my thought process would have been more along the lines of, *If they can't arrive at that conclusion themselves in their own hearts, it's not my job to point it out to them,* but I totally understand where Craig is coming from, ballsy as it was to put that comment out there. How sad it even had to come up.

Net result: there are only two families, Craig's and ours, that will be co-signing for financial responsibility. Exit our third family. It will now be split two ways instead of three. While part of me is sickened by Rob and Col's cold-hearted rationale, at some deeper level, I'm not at all surprised. In a way, it confirms a lot of what I've thought for a long time, but especially since our trip to Chicago.

Craig has also, prior to calling me, reached out to Mike in Las Vegas, and given him an update on the situation. Without any hesitation, Mike told him that we were all in, and whatever it took, we'd do what was best for Mom. My heart swells in total gratitude at the thought that Mike, 3,000 miles away, probably sleep deprived from late nights and the time change, heard Craig out and let him know that we'd still hold the line with him.

What further amazes me is that I had said nothing to Mike about the co-signing before he left for Vegas. I knew I could talk to him about it once he got home from the trip, and we had more specifics in hand. And, I wasn't sure how he'd feel about it. Instead, here he is, committing unequivocally without the two of us even having had the opportunity to discuss it ourselves. I can tell, even as much as the conversation with Colette has infuriated Craig, that Mike's willingness to do this without even talking to me has mitigated Craig's emotion. Mike has made MY evening, too, and his commitment means the world to me. I can't wait to talk to him myself later tonight. This is truly the ultimate Christmas present!

I realize, as I continue to talk with Craig, that there has been another irrevocable turn in the road for our family; one that makes me deeply sad, even though I can't say I didn't see it coming. Whatever Rob and Colette's motives that have led to their decision, I'm of the opinion that Craig and I need to accept it. We don't have to agree with it, but our anger and judgment isn't required, nor will it improve the situation. I feel like they're missing out on a wonderful opportunity for blessing through this commitment, but that's just my thought. The important thing is to move on, not to make this ugly for them, or to try to punish them for their decision. I verbalize this to Craig, but I'm not sure he wants to hear any of it. I hope he doesn't let this eat him alive with bitterness.

* * * * *

It's Friday, December 11th, and how I managed to get stuck planning the Christmas party for our entire practice at Highbridge, I'll never know. It was one of those things that quietly evolved, maybe due in part to my suggestions, in other equal parts to people being happy to let me take the lead. Especially from the standpoint that all my team members have been here longer, it defies logic. Maybe the rookie gets stuck with this kind of stuff. But, somehow, I am the delegate. I'm still a little in the dark on how our Christmas parties roll-I've only attended one other one (last year's, which was my first year working here), and it struck me as sterile and perfunctory, especially on the part of the doctors, who sat at their own table and made about zero effort to mingle. I guess I've been spoiled by Mike's company's Christmas parties over the years, which are warm, fun, and very enjoyable. They're also a testament to the deep friendships that have been built through the years, both in and outside of working hours.

Supposedly the doctors wanted to try something different this year, and after polling all of us, decided that they would close the practice following lunch on a Friday afternoon. The party would then be held AT our practice, (downstairs in our tiny eating area that hasn't been remodeled since the 1960's) everyone bringing a dish, the doctors providing a ham and meat tray, and then we'd play games. Upwards of 30 people crammed into a 12 x 14-foot space doesn't quite strike me as a recipe for a festive time, especially when the doctors already seem to prefer minimal interaction with their employees in a social setting. This could really be pushing the envelope. Never mind. I will do my best. I've planned games for Mike's Christmas parties before, and we've had a lot of fun with some of them, so my rationale is simple. If these games flop with this group of people, it's not on me.

Our business manager, Linda Robertson, has overseen things, and our clinical manager, Patsy McKiernan, and I have purchased what we need, including decorations, and organized the afternoon…still, I can't wait for it to be over. Being front and center, acting fun and seemingly spontaneous, is not my gig, especially when it comes to explaining the games. Yikes. One of the games we've decided on involves kazoos and four teams. Each person is given a kazoo, and each team draws from a basket containing the names of 30 random Christmas carols and holiday songs-some very well known, others relatively obscure. Each team performs their picks on the kazoos, those teams not performing identifying the song being played. Judges rate the teams on how well the song is played, and how quickly it's identified. It's a hilarious game to watch, especially when a group doesn't know a song and is forced to fake it.

Things get under way after we've gorged ourselves on food. Everybody brought in wonderful dishes. The kazoo game goes swimmingly, and people are great sports about joining in. Following that, we do a doctor's 'Brain Bowl' which is benign, and, I think, pretty funny. (I had made up all the questions, and at least the doctors laughed about them.) Linda had cautioned me beforehand about not drawing any attention to personal habits or mannerisms of the doctors;

apparently that's been a sore subject in the past. *Like I'd do that?*, so I keep it lighthearted and innocuous. After that we play a circle game with dice and gifts in the middle, then the doctors pass out our Christmas cards (enclosed are our bonuses-so nice!) and it winds down from there.

By three o'clock we are cleaning up, and my relief is palpable. My first Eastbridge Christmas party is under my belt as a planning committee member. Nice feedback from Linda and Patsy as we're restoring the kitchen to its normal state, which makes me happy. People really seemed to enjoy themselves, even the doctors, and I'm so thankful it went well. On top of that, I'm thinking of only having to work two days next week, and I'm basking in the glow of all of this as I get home Friday evening.

I fire up the tree and pour myself a celebratory glass of wine, planning to sit quietly for a while, write a few Christmas cards, and then go to bed early since it's my Saturday to work tomorrow. Mike will get home in the morning while I'm at Highbridge, and his Christmas party is tomorrow night. I need to grab this peace and quiet while I can. So of course, the phone rings, startling me from my peaceful reverie, and instead of it being Mike or Craig, as I'd anticipated, it's unanticipated Rob.

Oh, boy, strap one on, I think to myself, but I greet him cheerfully. "Hey, stranger. How are you?"

Common sense prevailing, I know in advance this will probably be a very charged conversation. My guess is, at some level it will involve a discussion about Beecher's document of financial responsibility, as well as Craig and Col's exchange this past week, and it has the potential to escalate quickly. I make up my mind not to let this happen, and especially not to take sides. I can't stand the thought of making this family divide any worse than it already is. Rob is his usual flat-affect self, but I listen carefully and objectively, drawing from the vast reservoir of our relationship through the years. I do understand his overall frustration with Craig-after all, they've been many of my same frustrations through the years, but in this instance, I feel like his anger may be completely misdirected. He cuts to the chase right away.

"Craig called Colette Wednesday night, and got really shitty with her about signing for potential financial responsibility," he states sharply. "This isn't his decision to make or to control."

"No, it's not," I assent. "But I don't think he's trying to do that." My days of being concerned about expressing my opinion in our family have long since expired, and, like it or not, Rob needs to hear this from my perspective, even if he doesn't agree with it.

"Keep in mind, I begin, "that Col called him asking him to get Mom out of your place…all for valid reasons. That was a short month ago, Rob, and he's doing everything in his power to make sure this can happen as quickly as possible so your family can have their lives back. This is a requirement for all residents at Beecher due to the recent financial crisis, and we need to commit soon, for them to hold the cottage that Col and Craig selected. And, based on the discussion the three of us had when we met in Covington last Saturday, all of us decided that our families-the three of us-Craig, you, and me, would all cosign. All of us felt that Mom remaining with you guys is no longer an option. Okay, we all agreed… complete consensus…so why wouldn't Craig assume that you all were still good with it? Neither of you had called him to let him know anything different. So, he calls Colette to let her know that Beecher has the document ready to sign, and suddenly, you've changed your mind at the 11th hour. Put yourself in his place, Rob. He's trying to make this work for all of us, Mom included."

"Well, God love him for that!" Rob hurls through the phone.

Who is this guy? I'm thinking. Already, my mind is racing ahead. Rob is really upset about this.

"You know, Rob, you and Col are ultimately the only ones who get to make your decision about contributing or not contributing," I hear myself say. "If Craig wanted to, he could easily cosign completely by himself. Mike and I also feel like this is really important to do for Mom. But I don't want you to feel pressure from Craig or from me-only you can make that decision in your heart of hearts," I answer, (even as I'm picturing his '67 GTO under its dust cover in his garage). I'm trying my hardest to build a bridge, and to let Rob know I'm not judging him.

"Also," I continue, "my family is at a much different point than yours with Callie being completely out of college, and Kerry almost there. Your boys are a lot younger, and you've got a lot of expenses ahead of you. If it doesn't work for you, then it doesn't work. You have to do what's best for your own family."

"I think we need to keep looking," Rob states flatly. "There are other options that would be less expensive than Beecher Springs."

This, after all the time and effort Craig, his own wife, and myself, have spent gathering information, touring facilities, and meeting to hash it all out. Has he verbalized this to Colette? How easy to make this assessment on the back end, when Rob has done nothing to assist in the search process. That takes nerve, and I'm not giving an inch on this.

"I'm not sure how much Col has shared with you about our search, or about the discount Beecher Springs is offering right now on their entry fee," I respond, intimating that if she had, he would already be aware of how much legwork we've done, "but the three of us have done a pretty exhaustive search of places in the Cincinnati area within a 15-30 minute radius of Southwoods. Col was the one who found the special offer for Beecher in the 'Interlocutor,'" I state. "And after Col and Craig toured the cottages at Beecher last Saturday, I think they both felt like the decision was made. Also, keep in mind that Mom and Dad were on the waiting list there until they took their names off when they moved in with you, and Mom still has a lot of friends there."

"Name one!" he spits out. Rob is obviously not appreciating

the way I keep pushing back. It dawns on me that this may be the first time ever we've had a difference of opinion, and perhaps he hasn't bargained on me standing my ground. I laugh, in disbelief that Rob is really being this combative.

"Well," I begin, "there are some people from Good Shepherd-Charlie and Harriet Lewis, and Beatrice Odell; then Tom and Martina King that Mom taught with, Deedee and Jerry Mueller, the Westhusens, and Dad's Kiwanis buddy and his wife...um, Larry and Carol Parks... I feel like I'm missing somebody."

I'm literally almost flushed with the glow of my success, because I know, based on how disconnected Rob is from Mom, he has no clue who most of these people even are, while also realizing that he can't argue with what he doesn't know. I pause for a moment, then move on.

"Whatever you feel about this, Rob," I say, "I would ask you one thing. You, Mike, Col and I have always had a great relationship, and I don't want anything to jeopardize that, regardless of what decisions each of us makes regarding Mom's future. Please, please don't let that become a wedge between us."

Rob is totally quiet, so I continue.

"And, just a thought...as difficult as this might be for you, I would really encourage you to call Craig and talk to him about how you feel. I think it would really help you, and I know it would give him a lot more perspective. I know that you and I both have a tough time dealing with conflict, and being able to verbalize our feelings about it...Mom and Dad weren't the best at modeling conflict resolution, and it's taken me a long time to learn how to do that in a healthy way. But I've talked to Craig in the past about some of my feelings towards him, and I think you'd be surprised at how easy it will be. Craig doesn't have to agree with you, but I guarantee you he'll listen. Then, at least, you'll have the satisfaction of having let him know how you feel and why. You owe yourself that, especially if you feel he was unfair to Colette."

This is also grown-up speak for 'Man up' and 'Don't put me in the middle, deal with it yourself', but I also know that it's valid advice across the board. I've had to learn these lessons myself, and it's always easier to complain to someone else than it is to own the situation yourself. This tendency of Rob's distinctly reminds me of how Mom deals with troublesome issues…there's an eerily close similarity. If Rob is looking for understanding and clarification, I'm willing to provide that. If he's looking for an ally in me, the office is closed for business.

"I'm not sure that's such a good idea," Rob says, but in a much softer tone.

I can tell the bite is gone.

"I think I'd like to talk to Mike before I call Craig. Will he be around this weekend?"

I explain that he's at the power show, telling Rob that Sunday would be the best time to call, and as we get to the end of the conversation, I wonder if he feels more peace having talked to me. He wouldn't have called me in the first place if he hadn't thought I'd deal with him in love, and it touches me that he wanted to reach out. At some level, I know even this call has been difficult for him.

"Listen," I end the conversation, "I love you and Col, and I hope you know that. Take care of yourselves, and give Mike a call, but please plan on calling Craig. He needs to hear from you as much as you need to level with him."

I sit in silence after I hang up, lost in thought. So much sadness, so much anger, so much of it stemming from our lack of ability to say what we really want or need to say, over the years. When does it end? Did I do anything to help that cause tonight? There's a fine line between owning other people's emotional baggage and pointing them in the right direction, but somehow, the words I spoke tonight feel about right to me. This day has made me very, very tired.

* * * * *

The rest of December flies by. My time off is glorious. It's filled with activity and rich with the satisfaction of doing things I enjoy. I bake, make fudge, do some Christmas shopping and buy for our family that we are 'gifting' through our practice. There are also my five Christmas concerts at church, spread out over a ten day stretch, which is my heart's springboard to everything else in the month. As the earlier tumult fades, I feel a deep peace within myself, and the joy of knowing that I celebrate the birth of a baby who came to show the world what true love really looks like.

Towards the middle of December, Craig calls to let me know about a recent development with Colette. He had fielded a call at work from June Hettinger, the head of the Financial department at Beecher Springs, wanting to give him a heads up on a phone call she'd received from Col. About ten days after Craig and Colette's meeting at Beecher, Colette had called her, wanting to meet with June alone, seeking full disclosure of Mom's finances. June had been very uncomfortable with the call, she told Craig, and had made it clear that since Colette was an in-law, not one of Mom's children, Beecher's policy prohibited doing that. Suggesting that if Colette brought Rob with her, they'd be within policy guidelines, Colette declined. Why wouldn't she have wanted Rob with her? What in the world is she trying to find? That incident, as well as the underhandedness surrounding it, really bothers me. This is a side of Col I wouldn't have thought existed, and the reality that she could do this puts a lot in question. It's also a trust breaker for me, and I realize I've lost a lot of respect for her in the course of a short phone conversation.

Rob never does call Craig, nor does he call Mike the weekend he and I spoke. Instead, he called Mike the third weekend in December, after Kerry was home from UK, finals behind her. We'd all been eating dinner, Mike excusing himself as soon as he realized it was Rob, and going upstairs, not wanting Kerry to hear any specifics. The call doesn't go well. Things obviously have been festering ever since Rob and I talked. He's extremely negative about the entire situation, including Mom's finances (an issue which he hadn't raised with me). Blatantly questioning the dollar amount that Mom currently has left, he states that it should be far more than that, commenting to Mike that 'something's not right'.

His acidic statement, "Now that it's about money, I'm involved!" sets the tone for the entire accusatory conversation.

He even goes so far as to tell Mike that he's certain Craig has changed the will and trust, both absurd accusations.

Mike, remaining as objective as he can, tells Rob that he doesn't believe that's the case, and encourages him to call Craig, much as I had. When Mike and I talk later that evening, it's clear to both of us that Rob firmly believes Craig has mishandled Mom's money, yet the claims he made are ludicrous, especially from the standpoint that all Rob needed to do was talk to either Craig or Tom Peers, Mom's financial planner, for clarification. It's as if he's created this myth of financial impropriety in his mind and decided to embrace it as truth, yet has nothing to prove its validity, other than, perhaps, wanting it to be true. These juvenile claims are based on some of the most simplistic premises I've ever heard, and I can't believe Rob, as intelligent as he is, would be naïve enough to believe them himself. Sadly, I guess he does, and I wonder how much Colette is feeding this firestorm of fiction? Where is Rob's integrity in all this?

As we're sitting on the couch later that evening, Mike filling me in on what transpired, he recounts a point in the conversation where Rob asked him, point blank, if Mike felt that Rob and Col should be signing the document of financial responsibility with us. Mike has never been one to sugarcoat things and is usually very honest; sometimes brutally so, if the situation warrants it. In this case, he didn't waver, and answered Rob with a direct 'Yes', that he did feel it would be the right thing to do. The discussion had deteriorated from there, Rob obviously not happy with Mike's response. I think he had hoped that Mike would somehow come down on his side. Rob became defensive, claiming we had done very little to take the load off them with Mom living there, at which point Mike had succinctly flung back, "I'm not here to clean up your mess."

Probably not the most sympathetic comment to make, given the circumstances, and Rob had abruptly hung up. In some respects, it's hard for me to hear about this exchange. I had really hoped Mike would be able to create some middle ground for Rob, rather than alienating him further. But in fairness to Mike, he is responsible for his words and his own set of feelings towards all my brothers. My trying to control his relationships with them would be anathema to who I am. Still, it drives the wedge between all of us even deeper.

It certainly doesn't make things better for anyone when Mike relays this conversation to Craig. Would it have created less rancor if Mike hadn't shared Rob's accusations? I sincerely doubt it. Craig already knew that Colette questioned him, based on her wanting full disclosure of Mom's financials from Beecher, but I feel like this is the straw that breaks the camel's back for Craig, and I can totally understand it. He's livid that his integrity is being questioned by a brother who has never once shown any interest in sitting down with him to familiarize himself with Mom's finances.

At this point, Craig decides it's time to go on the offensive. Meeting with Mom's lawyer and Tom Peers, he provides Rob with full disclosure of all of Mom's financial documents, which clearly show nothing has been altered or subverted in any way. Sending them via email to Rob, Craig lets him know exactly how he feels.

In addition to some paragraphs he includes spelling out some of the legalities in Mom's trust, there is this:

'I also realize that assaulting and attacking me personally has become very habitual for you, and that it probably feels natural at this juncture. Perhaps the next time you feel the need to question my intentions, ethics, integrity, morals, and values you will behave like a man and have the courage to say it to my face. Your unfounded, nonfactual, and emotional accusations are beyond comprehension.'

Craig sends us a copy of the email and disclosures as well, and reading it breaks my heart for every single one of us in our family. (Save Donny, far removed from all of this, and distance isn't sounding so bad at this point.) For my Mom, because if she had any idea this was transpiring, it would kill her. She'd blame herself for causing the problem based on her desire to be at Beecher. For Craig, because I can only imagine how much it must hurt to have his integrity questioned by the brother who was his best friend all through childhood. For Rob, because he has become the unhappiest human being I know; angry, adversarial, and too much of a coward to even talk to Craig one on one. And for me, because my family is dissolving before my eyes. The bridge is burning, and I can't imagine us ever finding our way back to any kind of reconciliation. It's not a good turn of events for any of us. And this is supposed to be the season of peace on earth?

All of this recedes into a more remote chamber of my heart once Callie arrives from Nashville. I've also been able to talk in depth to Kerry about it in the ensuing days, and have felt her empathy and support. Having both girls back home again is a blanket of completeness that I get to wrap around my sore heart. It's good medicine.

Over the years, we have developed a family tradition of going out to dinner on December 23rd, and we usually exchange a few gifts that evening. Christmas Eve is always a big travel night to northern Kentucky to be with Mike's family, and this is an opportunity to be 'just us'. All of us have come to look forward to it, and I think it may be the girls' favorite part of Christmas. It's a time to relax, to celebrate as a family, and this year especially so as Kerry has come through such a tough semester with a 3.8 GPA. Callie's happiness in her relationship with Andy is another facet that figures in, as well as Mom's upcoming move to Beecher. Both girls know how much I have wanted to see this happen, and in many ways, I think they're as excited for Mom as I am.

Craig ends up being the one to share the good news with Mom. I would have loved to have been able to be there to witness her reaction, but I haven't been back to Cincinnati since our meeting in Covington. Craig and I had both wanted to tell Mom as soon as possible, knowing how it would lift her spirits. Meeting her for lunch in one of our favorite family restaurants the third week of December, he relayed the exciting news.

As he recounted the story to me, they sat down, ordered their food, and after some small talk he'd asked her, "If you could change anything in your life, other than bringing Dad back, what would it be?" Quite the Pandora's Box…of course Mom could have responded by saying anything!

Her resolute statement had been, "I wish I could live at Beecher Springs."

Craig had replied, setting her up perfectly, "What if I told you I could make that happen?"

Then he launched into the whole story, telling her how we stumbled across the ad for the discounted entry fee in the Interlocutor. He described the cottage we'd found, how much she was going to like it, and that it will be ready for occupancy in in February.

At the end of this news, he had said simply, "Merry Christmas, Mom." At that point, she had started crying in happiness, and some of the people around them started giving Craig dirty looks, thinking he'd said something to upset her.

As much as I would have loved to witness this firsthand, deep in my heart I'm happy he got to be the one to give her this news. He deserved to be. Having been the one on the front lines, especially in terms of dealing with Rob and Col's withdrawal of support, I can't begrudge him being the one to provide Mom with this joy. Once I knew he'd broken the news, I called to congratulate her, basking in her reaction.

"I still can't believe it's true," she said. "But I worry you kids aren't telling me everything. I hope you're being honest with me."

I assure her (as I'm crossing my fingers) that there's no 'foreign aid' happening, and that the discount we found in the Interlocutor helped significantly. To allay any suspicion she might have in terms of thinking Colette has fueled Mom's need to move, I make sure to frame it up as a way to get her back closer to Southwoods for her own driving ease.

"This'll shorten your routes everywhere," I tell her. "You'll be back with all of your friends, and surrounded by new ones in your cottage, with all kinds of activities available. You'll also be 10 minutes from Good Shepherd, and you can pick up the threads of your life again without having to drive across the city. This is a dream come true for me, Mom."

Her response: "It's the best Christmas present ever."

We've scored big on this, and if I need any further confirmation at all, this seals the deal. June Hettinger has made it clear that the deposit will be due in mid-January, 30 days prior to Mom assuming occupancy of her cottage, so we'll be getting that together after the holidays. Basically, I'm on 'coast' through the end of the year, and it's a wonderful feeling.

We toast Mom's new life at Beecher during our family Christmas dinner, Callie stating, "To Gramma's freedom from her cupboard under the stairs," followed by Kerry's "To all the new friends she'll make at Beecher," with me adding, "God, thank you for blessing this from start to finish and for letting it finally become a reality!"

Mike waits a moment while we drink, then lifts his beer and says, grinning, "And to generous sons-in-laws!" We all burst out laughing, and I lean over and kiss him.

"And that's some MAJOR generosity!" I state emphatically.

Christmas Eve we attend our church's 3:00 service, which, on the heels of my five concerts at First Methodist, strikes me as a little on the loud, boisterous side. All the carols we sing with the worship band have a distinctly pop flavor, with techno arrangements. Heavily percussive Christmas carols is a reach for me after singing them with brass, strings, and harp. I try to focus on the meaning of the words, letting them penetrate my heart, knowing that this style of arrangement speaks to many people, even if I don't find it worshipful.

My favorite part of the service, and Kerry's, too, is the reading of the Christmas story from Luke. Jim Kennan, our minister, does this every year, sitting on the stage in an armchair and reading directly from the Bible in his lap. I close my eyes to better focus on Jim's voice and the images it creates, reaching across to Kerry to gently squeeze her hand.

"And there were shepherds abiding in the fields, keeping watch over their flocks by night. And lo, the angel of the Lord came upon them, and the glory of the Lord shone round about them, and they were sore afraid. But the angel said, 'Fear not, for behold, I bring you good tidings of great joy, which shall be to all people. For unto you is born this day in the city of David a Savior, which is Christ the Lord. And this shall be a sign unto you-ye shall find the babe wrapped in swaddling clothes and lying in a manger."

I can't hear these words without tears prickling my eyes. I love how God, in His infinite wisdom, made sure it was the shepherds, the scum of the earth and the utter outcasts of that society, who got to be the first responders in hearing His message of world upheaval. He knew in advance that they would receive it in simplicity and joy, carrying it forward from those dark hills into the hearts of others. NO spin, no pretense, no jockeying for power…instead, just the simple message of 'a baby has come into the world to save us-some angels just gave us the news.' God always works through vessels and hearts that are open, pure, and uncluttered. And, light always shines the brightest in dark places.

After the service, we head up to northern Kentucky for Christmas Eve with Mike's family. His sister Michelle and brother in law Steve have opened their home to all of us for years, in an incredible act of generosity. This is always a high power, megawatt evening of fun, with screaming people packed into Michelle's kitchen, and kids running everywhere. As Mike's entire family has continued to grow, with his nieces and nephews marrying and having children, there are now easily 50-55 people who will potentially show up at any given time over the course of this evening, and it is the single time of the year when all of us are together. We usually stay until around 11:00 and then drive back to Louisville.

Through the years, that dark, late ride home in the waning hours of Christmas Eve has become a precious time for me. Usually both girls end up falling asleep at some point, which leaves Mike and I quietly riding. There is the occasional house decorated with Christmas lights that's visible from the interstate, but mostly it's the dark hills, often bathed in pale moonlight, some years cocooned in snow, that are the constant. It takes me back to the fields those shepherds kept watch in 2,000 years ago when it was more than just starlight that filled the heavens.

* * * * *

Our Christmas day is slow, quiet, and relaxing, and none of us even surface until well past 10 AM. There's beautiful, cold sunlight pouring in through the windows, the trees stark and vivid against the sky as I get our brunch together. We loll around in the great room, opening the stockings that I stuff every year (which is one of my favorite things to do for the girls), then Kerry and Mike both curl up for naps. Cal and I don sweatshirts and sock caps, heading out for a long walk in our neighborhood while they sleep. I call Mom when we get in from our walk, and it sounds like she's had a fun day being with Col, Rob, and their boys. This will be her last Christmas in their house with them, and I'm glad she had the opportunity to be with them today. We eat a late dinner as the sky fades from violet to black, watch some movies, and I'm thankful for such a day of peace.

Two days later, on the 27th, Callie and I drive up to Cincinnati to see Mom. I'm supremely irritated because Kerry's Jeep has been stalling out, stranding her at work one of the times, and she and Mike stay behind to get it into the shop. I know it needs to be addressed; it just disappoints me that we all can't go together to see Mom. Cal and I leave Louisville around 2:00, hitting Cincy two hours later. I'm curious as to what Colette's attitude towards me will be, given everything that has transpired, but I should have known she'd make herself scarce. Cal and I see her briefly when we arrive, but she and the boys are headed out somewhere, Rob isn't around at all, and I get the distinct feeling she wants to minimize contact as much as possible. I had brought her a ceramic snowman, and I quietly leave the gift bag up on her counter after they leave-who knows, she might just take a sledgehammer to the poor chubby guy.

Mom seems to be holding the line securely, and I can tell she's very happy we're here. When she's excited, she always moves with a certain suppressed energy, and she's got that spring in her step this afternoon. Her mini Christmas tree is set up on her drum table, lit and decorated, and there are numerous packing boxes in corners and lined up against the outer walls of the kitchen.

"Geez, Mom, are you ready to move, or what?" I ask her, laughing, as I look around.

She explains to me, very seriously, that she's starting now, so she can 'take her time getting organized' and is filling the boxes with things she knows she definitely wants to take. Mom is a bona fide child of the depression…she throws nothing away, ever, and I find myself thinking this will be a monumental task for her. There's so much that will need to be gone through and weeded out, and I know she'll struggle with letting go of anything. I really need to come back up and spend an entire weekend helping her do this in January. Callie asks if there's anything we could help her go through while we're up here, but her response is classic Mom.

"No, I just want to enjoy our time," she says. "I have the

whole month of January to work on this."

On one side of the couch, Mom has made a big stack of photos she's gone through already, most of them the girls in various phases of growing up, and she invites Callie to look through them and take whatever she'd like, for either herself or Kerry. Cal is sorting through them and thoroughly enjoying herself when Mom brings her a small stack of presents from her coffee table.

"Can you tear yourself away from those pictures to see what Santa brought you?" she asks Cal teasingly. "He delivered these a few nights ago." She picks up several more, turns them over and searches for her fragile writing on the bottom of the packages that indicates whose gift it is, and brings three more over to me, placing them next to me on the couch. "And these are yours," she tells me.

I think of the trouble she's gone to buying and wrapping these, and for some reason it makes me want to cry- probably because it's so important to her to do this for us. She knows I love Yankee candles, so the first one I open is a large 'Cranberry Chutney' Yankee-one of my favorite scents. There's also a big sampler of various flavors of coffee, and a cute oversize earthenware coffee mug.

"As you can see, I've completely given in to your addiction to caffeine," she remarks, smiling. Years ago, she hammered on me constantly about giving up caffeine, and I gave her perfect lip service even as I continued drinking it in mass quantities. It's my only vice, along with an occasional cigarette with Michelle, and I don't have any plans for giving it up (the coffee).

"If you can't beat 'em, join 'em?" I tease her. Mom has never drunk any form of caffeine, probably due in large part to Gram's not drinking it, based on her Mormon beliefs.

"I suppose," she answers. "Besides," she adds, "and I tell you this every Christmas, you're the easiest one to buy for."

"Well, thanks, Gramma," Callie interjects. "I thought I was."

Mom considers this. "You ARE becoming easier," she acknowledges, "Because now all you and Kerry seem to want is a check. You know how impersonal I think that is…I hate to give you just that. So, Santa took some liberties, and you have your Mom to blame if you don't like these."

She hands Callie a card, and stacks three other wrapped packages on the footstool near Cal's chair. "Open the card last," she instructs.

She's given Cal a darling necklace with matching earrings, in a very eclectic black and silver weave. There's a beautiful asymmetrical silver piece hanging from the chain, and it's one of those timeless pieces Cal will be able to wear forever. The earrings are smaller replicas of the hammered silver piece.

"Mom, you have such an eye for this kind of thing," I comment, as Cal puts it on.

Mom laughs. "Not really. Sadly, I just buy what I like, and hope the person I'm giving it to likes it as much as I do."

The second package, the largest, is a beautiful grey, bronze, and taupe pillow that Callie can put on her new couch, which is a grayish taupe color. I had given Mom the colors back in November, suggesting it might be something Cal would like but not buy for herself. When she gently tears the wrapping open, I can tell she's genuinely touched.

"Gramma, this is beautiful!" she exclaims, lifting it up in the lamplight. "It'll be perfect for my couch. Where'd you find this?"

Again, typical Mom. "Well, it's a long story. I went to Target first and didn't like any of their selection, so I stopped at Pier One and they had a much better assortment. Their salesgirls were very helpful."

I think of where the closest Pier One is to Mom, and quickly realize the nearest one is at least half an hour from here. Unbidden, a lump forms in my throat as I picture Mom, worried about her peripheral vision, doggedly getting on the interstate to find just the right pillow for her granddaughter.

I glance over at Callie and our eyes meet. I'm sure she knows exactly what I'm thinking, and she stands up and walks over to the chair where Mom is sitting.

"Gramma, you're the best," she says, leaning down to hug Mom. "Only you would take the time to do that."

Mom glows, and retorts, "I do things like that for people I really like."

The final, smaller box is a collection of beautiful monogrammed 'C's in black, gold, and fuschia; each one a different pattern. "You outdid yourself, Gramma," Cal tells her, grinning from ear to ear. "Thank you so much. Kerry's really going to regret not being here."

"Well, I miss her," Mom comments. "And Santa has some things for her, too. Can I trust you to take these home to her?" she asks Cal, gently placing three packages and a card into a Macy's bag.

"I suppose," Cal says airily, "for a hug."

Now it's Mom's turn to open her gifts. I bought her a coordinated warm-up suit in shades of coral and turquoise, with both a long-sleeved pullover with a zip up top, and a short- sleeved print knit top. She rarely, if ever, buys clothes anymore, because I think she worries about spending the money. This way she doesn't have to feel guilty about having something cute and new to wear.

"I really like this," says Mom, gazing down at the articles of clothing in the box. "They'll be perfect for Beecher Springs when I'm out and about."

I love it that Mom is already picturing herself in her new digs, replete with new clothes. This move is long overdue. We sit for a while and talk, Mom asking Cal a lot about her job, her travelling, and Andy, bluntly asking her if "it's serious".

Cal grins and tells Mom, "I'd say it's seriously good, with seriously good potential," and Mom nods sagely.

"That's serious, then," Mom pronounces, and she and Callie both go off into gales of laughter.

This is so good for Mom, I think to myself.

We head out to dinner around 6:00, to a nearby bar and grille that Mom and I have frequented a lot these past few years whenever I'm up here. Cal and I tell Mom she has to order a drink, and she gets a strawberry daiquiri, Cal orders a beer, and I get a glass of wine. Mom seems so completely present and so relaxed-it warms my heart. Somehow, we get on the topic of Dad, probably started off by Callie reminiscing about all the hand-crafted pieces Dad used to make for her at Christmas, from her first hobbyhorse to her special desk that she still has in her condo.

"Did you have any idea that he was that good at woodworking when you were first dating?" Cal asks Mom.

"None whatsoever," Mom answers, "and even if he was, I'm not sure he would have volunteered that information. That came much later. When we first started seeing each other, my main concern was being sure there would be a next date."

And from there, Mom begins talking about some of her first dates with Dad. She's shared a lot with me over the years, especially the night we were at The Bend when she was in Louisville last summer, but I love hearing her adapt her narrative for Callie, and Cal is listening raptly. There are some details I'd not heard before, nor have I heard Mom weave this narrative with such relish. Her eyes sparkle, and her vocal inflections are extremely animated and uninhibited.

Mom and Dad truly idolized each other, I think yet another time. *They were meant to be together from the minute they climbed Long's Peak in that big group.*

I think again of how difficult it has been for Mom these past six years without Dad, yet how she has never once complained about being lonely, but just bravely made the best of the situation. Seeing her this vibrant gives me so much hope for her being able to start a whole new life at Beecher, surrounded by friends, activity, and familiarity.

We wrap up dinner reluctantly. I hate to see this evening end, and I wish we could spend the night. After hugs and goodbyes, Callie and I head out as a fine, grainy snow is beginning, and I pray the roads don't get bad on the way. Mom made me promise I would call her as soon as we got home, which should be around 10:30. By the time we junction onto 75-South in Kentucky, the snow has picked up, and is coming down in earnest, but in wind driven sheets that are slicing sideways across the highway, making it difficult to see the lines between lanes, especially with all of the refracted light from other headlights.

I decrease my speed and try to stay behind another car, so at least I have some rough definition of where the lane is in front of me, but it's getting dicey. If 75 is this bad, what will 71 be like? It's pretty much of a white-knuckler for me, and my stomach is in knots. But, luckily by the time I pick up I-71 South, the snow has really tapered off. Hurray-it looks like we're home free, and I always breathe easier on 71 anyway, even though it's more remote, because traffic isn't nearly as heavy.

Cal and I talk at length about the evening, and one comment she makes about Mom stays with me. "I cannot wait to see her shine at Beecher Springs," she says emphatically. "She has so much to offer, Mom. She's such a fun lady! You can tell how much she loved life when she was younger. Hearing her tell those stories is priceless...I can see her through a totally different lens of perspective!" And Cal couldn't be more accurate. It's time for Mom to shine.

The final days of 2009 are quiet and uneventful, with Kerry packing up and returning to UK, hopefully with all her Jeep issues behind her, and with Callie headed back to Nashville the day before New Year's Eve. I return for a few more days of work, with a half day on New Year's Eve, and savor what is left of this special season. 2010 will bring its own unique joys and challenges, and I feel ready to move into that stream of events.

Chapter Five

A WHOLE NEW WORLD
(January – April 2010)

"I love it, Mom!" I'm saying to her as I'm standing in the middle of her new living room, looking around at everything. "This is wonderful!"

She's been in her 'cottage', as they're called at Beecher Springs, for a week now. Last Saturday was her move date, while Mike and I were in Cabo with customers. Craig and Loire ended up not being a part of the move, either, because they were in Chicago with Loire's family. My hope had been that we could all help share that responsibility, calling Colette in late January to try to coordinate with her. I knew we'd be gone the weekend of February 14th, because of Cabo, but we were available any other weekend. As it turned out, Rob and Col ended up moving Mom completely on their own. Maybe they wanted it that way after everything that had transpired in December, and, if so, they got their wish. Col had been unsure of Rob's on-call schedule when I spoke to her, and though our conversation had been civil, it had also been brief.

We'd left it that she'd call me once she knew what weekend worked best for Rob, but she never followed up. Looking back, I wonder if I should have been more direct with her about everything that had happened, but I just didn't have it in me. I'm sure she knew Craig had copied us on the email he sent Rob; that was easy enough to see, and other than that, it's anybody's guess as to whether she knew Rob had called both Mike and me in December. Nor did I want to stir the pot by getting into a discussion with her. I was still trying my best to understand and respect their decision not to cosign with us. Bringing it up could well have put Colette on the defensive. By this time, Mom's move was a done deal anyway, and my thought process was to make it as easy on all of us as possible. Rehashing everything seemed to serve no purpose other than inflaming an already ugly situation. And, no matter what, Colette's request had been fulfilled. Mom was out of there.

It bothered me that Colette didn't ever call me back, but if that's how she chose to play it, okay. It probably worked out better for me to be here with Mom this weekend anyway, and I'll be able to help her so much more now that everything's moved. When I asked Mom how it all went, she relayed to me that Rob threw his back out on the second piece of furniture he lifted (Mom's dresser, with all the drawers taken out), which left only Colette and the boys to finish the task, since they had hired no movers. (Mom had desperately wanted movers; I know she hadn't wanted Col and Rob involved, other than carrying an occasional box upstairs.) I had mentioned movers to Colette the night I had called her, hoping to take the brunt of the move off them, but she hadn't liked the idea. Or, more importantly, maybe she had known Rob wouldn't like the idea.

"You know how movers can be," she had told me. "They're so careless. They might ding up the walls or scratch something," so I assumed there was a reason they didn't want movers involved. And, over the course of the past week, Mom has made a couple of trips back and forth with extra smaller loads, but even that has overwhelmed her. I can tell how tired she is, and how much still needs to be unpacked and organized. This is a huge transition for someone at 82.

I look around the big living area, which is really more of a great room. All of Mom's family room furniture is at the front of the room, as you come in her front door. Her two-section couch, which is more of a wrap around, lines the big front window that looks out over the parking area, and then angles right down a long wall into the center of the room. In its usual spot in front of the couch is the round coffee table we grew up with. On the farthest wall of the room, rising to a bank of windows that runs across the apex, stands our old kitchen table and its five spindle chairs. (Craig always ate on the window seat, which functioned as our sixth chair.)

"Does it feel like home yet?" I ask Mom, wondering what it's felt like to be here this week. I hope it hasn't been a letdown.

"I'm getting there," Mom answers. "I love being back on this side of town, so that's definitely helping. There's still so much unpacking and organizing to do, though, and I just can't summon the energy. All I want to do is lie down and nap."

"This is a big transition, Mom," I state. "Unpacking and settling into a new place is a huge job for anybody. That's one reason I came up this weekend. I'm going to be your unpacker. You can just order me around and tell me where you want stuff."

"No," Mom replies, "you've been working all week. This is the last thing you need to be doing with your weekend. You should be at home with Mike. We're just going to take it easy this weekend. I had your bedroom completely clean and all ready for you, and then Rob came over unannounced this morning with a truck he'd borrowed from someone-it might have been Clyde's (Col's father), and he carried in load after load of things I'd planned on going back for a bit at a time. He just threw it all here in the living room and your room, and then left."

Craig had called me at lunch today to tell me about this latest fiasco. Apparently, as Mom had said, Rob had brought what sounded like all the rest of what she had left behind, not even bothering to call her to tell her he was on his way, pulled up and started unloading box after box of her stuff, piling it in her living room and the guest bedroom-the room Mom is already referring to as 'my' room. My guess is that Rob was in one of his tight-lipped, clenched jaw-type of moods, and probably offered no help to Mom whatsoever in terms of asking her where she wanted the boxes to be put. He left as soon as he had unloaded everything, and Mom immediately had a meltdown. She had called Craig at work in tears, explaining what had happened.

"She worked so hard all week to get everything put away and to have the place looking nice for you," Craig had told me when we spoke earlier today. He had known I was coming up to be with Mom this weekend. "I think she was more upset about him trashing 'your bedroom' than anything else! She told me, 'He completely messed up Bet's room, and I had everything perfect for her.'"

Knowing the effort Mom's put into getting the place the way she wants it, it breaks my heart, and I know it must have exhausted her. The simple fact that she wanted 'my room' just right for me touches me, too. I know she wanted it to feel cozy and welcoming, not to be lined with boxes that needed to be stepped over and unpacked.

Craig, in an act of supreme kindness, had taken the rest of the day off, driven down to Cincinnati, and helped Mom determine what was in the boxes, labeling each one for her, and deciding where to store them until they were unpacked. Most went in her garage; some went in the guest room closets, and a few still line the walls of the guest room. He had moved everything until the living room was clear again, and Mom had calmed down. He was furious when he relayed the scenario to me.

"What an asshole!" was his blunt assessment. "Why would he do that to Mom? It's like he couldn't have made it any clearer to her that they wanted every trace of her out of that house as soon as possible!"

It does seem very cold and unfeeling, and I find myself wondering if Colette had totally driven the whole situation…I could hear her saying, 'Rob, get all of your mom's stuff over to her today…I don't want it sitting here indefinitely, and I don't want her coming back for it, either.' Who knows? Less and less would surprise me in terms of what they do. Then, my ability, even after everything that's gone down, to give them the benefit of the doubt…maybe they just wanted to save Mom all the trips back and forth.

"I know, Mom…Craig told me about it," I say. "I'm so sorry that happened. But you don't need to worry about my bedroom. You know I'll like it no matter what. And I can certainly unpack anything that's in there tomorrow." I look around and grin. "I just can't believe you're really here! I'm so happy for you!"

And I am. I drove up after work tonight-my first drive ever in darkness for the entire way here, but I'm determined to give Mom a full weekend of my time, both to be with her for companionship and to help her get organized. Now that this move is real, and she's no longer at Rob's, I feel a giddy sense of release for her that is amazing to me. Part of it is that, from here on out, I can come here whenever I want and visit. It's solely Mom's place now. She can do whatever she wants whenever she wants, and there's no more walking on eggshells, or feeling like she's putting Rob's family out. And, she's back close to everything important in her life- Good Shepherd, her beauty shop, the bank, her favorite restaurants, and most of all, her friends.

I'm ecstatically happy for her, and I want this to be a place she is comfortable and at home in-a place that fills her up. But, now that she's here, I don't want her to feel like we've washed our hands of the situation. This new chapter can't be an excuse for us to say, 'OK, she's good-she'll make new friends now, and she's close to her old ones again.' God has impressed on my heart the absolute need to be that bridge moving forward even as she's building her new life. You can never NOT need your family.

We talk for a little while, and then I wash my face in "my" bathroom off "my" bedroom, put my PJ's on, and we curl up on the couch and watch the news. I stretch out, propping my head up on a couple of sofa pillows, and realize how tired I am. Fifteen minutes into the news, I can't keep my eyes open. I kiss Mom goodnight and trudge into my room. Mom follows me in, and for a minute I think something is wrong.

"I've come to tuck you in," Mom announces. "It's the least I can do on your first night here. And…oh, wait a minute." She seems flustered about something. Turning on heel, she leaves the room, and I lay in bed waiting. In a few minutes she returns.

"These were supposed to be laying on your pillow, and I forgot to turn your bed down," she states, somewhat sheepishly. In her hand are several Andes mints-she knows I love them. I burst out laughing.

"Oh, my gosh, Mom, you are the best," I say, sitting up in bed. "Here, lay them on my pillow and I'll act surprised."

"Well, it's a little late to act surprised," she tells me drily.

I pat my pillow. "Right here," I motion. "My eyes are closed and I'm waiting."

I can feel Mom lean over and arrange them on the pillow, then straighten back up. I open my eyes.

"Will you look at this?" I say in feigned surprise, picking up the three mints. "This is one classy establishment I'm staying in. I knew this place was a wise decision!"

Mom is enjoying this. "The meals may leave a little to be desired, but I hear the occupants in the south are pretty fond of this site."

"Yes," I answer. "It has quite a reputation down there."

She leans down to kiss me goodnight. "It's nice to go to

sleep with someone else in my house," she tells me.

I smile. "It's nice to be going to sleep in your house," I respond.

She flips my light out and quietly shuffles into her own bedroom. I snuggle into my bed, thinking to myself, *Yeah, this is going to be good for Mom.* In the distance, I hear the melancholy wail of a train whistle, and I can feel myself smile in the dark. That's my favorite nighttime sound from childhood, and it feels like a benediction. *Even better,* I think. I'm asleep in three minutes.

* * * * *

I wake up the next morning on work schedule time out of a deep, blank sleep, and it takes me a few minutes to remember where I am. I'm happy all over again when I think of what this means for Mom, and when I spot the three mints lying on the nightstand. I stretch luxuriously in bed, arms up over my head. The place is quiet. I can tell Mom is still asleep, so I decide to stay in bed, too. She needs to sleep as late as possible. I wonder if it's been hard for her to sleep here knowing she's all by herself now. I'll have to ask her later.

I can see the sky through the row of windows that run along the top of the cottage, and it's beginning to lighten. Versus the inky black of night, it's just a pale pearly grey now. I hadn't thought to check last night before I fell asleep. It didn't even occur to me that the high windows were in here as well. I feel another rush of pleasure thinking that I can look up at the sky tonight and maybe see the moon and stars if it's clear. I really like this place.

I think back over the past month, and I'm glad it's past. It's been stressful-both in terms of work and tying up all the loose ends with Beecher Springs to ready Mom for her move. I had hoped against hope that Rob might have a change of heart about co-signing with us, but that wasn't to be. The last time I spoke to him was the night he called in December to tell me they'd 'done enough for Mom'. My guess is that Rob did not get the type of support he was looking for from Mike or me. Instead, he got my objectivity, and Mike's honesty. And, even though I had strongly encouraged it, he never did call Craig. Now, based on Craig's scathing email to him, I know that will never happen. I still think Rob and Colette truly believe there has been financial malfeasance regarding Mom's estate where Craig is concerned, and that Craig has somehow altered the will, which is beyond ridiculous. So, based on that premise, Rob isn't about to give a thief more money. If anyone had told me a decade ago that things would play out this way, I wouldn't have thought it possible. It's progressed from bad to deplorable to downright ugly, all over what should have been an easy decision to do the best we could for my mom.

In a sick way, but I know Craig shares my feelings, I almost relish the fact that Rob has decided not to participate in sharing any responsibility, because that choice eliminates him from having any further say in Mom's living situation, other than something medical if she's unable to make a decision for herself. Craig and I never had a say in her moving to Rob's…finally we get to be active participants in a decision that will benefit her. That's very freeing, after so many years of my hands being tied. I'd still rather have had all of us reach a consensus, though. I doubt things between all of us will ever be the same.

The other thing that has weighed on me all through January is Mom's suspiciousness about her finances covering the move. She may be forgetful, but she's far from stupid, and she's remarked numerous times to Craig and me (and, I'm assuming, to Rob and Colette, too) that she can't believe she's in a cottage as nice as the one in the Knolls. Craig and I have had several conversations about this, because it's imperative to us that Mom never, EVER find out that we co-signed the document of financial responsibility. First, it would kill her to know we did that; secondly, she'd opt to go somewhere much less expensive (what Rob was pushing for) when Beecher Springs has always been her first choice. Third, if she knew the decision had created this huge rift in our family, it would sicken her, even though the cracks in the foundation were there long before this decision ever arose.

Craig and I have emphasized the amount of the discount Beecher Springs was offering, implying that it was significantly larger than it was. At one point, Mom had said to me, "Betsy, promise me you're not using any of your money for this. Promise. I couldn't bear knowing that, and it wouldn't be right."

"None of my money," I had stated. "But all of yours." We'll say that it's Mike's money, not mine, which, since he's earned far more than I have in my lifetime, literally makes it a sort of semi-truth.

"I think you're hiding something from me, Bet," Mom would say over the phone when we'd talk. "This is just too good to be true."

"I am hiding something from you," I'd say. "I'm hiding how incredibly excited I am about you moving to Beecher Springs."

Craig, too, did the same song and dance, asking her if she really thought we'd cough up that amount of money when we had kids to raise. Our biggest concern was that Colette and Rob would tell Mom the truth, under the guise of clearing themselves. Something along the lines of 'Here are OUR reasons for NOT cosigning; here's why we DIDN'T agree with this decision.' (Even though Col had been the one to suggest Beecher in the first place.) Maybe the biggest reason they didn't blow the whistle was that they knew it would keep Mom with them for a longer period while we looked at other alternatives. I'm thinking about all this now as I'm lying peacefully in bed on my back, watching the sky lighten. It's now a white-grey, with the faintest pink tinge to it. The digital clock Mom has on my round night table reads 7:27.

Towards the middle of January, prior to the phone call

about what weekend to move Mom, I had called Colette to confirm for sure the fact that they would not be not cosigning. I received my negative confirmation in no uncertain terms. Very accusatory towards Craig from the start of the conversation, I had stopped her, and much as I had done with Rob, tried to be very open and truthful. I completely accepted their decision not to contribute, I told her, but it had caught Craig off guard when he had called her to finalize plans. It might have been more considerate, I had suggested, to have called him as soon as they had decided not to do it, versus leaving him to make false assumptions. I even went as far as to suggest that Rob should have been the one to call Craig and shoot straight with him. I could tell that Colette didn't like hearing my differing opinions, and it had occurred to me that, like my conversation with Rob, this was the first time ever I had openly disagreed with her. I'm sure my calm frankness was a little disconcerting to Colette, especially for someone who was usually the one in control. Oh, well. I had said what I needed to say, and it felt pretty good. I think at this point, they just want to be free of all of us, Mom included.

By now, my head is hurting from lack of caffeine, which is sad, but a fact of life, because usually my first sip of life juice occurs around 6 AM on a workday. My body is starting to go into panic mode. I lay a few more minutes, then quietly get up and slip into a pair of yoga pants and a sweatshirt, thinking I can sneak out to the kitchen to try to locate Mom's coffeemaker and the coffee she always keeps for me. Just as I step into the kitchen, I hear her soft padding out of the bedroom. She's still in her blue nightgown, and, as has been her practice for years, her hair is wrapped in several long strips of toilet paper wound around her head (supposedly to hold her permed curls in place), secured with long silver hair clips. How they manage to stay in place without jabbing her eyes out in the middle of the night is an unsolved mystery.

I can't help myself. I look at her and start laughing. "Well, good morning, my little banshee!" I greet her.

"What's that supposed to mean?" Mom asks, somewhat testily, looking at me with her eyebrows raised.

I motion to her hair. "Nice wrapping job," I comment, smirking.

Mom reaches up with her hand to check the toilet paper, as if to be certain it's still there. "A necessary evil," she answers, and then asks me, "How did you sleep?"

"Like a baby," I reply. "I was asleep as soon as my head hit the pillow with my mints."

"Were you too hot or cold?" Mom asks, and I know she wants to be sure I had the perfect sleeping temperature.

"Baby Bear," I tell her. "Just right."

She nods. "Good." Then, noticing my opening and closing of cabinet doors, "Oh, Bet, are you looking for my coffeemaker?" She sighs heavily. "I have no idea where it is. I should have thought of that last night before we went to bed. I'm sure it's packed."

Not good for my headache and I feel myself growing irritated. *This isn't Mom's fault*, I tell myself. Instead, I realize I can walk over to one of the adjacent main buildings that has a coffee shop in it and get coffee there to bring back. Problem solved, and I walk over with my wallet in the brisk morning air, passing an amazing model train display in one of the alcoves in the main building. It's a large-scale replication, complete with lights and a full-bodied whistle. The tracks it runs on traverse imitation mountains with tunnels cut through them, the train disappearing in blackness only to emerge further down the range, then climbing the tracks that scale the outside of the mountains. The front of the display is a model village with an Austrian flavor to it, the train chugging importantly through the business district of the small community. I stand watching it, spellbound.

After I order my two large coffees, I come back again to watch it, standing quietly, coffee sack in hand. There's something hypnotic in the motion of the locomotive. I have no idea how long I've been there when I hear the soft clink-

clink-clink of a walker coming towards me. It's a frail little elderly man, dapper in a red and black plaid flannel shirt and a Cincinnati Reds ball cap.

"Fun little exhibit, isn't it?" he asks me, nodding toward the train. "My grandchildren love it!"

I smile. "I can see why," I answer. "It's beautifully done. And I love the tunnels."

He nods and grins. "My grandkids worry about not being able to see it when it disappears in the tunnels-they're always so relieved when it pops back out again!" He chuckles. "You have a good day, hon," he tells me, and I thank him and tell him to do the same. This simple exchange fills my heart with warmth, and I wonder if everyone is this friendly. Mom is absolutely going to love this place.

Once I get back to her cottage and the coffee begins to lubricate my brain synapses, I feel myself coming to life. Mom has only made one trip to the grocery store so far, buying just some basics, so I use what she has for our breakfast, making us scrambled eggs and cheese with toast. We both eat like lumberjacks, composing a lengthy shopping list as we eat. That's something I'll probably need to monitor each time I come up now. I also offer to reorganize the kitchen, having Mom tell me where she wants everything, being sure the items she uses most are within easy reach. I could tell, just in looking for the coffeemaker, that things have been put away very haphazardly, and this is as good a place as any to start.

There's a fair amount of storage space in her kitchen. It's galley style, with a ceramic tile floor, and the sink is in the middle at the far end of it, under a window that looks out on the parking area like the window in her living room. I pull all the boxes that appear to have any kitchen items in them into the living room, slowly unpacking them as I go. Cupboard by cupboard, shelf by shelf, I organize and fuse in the items that have been unpacked. It's already apparent that Mom is going to have to consolidate; she hasn't used some of this stuff in years. This is where it gets sensitive, because

I don't want her getting agitated, thinking I'm getting rid of her stuff. The simple fact of the matter is that some of it HAS to go. She's a packrat, and this is the perfect opportunity to de-clutter as I unpack. I'm contemplating the best tactic to use with Mom.

I devise a system that I think will work. If it's something I know has no sentimental value to her, or is very much like something else she has, like duplicate kitchenware, I ask her if I can have it, and I've started a packing box for me. Callie or Kerry might also like some of these items, and what we don't keep will go to Goodwill in Louisville. Part of me hates being this calculating about it, but I know this task would completely overwhelm Mom, and she lacks the energy for it.

While I tackle the kitchen, she 'unpacks' a couple of the boxes, but what I notice more than her unpacking is her aimlessly unwrapping objects, setting them down, and then coming back later to pick them up and look at them again as if she's seeing them for the first time. A few of them she brings in and sets on the counter, saying politely, "You might want to find a good place for these." And I do. The majority end up spread out over the surface of the couch. I'm so, so glad I came up to help with all of this.

Around 1:00 we break for lunch, and I make us peanut butter and jelly sandwiches and chicken noodle soup. (Mom was always a big Campbell's soup fan.) One thing I had done before I made the trip up here was to pick up several packets containing change of address cards. I had gone to Target and spotted them on an end cap, immediately knowing they'd be a great idea for Mom. My hope is that they generate numerous phone calls and some 'welcome to your new home' cards. And, too, it's a reminder to all her friends that she's 'back on the block' again. After lunch, we take a break from unpacking and crack into a packet of the cards.

"Get your address book," I tell Mom, "and we're going to go through it, person by person. You tell me if you want me to send them a card or not."

I know she's reached the point where she no longer likes to write. Her manuscript is shaky and spidery, and she has a lot of trouble forming her letters. There's no justice. Back in the day, she was the Queen Card Sender, cards addressed in advance, and in a file holder that was divided into months of the year, so no niece, nephew, friend or relative was forgotten. Mom deserves this reverse consideration now.

"You read me the addresses," I suggest, "and stamp all the envelopes."

We do about ten of them, and I can tell she's whipped. Sometimes recently I forget that what is relaxing for me is a huge effort for her.

"Lay down and get your feet up for a few minutes," I tell her. "Just close those eyes for a baby nap. I'll fill out the insides of the cards, so we can stuff these envelopes."

"Oh, I shouldn't sleep while you're working," she protests. "I feel so guilty."

I look at her and slide my glasses down my nose for effect. "Don't make me send you to your room," I admonish her. "Get over to that couch, close your eyes, and stop talking to me."

She does get comfortable on the couch and is asleep instantly. I quietly work on the cards for the next hour, just savoring being here and knowing Mom is happy and resting. I also flip ahead in her book, continuing to address cards to friends and relatives I know she'll want to include, filling out each with Mom's new information. I'm almost through an entire pack when she wakes up.

"I'm on a roll," I tell her. "You're going to be deluged with phone calls and social invitations."

"That would be nice," she replies. "I won't know how to act."

We decide to go to her 5:30 worship service at Good Shepherd. Anything I can do to encourage her to keep up her routine and to get out, I'm going to be all about it. I figure we can grab dinner afterwards somewhere. This day has truly flown. I offer to drive, because I know it'll be completely dark when we return home, and we leave for church around 5:00. It delights me to drive this route to Good Shepherd, especially through Preston Park, a huge greenbelt area which rims the church, knowing how close it will put Mom from now on.

As we turn onto the main road once we leave Beecher, I comment on how cold it is. Mom says nothing in response, and then, after a few minutes have elapsed, apropos of nothing, asks, "Where are we going again?"

I'm flummoxed. Yes, there's been a definite decline in her since Christmas, when Callie and I visited her in Cincinnati at Rob's. She's moving much more slowly, and seems to be having trouble focusing, but this totally comes out of left field.

"To church, remember?" I answer, as calmly as possible. Wow. I'd better start keeping track of this. Is this just a fluke or the new normal?

We get to church, settle into one of the front pews, and I soak up the peace of early evening. The sky outside is streaked with purple and magenta as the final rays of the sun sink below the horizon, casting long beams across the altar and the first few pews. I love gazing out the huge floor to ceiling windows on the left side of the sanctuary that overlook Preston Lake. Good Shepherd sits on a high hill that slopes down to the park road, and the bare trees are stark against the darkening sky. I used to stare out these same windows when the sermons bored me as a kid, and I think God spoke to me through the glorious views outside those windows as much as He did through any sermon I ever digested.

Good Shepherd has a very special place in my heart. Mom and Dad became members here shortly after they were married, when it was a small, several years old mission church. It's the church I grew up in, leaving it only when we were transferred to Louisville. The congregation is like extended family, and there's a deep sense of community and support. I'm indebted to them, as well. They have taken such good care of Mom since Dad passed.

The service is simple and beautiful. After all the contemporary praise choruses we worship with at home, these old hymns are such a gift to sing. I enjoy both types of music, but these are my roots, because they're what I grew up ingesting. I know Mom is not a Pastor Morehouse fan (their recent new minister), but I genuinely enjoy both his message and delivery. I quietly thank God for allowing Mom to finally get to Beecher Springs, and for our time together this weekend. We talk with people after the service, lots of Mom's friends coming over to tell her hello, and to greet me. I make sure to mention Mom's Beecher move to all of them.

"I'm helping her unpack and get everything shipshape," I tell Sherry Castille, one of Mom's old friends. "I'm her concierge service."

Sherry has the best laugh, and it rolls right out now. "Betsy, I'm glad she's got her own place finally," she tells me. "She's so much closer to all of us now. Joan," she says, wrapping her arm around Mom's shoulder, and squeezing her, "We better see a lot more of you now. You were too far away."

I love hearing this, and I hope it encourages Mom.

"It is nice," Mom tells Sherry. "It took us no time to drive here tonight-no more interstate."

Sherry winks at me, and nods knowingly at Mom. "You had quite a drive before," she states. "You're going to love Beecher Springs, Joan. There's lots to do, and so many nice people there."

Back out in the car, Mom and I discuss where we want to go for dinner. Standard choices involve a local family owned restaurant called Barney's; then there's Stiver's, Vince's Pizza, or Chili Time. I'm really leaning towards Chili Time-chili sounds so good as cold as it is. I mention it to Mom, knowing she loves that restaurant chain and will more than likely agree that needs to be our destination. Wait for it… but Mom's comment is, "I don't think there are any around here, Bet."

I momentarily freeze, and, unbidden, feel a cold chill creep down my arms. Gently I say, "Yeah, there's one up at the top of Preston Road-by the 275 Interchange. Remember?"

"No, I don't think so," Mom replies resolutely. "If there was, it's closed now. But, to my knowledge, there's never been one there."

This is blowing my mind; it's almost like I've entered an alternate reality. For years after church on Sundays, Mom and Dad would go there, often with their friends Charlie and Margie Lewis from Good Shepherd. Charlie had loved his Chili Time, and Mom and Dad were more than happy to accompany them. Now, based on Mom's level of certainty that no Chili Time exists up this road, I'm starting to question myself. Could it have been another chili restaurant instead of a Chili Time? I know they used to eat there, because Mike, the girls and I often came with them when we were in town.

"But Mom," I hear myself protest, "You and Dad always used to meet Charlie and Margie there after church to eat, remember?"

"No, we never did that," Mom declares, again as matter of fact as if she's stating that it's raining. "There's never been a Chili Time up here."

By now, we're just a few blocks away from where I'll turn in to the Chili Time that isn't there, and part of me sincerely hopes it ISN'T there so that Mom will be proved right. Otherwise, we're farther down a dark path than I'd realized. I accelerate through a green light, reach the intersection where I should turn right, and put my signal on. There, high above us, is the Chili Time sign, lit up like the Fourth of July to be visible to travelers on the interstate. I shake my head in the dark, and quietly exhale.

And to complete the utter bizarreness of this exchange,

Mom says beside me, as if our previous conversation never even took place, "Here we are. Charlie and Margie Lewis loved this place. We used to meet them here all the time after church on Sundays."

What is happening? I get out of the car almost reluctantly, trying my best to process what has just happened. Is this dementia? It's almost like a time warp, but the thing that's most disturbing to me is that this entire conversation has only spanned a period of; maybe, three minutes...yet Mom can't hold what was said in those prior two minutes to relate it to what is taking place right now. How can she fail to connect what just happened? One minute there's abject denial that this restaurant even existed, let alone acknowledging that she and Dad met friends here; then a scant minute later, recognizing both the location AND acknowledging the history associated with it.

What does this mean? Do I question her on it? If I did, would she even have any recollection of our prior discussion? Add in her comment on the way to church asking where we were going, and I'm really concerned. Is she even carrying forward what we've talked about this weekend? Now I'm not sure at all, and I feel like there's been a seismic shift in the ground under my feet.

I decide not to say anything to Mom, because if she's having these cognitive blips, calling her out on them will only alarm her and put her on the defensive. This is shades of what Colette was talking about with the 5:30 AM doctor's appointment Mom claimed she had. And, if Mom's tracking this direction anyway, which obviously she is, I could see how a week of intense transition like this due to her move could really exacerbate the problem. No point in mentioning it. I just need to keep watching.

We order, and Mom gets a tuna sandwich-me, my beloved five-way. I'm getting my wallet out to pay for us as we finish up, and my head is down rooting through my purse, when I hear the waitress ask Mom, "Ma'am, why don't I get you a box for that? That's awfully messy just to put in your purse," and I look up to see Mom cramming the loosely wrapped remains of her tuna sandwich into her purse.

"Whoa, Mom-hold on," I blurt out. "You don't want that in your purse. That tuna's smelly. Let her get you a box."

"It's fine," Mom states. "I've wrapped it up."

The waitress is standing there looking torn, obviously reading the situation for what it is, and I make direct eye contact with her and smile.

"A box would be great," I tell her, and I can see visible relief as she moves to go get one.

"Now why did you put her to all that trouble?" Mom scolds me. "It would have been just fine in my purse."

Again, I try to find the middle ground without humiliating her.

"That tuna odor would linger, Mom," I tell her. "Plus, it would pick up germs from your purse-it could make you sick."

The waitress returns and puts the box on the table, making a cute comment about it being a safer mode of travel. I let Mom transfer her sandwich to the box, and she's able to close it securely. We pay our bill, I leave a substantial tip for our sweet waitress, and we drive back to Beecher. It has been the most interesting and unsettling of nights.

We tackle about eight more change of address cards, and then decide to watch some old Andy of Mayberry reruns. Mom seems completely herself the rest of the evening, which is somewhat comforting. We head to bed around 10:30, and I lay wide awake for a long time, thinking over today's events. Is Mom truly able to be here by herself? Today's events make me unsure of that. Will she settle in and be okay as her routines develop? Is she a risk to herself? I just don't know. And then there's her driving. What would have happened tonight if SHE had been behind the wheel on the way to church and forgotten where she was going? Especially if I hadn't been in the car with her at all? Troubling questions, all of these, and further confirmation of why I need to be up here for extended periods of time.

I pray in my head, first thanking God for Mike's willingness to make that financial commitment so that Mom could be here at all. I'm still amazed sometimes, when I really stop and think about what we've accomplished over the past three months. It makes me very happy. I pray for guidance forward, asking God to build in support that Mom needs even as she regains as much of her independence as possible. Therein lies our challenge. I have no idea what that will look like.

Show me, God, I pray. I gaze up through the skylight, see several dim stars shining, and my eyes eventually close in sleep.

Sunday is a kind of 'wrap up day'. I really want to finish the unpacking for Mom, and after I load up on three large coffees at the residents' center, (and watch the train again for a good ten minutes) I tear into what's left. By around 1:00, I have the kitchen completely organized and the boxes in my bedroom all emptied out. Four boxes full of things that I'm taking home go out to my Jeep, and I walk Mom through the kitchen in terms of what's where. She's mostly hung out in the living room watching 'Meet the Press' and then found 'African Queen' on a movie channel, which she's currently engrossed in.

"Bet, thank you for doing all of this," she tells me. "You know it would have taken me forever. It looks so good, and it'll be easy for me to find everything."

"Do you want me to make a list of what's in which cabinet?" I ask her, wondering if she'll even remember having this conversation. "I'm glad to do that if it'll help you when you're looking for something specific."

"Heavens, no!" is her answer. "You've done more than enough. If I can't find something, I can always call you."

I fix us Bisquik pancakes for lunch, and then we do another round of the cards. I've got all 60 addressed by the time we finish. The inside information is the only thing left to do, and then they can be mailed.

"What should we do for dinner tonight?" Mom asks lazily as we're finishing up the cards, with 'African Queen' continuing in the background.

"What sounds good to you?" I ask, reminding her that we're going to Kroger to stock up. "We can get whatever sounds good and I'll fix us dinner here," I suggest.

"Oh, no," Mom responds. "You've worked hard enough this weekend. Unpacking, cooking for me, and getting me organized…I'm treating you. I have an idea! Why don't you let me take you up to the Manor House for dinner?"

The Manor House is Beecher's restaurant for their residents and is also open to the public. Mom and Dad used to come with some of their friends who had retired here years ago, and it's very nice. In addition, they host group events and parties for the residents.

"That does sound fun," I venture. "I haven't been up there in years. Do you have to make a reservation ahead of time?"

Mom isn't sure, but she looks through some information lying near her phone, finds the number she needs, and calls to ask. This hardly seems to be the same person who denied Chili Time's existence last night. They assure her that no reservations are needed, and we can walk in at any point during the evening. I'm thinking that it will be helpful for her to go there first with me-maybe we'll see someone she knows. If nothing else, it'll be another chance to 'acclimate' with me along. I know she'd never venture up there solo.

Shopping at Kroger with Mom is relaxing for me. She can only move so fast, and we just take our time going up and down the aisles, almost 'browsing' for the things we need. Being here over the course of the weekend has reinforced to me that even the simplest tasks-the 'everyday living stuff'-is going to be taking far more time now, because of how much Mom's slowing down. I don't mind it a bit. This is where my innate patience serves me so well, and I love knowing it's helping Mom to have me with her. It gets her out, it gives her exercise and stimulation, and we get to be together. I let her push the cart and make all the decisions, the exception being a big canister of 'Chock Full 'O Nuts' coffee and a bouquet of flowers for her coffee table.

Our dinner at the Manor House is fun. We walk the half mile to it, even though it's cold, and it's surprisingly full for a Sunday night. It's a very warm, relaxing atmosphere with 1940's Big Band music playing in the background, and the buzz of conversation is inviting. We've just ordered our meal when a woman comes toward us, smiling and excited, and leans down to Mom, hugging her.

"Hello, Joan!" she greets Mom. "I couldn't believe it when I saw you come in! How are you? Is this Betsy?"

She looks very familiar, but I can't place her until Mom greets her in return. "Well, hello, Carol!" and I can tell she's genuinely glad to see whoever this is. "Bet, you remember Carol and Larry Parks, don't you? Dad and Larry were both in Kiwanis together."

Now the light goes on. "Sure!" I answer, and greet Carol, too. She and Larry have been residents here for at least six years. Larry has come up behind her, and they ask if we're visiting. I give Mom the floor.

"Oh, no," Mom answers, smiling. "I'm finally here for good. I just moved into the Knolls last weekend, and Bet's here this entire weekend helping me get unpacked. She's organized my whole kitchen for me!"

I can tell they're genuinely happy Mom is so close by. My parents used to get together with them a lot before they moved to Rob's.

"Joan, this is wonderful news, it really is," Carol is saying. "I didn't realize you were thinking about doing this!"

I can see Mom hesitating in terms of how to frame this up, so I jump in quickly, "That thirty minutes of interstate driving was getting old, and she missed doing more over this way. This move made perfect sense-now she's back close to friends, church, and everything else."

Mom looks at me gratefully. "It is nice," she tells Carol and Larry. "You remember, Bill and I had our name on a waiting list here years ago."

"I do remember that," Larry affirms. "Well, welcome back, Joan! It's great to have you here! We'll have to get the old gang back together for dinner soon!"

I'm smiling broadly. I'd completely forgotten how adorable these two were. No wonder Mom and Dad enjoyed them so much. The memory of them being at Dad's funeral comes back to me, as well.

Mom tells them, half-jokingly, "Look for my change of address card in the mail. Betsy's sending them to everyone under the sun."

I look at Larry and Carol and wink. "People need to know where to find her," I tell them. They laugh, and we talk for a few more minutes.

Dinner is delicious, and Mom and I walk slowly back to her cottage around 7:30. I hate it that it's Sunday night already, and I have a slightly sick feeling in the pit of my stomach. I really don't want to leave Mom. It feels like the weekend just got started. I pack a lunch to take with me in the morning, and we play a few hands of gin rummy and watch the news. I get the coffee pot ready to go for tomorrow morning, and we're both in bed around 10:30. I've made it clear to Mom that I'll be up to visit frequently. I want her to know she can count on me to be here on a regular basis. I'm sure she'll develop her routine over time and start doing more with her friends-Larry and Carol were testimony to that tonight, as were Mom's friends at Good Shepherd, but based on what I've seen this weekend, I feel strongly that she needs someone from our family checking in on her and spending more than just a few hours at a time with her.

The episodes of forgetfulness that I witnessed last night still concern me. I set the alarm for 4:45. I can shower, dress, and be on the road by 5:30, and that gives me two and a half hours to make it to work. Traffic shouldn't be bad that early in the morning…worst case scenario, I'm late getting to work, and that really wouldn't bother me. This whole trip process is going to be trial and error. Kissing Mom goodnight, I tell her how much fun I've had with her this weekend.

"It's been wonderful having you here," she tells me. "I've enjoyed it so much. You did way too much, but I thank you for everything. It really does help me to feel a little more settled in."

I lay awake for a long time, just staring up at the skylight. I so hope she will be happy here, and I feel like we're off to a good start. In the morning, there is one small glitch, or one huge problem, depending on how you look at it. I can't get any hot water out of the shower. I try leaving the water on for almost five minutes, thinking it may take time to pull from the water heater, but it's still stone cold. I turn it off, turn it back on, try just the hot water handle alone…nothing.

"Have you had trouble with this?" I ask Mom, calling her in from the kitchen, because of course she's up to see me off. "Am I doing something wrong?"

Mom has a funny look on her face, but I can't read her.

"Did it work for you earlier this week?" I rephrase my question. She only takes showers, never baths, so I know she's had to have used it.

"Well, um, uh, I really don't know how it works, Bet. I feel terrible that you don't have hot water."

Wait a minute. Is Mom telling me, in a round-about, embarrassed way that she hasn't taken any showers at all since she's moved in? That's a stretch of…nine days now. Oh my gosh. I look at her, straight into her eyes, and she looks back at me, and I know that's been the case. She's never been able to lie, and I can read this like a book.

"Oh, Mom," I sigh. "Why haven't you called someone? If I hadn't been such a European this weekend, and had showered yesterday, I would have known then! Didn't you want to wash?"

Now I'm not only concerned, I'm upset, because I'm wondering if this, too, totally slipped her mind and she hasn't even thought about it until now, when I'm calling her out on it. I can tell she's mortified, and I really need to curb my own temper, because I'm going to have to go in to work un-showered. Oh, worse things could happen, for sure… it's just not how I wanted my first trip here to end. Or how I wanted to show up at work today.

"Listen, do you want me to call somebody to come and take a look at this?" I ask her.

"No, Bet," she tells me. "I'll do it today. I just didn't want to bother anybody."

I feel like this is just a cover for something deeper, like her forgetfulness, because if it was something she had really wanted, she would have called someone immediately.

"Do you know who to call?" I ask her. "And do you have the number?"

"Yes," she answers, "I'll find it in the manual they gave me. I feel so badly you can't shower before you go to work."

"Yeah, me too," I answer flatly. "So, I need to throw my scrubs on here, and get some makeup on."

By the time I'm dressed and ready, I feel slightly better about my situation, but not at all better about Mom's.

"Promise me you'll call them and get somebody over here today to look at this, because you need to take a shower," I tell her one more time as I'm getting ready to hug her goodbye. "I'm calling tonight after work to check on you, and I want you to tell me you have hot water and a clean body."

She gives me her word she'll call, and I hug and kiss her goodbye wanting to throw up and cry at the same time. I never dreamed it would be this hard to leave. Her last words to me are, "Don't you worry about me-I'll get this figured out."

I think I may need to get some things figured out, too.

* * * * *

Mom does call maintenance about the shower, and they come over that same day and show her exactly how to work the faucet, so she has her first Knoll shower nine days after moving in. Better late than never, I suppose. With that behind us, and an occasional reminder from me asking her when her last shower was, (which aggravates her to no end) she seems to be remembering to do it on a regular basis. She appears to be settling in well, and as I call her over the course of the next three weeks, I'm amazed at the transformation I witness. For the first time in years, she is literally gabbing to me on the phone about her various goings-on instead of me carrying the conversation, and each time I hang up after we've talked, there's a huge smile on my face. Just about all her neighbors have come over to introduce themselves, bringing goodies, their names and phone numbers, and asking Mom to come join them for some event, whether it's a lunch, dinner, birthday party, or concert in Beecher's auditorium. Mom attends everything.

There are lots of times I call when she's obviously out, so I leave a message-something I haven't done in a long, long time. She's also started going over to Beecher's Fitness Center, where a trainer is helping her design a fitness program tailored to her needs. Three mornings a week now, she is working out, doing a series of stretches, reps with free weights, and spending time on the exercise bike, all monitored by the trainer, whom she really likes. Gone is her negativity, and in its place seems to be the Mom I remember from years ago; one who was never afraid to take the initiative. She seems to be making the most of every opportunity and doing a lot at Good Shepherd as well. Craig and I compare notes and couldn't be happier with what we're seeing and hearing.

Mom also speaks highly of Sally, the lady who comes to clean her cottage on Wednesdays. Not only is she thorough and meticulous, but Mom likes talking to her, and I guess Sally is fine with that as she works. *Boy,* I'm thinking, *we have hit a home run.* She informs me in one of our phone conversations that each month Beecher hosts a big birthday party at the Manor House for all the residents who have birthdays that month, and anyone can attend to help celebrate. Mom has been to both February and March's birthday parties with a group of her neighbors, who call themselves 'The Knoll Girls'! What an absolute hoot…she may need a curfew down the road! Admitting to napping a lot in the afternoons, she tells me, "this social schedule is wearing me out, but I enjoy it so much!" and I laugh.

"You go right ahead and nap!" I tell her. "And then go to your parties. That's why you're there!"

I think she's having the time of her life. There's a huge part of me that wishes this could have happened five years ago, giving her that additional time to build relationships and soak up all this activity. I do my best not to dwell on that.

Another surprising twist to all of this has been the amount of interest some of my co-workers have shown throughout this transition with Mom. Jeannie, who works in the back on the advice line, and Lynsey, my front desk teammate, as well as being mother and daughter themselves, ask me regularly about Mom. But along with them, several of the medical assistants who have heard me talk about Mom inquire about her. They really seem to enjoy hearing my stories about her settling in and becoming so social. Tia, one of the older ladies who works on the phone lines with Jeannie, (she's well into her 70's) is also very interested in how Mom is faring. I hadn't bargained on this support, and I generally don't talk extensively about my private life at work. Still, it means a lot to witness this level of caring. I'm beginning to feel like I have a support system at Highbridge, and I have to admit, that's a good feeling.

* * * * *

My second trip back to Mom's, in the middle of March, is another good one. I'm beginning to develop my 'visit template', and it already seems semi natural. It's working well with my schedule at Eastbridge, and I'm getting more comfortable with the drive. Now that I've driven straight to work from Cincinnati once, I'm not nearly as anxious about doing it. There's a peace I hadn't counted on in seeing the sunrise as I'm making the trip back down 71 in those early morning hours, and I know God's got my back on this.

I've altered this visit slightly, and am coming up on Wednesday evening after work, staying Thursday, which is my weekday off, then spending Thursday night and driving back Friday morning to work. Mom has made it clear she doesn't like the idea of my driving back early in the morning, and wants me to leave on Thursday, but I've explained that it's easier driving back early in the morning when traffic isn't heavy. Surprisingly, she hasn't pushed the issue.

The weather has brightened the past several days, and it's really starting to feel like spring. With the sunlight stronger now, crocuses are pushing up, and I went for my first walk during lunch yesterday. Our practice butts up to an older neighborhood that has a labyrinth of interconnected streets, and I've developed a couple of different walking routes, depending on how much time I have. Just having the sun on my face and hearing the birdsong is heaven. I'm hoping it's warm enough for Mom and me to sit out on her back porch. She has a big concrete square with a retractable awning over it that's perfect to enjoy weather like this. On either side of her porch are small flower beds, along with privacy walls on both sides-a nice touch.

Mom's got her heavy door standing ajar when I pull in at 6:45, so I know she's been waiting for me, and she comes right out to greet me when she sees me pull in. There's still light in the sky, and I can tell she's smiling as she comes towards me.

"You made good time," she tells me as I hug her. "How was your drive?"

"Not bad at all," I relay. "Music blaring the whole way and bridge traffic decent."

As we walk from the parking lot, I notice Craig has put two of her outdoor chairs on her front porch, and it looks cute and homey. I've splurged a little and bought her a housewarming gift-something I know she wouldn't buy for herself. It's a simple floral wreath made of silk forsythia, with spring green ribbon intertwined through the flowers, and a big bow to set it off. I had been sending flowers to Callie's office for her birthday in February when I spotted this and thought it would look pretty on Mom's front door. I got one for myself, too. Mom is delighted with hers. "What did I do to deserve this?" she asks, as I give it to her.

"Moved, unpacked, and never once complained," I tell her.

"You should not be spending money on me like this, Betsy. Your being here is more than enough," she remonstrates.

"Yeah, I know," I tell her. "I am pretty special. But I can't hang on your front door. This wreath is the essence of spring. When I'm not here, you look at it and think of me."

"I think of you anyway," Mom answers simply.

As it did in February, our time together flies. Mom seems so comfortable in this space already, and we slip into our leisurely routine, sleeping in on Thursday morning until almost 9:00. The area surrounding the cottages is always quiet, which is somewhat surprising to me. I make my pot of coffee, light one of Mom's candles, and we sit on the couch and talk for close to an hour before either of us makes any move for breakfast.

One thing that delights me over the course of Thursday is the number of times that Mom's phone rings. Three different times various friends call, all with invites to do things. A lunch tomorrow with Good Shepherd friends; a March birthday party at the Manor House and a 1940's style big band concert at the activity center. (Mom informs me that "all the Knoll girls" are going.) I love every bit of it.

We take a long walk in the early afternoon, since the weather is mild. This retirement community is huge. There's a lot of variety in terms of living options, and in the various styles of the housing offered. It truly runs the gambit. As we amble, Mom points out the areas where some of her friends live.

"Do you feel like you've settled in completely?" I ask her as we walk. I'm looking at some of the larger condominiums with multiple floors as we trudge up a hill.

"I do," she answers, with no hesitation. "I wish this could have happened a long time ago, Bet. There's always something to do, and everyone is so nice here. I really like my neighbors."

"That makes me so happy, Mom," I respond. "You deserve this, and I love knowing you're enjoying yourself. It seems like you've adjusted so quickly. Have Rob and Colette been to see you since they moved you in?"

"No, not yet," Mom replies. "But I'm sure with their work schedules, and the boys as busy as they are, it's hard to find a good time."

"Maybe you could invite them over to dinner," I suggest. "Take them to the Manor House like you did me, and they could see your place while they're here."

"I should do that," Mom agrees. "I honestly hadn't even thought about it."

Maybe she hasn't, but I sure have. It's been almost exactly a month now since Mom moved; they're in the same city and haven't seen her once since she left their home. It's unbelievable. Nor has Donny been over at all. I had called him back in January to let him know that Mom was moving to Beecher, and then again in February after I had spent the weekend with her, giving him her new address and phone number, and suggesting he stop by to see her place, even if it was just for a short visit. Nothing. He's only ten to fifteen minutes away; less distance even than Rob. I don't understand it.

Mom has a hair appointment in the afternoon, and I drive her to that and read while she's there. After that it's Barney's for dinner. I do manage to clean out the big hallway closet between our two bedrooms, and net a few more boxes to go back to Louisville with me. My next big project is going to be cleaning Mom's bedroom closet out, and that's going to be a much touchier project. Namely, because it involves her clothes…way, way too many of them. She's got stacks of them just pushed into her closet; not even hanging up, just resting on other clothes, layer upon layer. You can't even see what clothes are on the very bottom, let alone shoes or anything else on the floor of the closet. That is obviously going to be a big weekend project, so I'm targeting my next trip in April, after Easter. I already know I will need my arsenal of patience that day.

A week later, I call Mom on St. Patrick's Day to chat-I got home from work early and thought I'd check in. Apparently, her social calendar was too full to accommodate me.

As soon as the words, "Happy St. Patrick's Day," are out of my mouth, Mom's rushed response is, "Bet, I'm going to need to call you back. The girls are going to be here in just a few minutes to pick me up for our St. Patrick's Day party, and I need to get ready. I'm sorry. I'll call you back another time."

"No problem, Mom," I answer, fist pumping the air. "Enjoy your party!"

"I will!" is her response. Click. She's hung up.

I can't wait to tell Craig this. Someone is really living the vide loco. I also thoroughly enjoy recounting this to Liz, Lynsey, Tia, and Jeannie the next day at work. All of them find it highly amusing, but I can tell they're also happy Mom is having such a good time.

"Long live the Knoll Girls!" Liz exclaims, giggling, after I tell her the story. Indeed.

* * * * *

Saturday, April 10th…and I'm standing in the middle of Mom's bedroom at Beecher Springs, surrounded by stacks of clothes piled high on her bed. A Stiver's double cheeseburger on a paper plate is sitting on her nightstand waiting for my consumption. I drove up after working until 12:30 today, doing a drive-through on my way. Lucky for me Stiver's is right down the road.

"I'd say you've got quite a wardrobe going on here," I comment, looking around me at clothes that easily date back into the early 1980's. This is not a task I've looked forward to, and I can tell already Mom is going to be pressing me on this every step of the way. I hop over a pile of sweaters on the floor and take a big bite of my cheeseburger. I'm starving.

"What are you going to do with all of these?" Mom asks suspiciously, as if I'm going to cast a spell to make them disappear.

I hesitate to answer, and the words 'Burn them all' aren't far from my lips. "Well," I answer slowly, "I think I'll divide them into piles first. Let's separate your pants, your blouses, your sweaters, matching sets, and see everything we've got. Then we can start weeding out if we need to."

I throw the 'weeding out if we need to' purely to plant a strong visual…knowing full well that we'll be doing more than our share of that. This is the biggest mess I've ever seen, and after getting up at 6 AM this morning, working a half day and then driving up here, I can feel my energy level flat lining. I'm still in my scrubs from work-they're always comfortable to drive up in, and I'll leave them on for this entire project. I know I could put this off until tomorrow, but I'd rather tackle it today, get it done, and relax all day tomorrow with Mom. I want to drive back Monday morning knowing that she has a clean, organized closet where everything she has is clearly visible to her.

Needing to start somewhere, I dive in on one of the stacks on her bed, separating it into various categories of clothing, creating piles of different types around Mom's bedroom. I use the carpet, her armchair, and clear a spot on her bed for some jackets. Mom's closet has one long rod down its length, with a shelf above the rod (I'm picturing folded sweaters and her extensive collection of purses up there), and there will also be storage space on the floor once it's cleared. I can even buy a shoe organizer if we need one. Unlike my unpacking the various kitchen boxes, when Mom wandered around not paying much attention to what I did, she is homed in on this like a surveillance expert. I pray a silent prayer asking for patience, knowing how stubborn she can get, and knowing, too, how acidic I can be when I get irritated with her.

Some of her nicer pants and top coordinates I automatically hang in the closet next to one another, mainly so Mom can visually see they go together. That way, there's no worry about 'finding their match'. Over the years as she has slowed down, Colette and I have both taken to giving her clothes for Christmas and her birthdays, which she really seems to enjoy. She used to be such a shopper in her earlier years. Her gifts to us were legendary back in the day, but I think shopping for herself has become overwhelming to her at this point.

I make sure I'm checking with her every step of the way as I hang these pants and top go-togethers back in her closet. Her input is critical on this and she needs as much of it as possible. Getting six or seven of these ensembles back into her closet really helps get the process underway, because it makes the 'spare' articles of clothing much more visible. I take another bite of my cheeseburger, chase it with Diet Coke, and start looking around the bedroom for all the stray pairs of pants-pulling them out from their respective piles. This will be my next step.

"What's happening to the ones you're pulling out?" Mom asks, with a note of agitation in her voice.

"I just want all your pants together to see what you've got here, and how to best organize them," I answer, and she actually goes through several of the piles and pulls out three different pairs to help me, plopping them on the stack we're creating. When we're finished finding all the random pairs, our total is 14. Wow. Just a tad excessive, with six pairs already in the closet, three of which are navy. Of the 14, eight pairs are navy. Oh, my...Goodwill is going to love me. Mom, not so much, probably. For the time being, the fate of the extra pants will not be determined. Instead, I'm going to work on getting Mom's warm-ups in the closet. She has a fair number of those and will probably want to hang on to all of them.

"Let's do your warm-ups next," I suggest, and then we'll see how much space we have left."

We locate all hiding warm-ups in our stacks, and I group these in 'top-bottom' units so the pants are hung underneath the top, to save room in the closet.

"Does this work for you?" I ask, modeling the 'one hanger' idea.

Mom gives it the once over. "Looks fine," she affirms. "I just hope I remember the pants are underneath the top."

I start laughing. "Well, look," I giggle, tugging on the legs of the pants hanging down below the edge of the top, "right down here-you can always see the pants hanging out at the bottom. No guesswork involved."

Mom looks at me sheepishly, and smiles. "Well, alright. I guess that is pretty easy to see after all," and we get those into the closet. So far, so good.

I see a 'Grandmother' sweatshirt that Colette had made for her with all of the grandkids' pictures appliquéd on, and I know that's a keeper. It goes into the closet next to the warm-ups. Coming across a couple of windbreakers and a heavy blazer that could probably go out in the coat closet in the great room, I suggest this to Mom.

"Sure," she shrugs. "I'll put them out there." While she's out of the room, I start on her random blouses. Man, I forgot how popular blouses and button up shirts were in the 1980's, especially blouses that you wore under suits. And, true to form, Mom has a bunch. This is where we'll really have to start weeding. I come across two beautiful plaid skirts that I know she'll want to keep-when Mom and Dad visited the British Isles (also in the 1980's) Mom located the clan plaids of her father's family, both his mother and his father, and had wool skirts made of each of the plaids. She had proudly worn them to church countless times, and I probably treasured them as much as she did. Those go into the closet as well, along with Mom's favorite Ultrasuede suit (navy, of course!). Shuffle, shuffle, shuffle, and Mom's back from the great room.

"Hey, I put your two Scottish plaids and your navy suit in," I inform her, so she knows they're safe within. We finish the blouses and shirts, work our way through the other oddball pieces, get a good pile of sweaters going, and finally, about an hour in, everything has been organized into stacks. Now comes the hard part. The closet is almost full as it is, but I know Mom's not going to let of go of all these remaining piles easily. I bring an empty packing box in from the garage and take a deep breath.

"So, your closet's almost full," I suggest, "and you can certainly put some extra shirts and odds and ends in the guest closet, but we really need to scale these stacks down. Let's start with your pants. You've got three navy pairs of pants in your closet already, which gives you some variety, and eight navies in this outside stack. Do you want to pick one or two more navy pairs to keep, and then we'll give the rest to Goodwill?"

I can't think of any softer way to frame this up. I look at Mom, and I can tell she does not like this one bit.

"I don't like giving any of this away," she announces bluntly. "Each of those pairs of pants is slightly different."

Ohhhhh, I knew it would come down to this, and I don't feel prepared for it. At the risk of hurting Mom's feelings on this, we need to find some middle ground. She won't wear half these clothes.

"Well," I hear myself say, "then pick your three favorite pairs from the stack instead of two. That'll give you six pairs of navy pants to keep."

Mom looks at me with a hard, steely gaze-in that way that only she can, drawing herself up to her full height of 5'2", squaring her shoulders haughtily, and says, "Here's the difference, Bet. You wear those scrubs every day," (vaguely waving at them in a gesture of abject dismissal) "and that works for you, but I'm going to be out and about every day here. People are going to see me. I need these clothes."

At this pronouncement I can't help myself. I haven't seen this side of my mom in a long time, and it catches me so completely off guard that I fall onto her bed, oblivious to the stack of shirts that go sliding, and burst out laughing. Mom glares at me, highly irritated that I'm not taking her seriously.

"Sorry," I choke out, still on my back on the bed. "I didn't realize people here took pictures of what you wear each day. MOM! Seriously! Most of these people can't remember what they ate for breakfast, and you're worried about someone noticing that you're wearing the same pair of navy pants? Come on!"

This, as soon as it leaves my mouth, is grounds for recall. I shouldn't have said it; it was below the belt, and Mom can't fight back at my level. But this is the side of her that pushes my buttons-that 'appearances are everything' mentality. In her mind, she has a reputation that must be upheld. I get that this is a whole new chapter of her life, and that she wants to put her best foot forward. Still, this level of self-absorption is beyond me. The closet is already chock full of her clothes.

I sit up on the bed and push my hair back, trying to regain composure without saying anything else sarcastic or derogatory. *Better shift gears*, I'm thinking. I decide to quietly start work on the pile of sweaters. There are several that are borderline duplicates that, with Mom's agreement, we decide can go in the Goodwill box. The other four Mom wants to keep. Folding them, I stack them on her top closet shelf.

"Can you reach these?" I ask her, knowing I'm a good three to four inches taller than she is, and wanting to be sure they're in an easy access spot.

Mom looks up at where I've placed them, and says sulkily, "Yes."

Oh, brother, I think, *is the rest of the weekend going to be like this, now that I've stepped on her toes?*

"Mom, listen," I say gently. "I'm not trying to make this hard on you, and I'm not forcing you to give away your clothes. I'm just trying to help you scale down a little bit, because you have much less closet space here than you did at Rob and Colette's. When I leave Monday morning, I want you to feel organized, and to know exactly what you have and where it is, instead of having all this stuff just piled in your closet, not even hung up. You couldn't even tell what was buried underneath these piles of clothes."

But already, I feel like I've slipped into a scolding mode where Mom probably feels badly that she hasn't organized it herself.

"Let's just take some of the pieces you don't wear much anymore, or that you have two of, and get rid of a few of them. That way, you'll be able to enjoy what you have, and other people can enjoy what you've let go of."

Mom says nothing, so I'm not sure whether she's still angry or just processing, so I leave it alone. I start on a pile of random skirts, and several pairs of culottes, which mom has long ago stopped wearing because of the varicose veins in her legs. They go in the giveaway box. I get to a couple of old sweatshirts and hold them up.

"Keep or go?" I ask her quietly.

"Keep," she points at the green one, "Go," at the black one.

I notice she's deliberating over the pile of navy pants, and slowly places three pairs in the giveaway box. That's a start. *Now three more*, runs through my mind, but I don't say anything. With her blessing, I put a bunch of old belts in the box, also several scarves, and a stack of knit shirts she's easily had for thirty years. By around 3:00, as the April sun rounds the back of her cottage, we have two boxes and a garbage bag full of clothes Mom is parting with. I have surreptitiously buried two more pairs of her navy pants at the bottom of one of the boxes, hoping she won't miss them. I shouldn't have, but I did anyway. Then I hung the two remaining pairs in the closet. Surely five pairs of navy pants will satisfy the paparazzi.

As we're working, Mom offers, "You know, there's a thrift place here that sells clothes the residents don't want-almost like a consignment shop. They sell them to other residents, and, I think, to the public. I could take all my clothes there."

"You could," I answer noncommittally.

But you wouldn't, immediately echoes in my head. *You'd wait till I left on Monday, and then just unpack everything we've gone through and smash it right back in your closet.* I know her too well. I feel horrible for doubting her, but she wouldn't be caught dead taking her clothes to this consignment place to sell. Instead, I have an idea. Maybe I can call her bluff.

To test the waters, I say, "That's actually a really good idea. Let's throw the boxes in my Jeep and we can run them over."

Surely, I'm thinking, this thrift exchange will be open on a Saturday afternoon.

"I don't think they're open on Saturday afternoons," is Mom's swift answer…Too swift. "I think just Mondays through Fridays."

My answer: "Ahhh, okay."

So, instead of taking them out to my Jeep, I move them into the guest room. There is a slow-emerging plan taking shape in my mind. I'm not proud of it at all and it's downright sneaky, but it might work.

Mom's closet is full, it's organized, and she has all her newest and most recent clothes organized, as well as some of her vintage pieces. I even put a few of her dressy dresses and a nice wrap she has in the guest room closet, even though I know she'll probably never wear them again. And, have mercy, even her elastic stretch waistband jeans have been spared, and they're making friends with her navy pants. We're down to sorting through her shoes, and decide three pairs can be given away, then I organize the rest on the floor of her closet, stack her purses in a row next to the sweaters on her upper shelf, and it looks marvelous. This needs to be featured in a closet do-over article! I make a mental note to bring a shoe organizer next time I come, and I know this is a vast improvement.

"What do you think?" I ask Mom, standing in front of the closet and peering in. I'm curious to hear her response.

"It'll do, I guess," she answers, somewhat less than enthusiastically, but I can tell her irritation has dissipated.

Thank goodness. I walk her through how I've organized everything, showing her what's where, reminding her where her plaid skirts are, her 50th wedding anniversary dress, moving across the rack to her jeans, extra navy pants, and sweatshirts.

"It's very user friendly," I tell her, laughing.

"Well, I do thank you for doing this, Bet," she says graciously. "You're the only one who would have taken the time to do it."

"It'll work for you, I think," I respond, "and I think it'll be easier for you to find things in the long run."

But, even making that statement, a part of me feels like I've robbed her of something-definitely her power of decision making, maybe, but something else I can't quite put my finger on. I can tell this has really worn her out, and we settle on the couch in the great room, just to rest for a little while. She stretches out and is asleep immediately. I read for about 10 minutes, and when she starts snoring gently, I know I can begin to execute my plan. I feel terrible and guilty doing this, but these clothes MUST go, and I'm not taking any chances on leaving them here. Regardless of where Mom claims she'll take them, they need to disappear via ME. They're not safe in my Jeep, because we'll be driving in it all weekend, and Mom would clearly see the boxes and bag in my trunk. That would prompt her wanting me to bring them back in to her cottage so she could take them to 'Reruns'-the name of the thrift exchange. That can't happen.

Here's my dastardly plan: outside Mom's back porch, and over to the right of the row of cottages, directly behind Breck, (the assisted living building) is a random grove of trees. I can see them as I stand in the guest bedroom looking out the sliding glass door. There are several pines, and another deciduous tree with still bare branches. My plan is to quietly slip all three of these bags/boxes out there, basically hiding them behind the pines, and then, on my way out on Monday morning, when it's dark, to stop and throw them in my trunk: Destination Goodwill in Louisville. That also saves Mom the hassle of dealing with them. (Pure justification on my part.)

The weather is supposed to be beautiful tonight and tomorrow, so I know there's no risk of the bags being rained on. Just in case, I quietly take a dry-cleaning bag off one of Mom's dresses, remove one more pair of navy pants from her closet, fold it and imbed it deep in the box of clothes, and then cover the box tightly with the bag.

Now, as silently as a thief in the night, I remove the security rod from the track in the sliding door, quietly unlatch the handle, and try to open it. Of course, it sticks. I wonder if it got painted shut when they repainted the place for Mom. I desperately need this door to open. I take both hands and placing them up and down on the handle, throw my entire body weight back as I tug. This time, it gives with a giant slurping sound as the seal breaks. I stop cold for a minute, wondering if Mom heard it. Tiptoeing out into the hallway, I can see her still motionless on the couch. Okay. Commence plan.

One by one, I silently carry the bag and the two packing boxes out to the pine trees, placing them on the far sides of the trees, where they're totally hidden from the view in the guestroom, should Mom look out. I push them all together, and hope none of her neighbors have seen me do this. It's the act of a madwoman, and I'd hate for one of them to mention it to Mom. Come to think of it, none of them know who I am, so, unless they see me slipping back into Mom's cottage, I should be safe doing this. After my three trips out, I slip back in through the guestroom door, gently closing it, and latching it shut with my thumb. The security rod will have to wait. I'm afraid of it dropping into the track and clanging, so I roll it under the bed with my foot. I'll deal with that another time.

Mom is still asleep at 4:20, and since she had mentioned wanting to go to church tonight, I figure I'd better wake her. "Oh, sleepy head," I intone, "can you hear me?"

Her eyelids flutter open and she looks at me, and then looks around, as if she's alarmed. "What time is it?" she asks me, lying completely motionless like she's afraid to move.

"About 4:20," I answer. "Do you still want to go to church?"

"Oh, yes," Mom answers. "I told Nancy we'd meet her there and maybe the three of us could go out to dinner afterwards."

"Sure, that would be fun," I agree. It delights me that Mom has taken the initiative to make plans, knowing I'll be fine with whatever she wants to do. (In some small way, it makes up for how I feel about the clothes heist.)

She changes clothes, I throw on a pair of jeans and a sweater, and we head out, me driving. This time I notice there are no questions about where we're going, so either she remembers, or she's not concerned about it.

"What did you do with the boxes of clothes?" she asks point blank as we turn onto the park road. Oh, crap. I hadn't bargained on this coming up again-at least not now.

"They're at your place," I answer. Technically speaking, they ARE. They're just not INSIDE her place.

"Where at my place?" she persists. "I didn't see them anywhere before we left."

"Yeah, they're there," I reiterate. I really don't want to lie about this and make it worse.

"Did you put them in your room?" she asks pointedly. "Because I didn't see them in there."

Why can't she be as forgetful about the clothes as she was about eating at Chili Time with Dad and the Lewises?

"They should be there," I answer, hoping that maybe Mom will think she overlooked seeing them.

"You know, Bet, I really want to take those to Reruns," she states.

"Okay," I reply. "We can talk about it when we get home."

Hopefully, by then, she will have forgotten about them. I'm happy as I pull up the steep hill to Good Shepherd. What a difference two months makes with Mother Nature! The bare trees on the hills in February have blown up into a haze of lime greens and green-golds, and you can barely see the lake anymore because of the thickening foliage. It's a soft, warm evening as we walk into church to find Nancy, and as we slide into the pew where she's waiting for us, I feel so blessed to still be able to share this with Mom. I absorb another good Pastor Morehouse message on Matthew 3 and John the Baptist's baptism of repentance versus Christ's baptism of the Holy Spirit. He does a great job describing what that should look like in our own lives; it's very meaningful, and there's a lot of meat in it. Later, as we take communion, and I watch these familiar, dear faces file by me, I wonder where all of them stand in their feelings towards him. I pray silently that they can extend grace to him even as he is willing to respond to their requests for less change; perhaps at a slower pace. Everyone needs to be willing to meet halfway. I'll be curious to talk to Nancy at dinner and see how she feels towards him. I know she and Mom shared very similar feelings towards the changes that are being made in the music program, but I wonder if Nancy has been able to move beyond that. I'm not sure Mom has. In her mind, he's taken away her Sunday morning service.

After worship, we linger out in the fellowship area, the rays of the sinking sun filling the room with filtered light as it pours through the trees. With its views of the trees and the lake, the placement of this room is perfect, and it feels like you're in a lodge on a mountaintop. Mom is chattering away to the Reinholds, a family I grew up with here. I can tell folks are genuinely happy she's back and that sense of reconnection is so evident. I don't think she's missed a Saturday night service since she moved from Rob's. Nancy, the Reinholds, Mom and I stand in a big circle yakking away for a good half hour, them wanting to know how my job is going; how Callie and Kerry are, when I'm heading back, and always, 'Be sure to tell Mike we said hello'. It's such a feeling of being loved and valued. Never mind that I've been gone from this church 25 years. That sense of deep extended family never changes.

Dinner with Nancy is enjoyable and gives us a chance to catch up in even more depth. She's been Mom's closest friend at Good Shepherd for years, dating back to when the two couples used to do so much together before her husband and Dad passed. Nancy was also my confirmation teacher in 7th grade, and I've always had a lot of respect for her. There's a peace to her that is vast, and she's one of those people who makes you feel stronger just by being in her presence. Spending this extra time with her is a gift. We end up at Barney's, order, and then digress into discussion about Good Shepherd and the changes that are taking place. Nancy confides that she's thinking of transferring her membership to another Episcopal church she's been visiting since January. It's further from her home than Good Shepherd is but is very liturgical and they sing all the old hymns there. I realize how deep-seated Nancy's dislike of any contemporary praise music is, and even though I don't personally agree, I respect her opinion. Her faith and integrity count for a lot with me.

Having been a musician all my life, as well as having lived through this type of transition in one of our previous churches in Louisville, I can see this issue from both sides, and I know how bitterly divisive it can be. I've never had a problem with the contemporary music, and it speaks to me in a way the hymns don't. That said, many of the hymns possess a reverence and theology that some of the contemporary choruses totally lack. They're not always well written, and they have a tendency toward banality and repetitiveness. But, on this, I need to put myself in Mom and Nancy's shoes. This is all they've ever known, and I think it's far too late for them to feel like they want to give it a chance. They need the comfort of those hymns, and the style of worship that has fed them for decades to be the bedrock in the final years of their lives.

Further, in listening to them talk tonight, they feel like Pastor Morehouse has turned a deaf ear to their concerns, especially because they're no longer big financial contributors. Basically, they feel they're being steamrolled. Paul and Jackie Theiss, another couple both Mom and Nancy have been close to for years at Good Shepherd, have already left and joined the church that Nancy has been visiting. I hate it that Mom is having to deal with all this change and transition, especially as she's close now and wanting to become more involved. I'm sure she's feeling some degree of pressure to decide, too, especially as many of her closest friends have left or are considering it. Nancy offers to pick Mom up next Sunday morning and drive her to St. Luke's so they can worship together, and Mom can see what it's like there first-hand. I'm surprised to hear her agree to it.

"It sure can't hurt," she tells Nancy. "I just feel like

Morehouse (I'm amused by how she drops his title in complete disrespect for him) could care less about any of us who don't want what he wants. I think he views us as a nuisance."

He also may view the implementation of the contemporary service and its style of music as a survival issue for the church. This is a congregation where the liturgy hasn't changed since I left...but I don't say any of this. I get where Nancy and Mom are, but sadly, it sounds like they're in a small minority. We finish up our meal, talk some more about what Callie and Kerry are up to, as well as Nancy's granddaughters, who are roughly the same age, and then make our way home.

"I'm so glad you've kept in close touch with Nancy," I comment to Mom. "She's such a great person. I love spending time with her."

I see Mom nod in agreement in the dark. "The thought of her possibly leaving Good Shepherd makes me sad," she muses. "It wouldn't be the same without her. But, Bet, I just can't see pulling up and starting all over somewhere else. Even if I do like St. Luke's when I visit, your dad and I put so much work into Good Shepherd back when Pastor Williams was first called in the 1960's. I just feel like it would be disloyal to walk away from that. Plus, St. Luke's would be a much longer drive for me, and in bad weather I couldn't go at all. I think I'm just going to sit tight and see what happens."

I respect Mom for this measured approach and tell her there's no need to make a hasty decision.

"Stay in prayer about it, and keep attending your Saturday night services faithfully," I tell her. "You know, Mom, God's purposes for you in this may be totally different than for Nancy or the Theisses. I know you miss Paul and Jackie not being at Good Shepherd anymore, but a lot of the older members like you are still there. It's not like you're the last man standing. Still, I wish you didn't have to deal with all this. It's really hard on your entire congregation."

I try to peek at the hidden clothes bags as we drive by, but I can't see anything in the dark. Maybe somebody has already discovered them and taken them off my hands...Fine by me. Mom and I play a few hands of gin rummy, watch the news, and thankfully there is no further mention of the clothes. We hit the sack a little before 11:00. I lay in bed replaying the day and gazing up at the skylight. I'm struck by how much upheaval Mom has had in her life recently. She's really been through it, in her move here, Rob and Col's bizarre behavior, and the changes at Good Shepherd. I can't imagine how that must feel at a time when all she probably wants is consistency. She's such a quiet fighter, in her own way. I can see a thin sliver of moon sailing up at the top of the window panel, and I follow it slowly across the sky until I'm asleep.

I'm awakened by profuse bird song the next morning, and the room is awash in sunlight. Wispy clouds are stringing themselves across the skylight, and I turn to look at the clock. It's 8:42...wow. I slept in this morning. I get up and throw a sweatshirt on and can smell coffee already made as I open the curtains of the sliding door. *I need to replace that security bar sometime today*, I remind myself. Mom's already up, reading a magazine on the couch. She looks up and smiles at me.

"I tried to be really quiet," she greets me, "but I did make your coffee for you. Strong-the way you like it."

I ask her how long she's been up.

"Not that long," she answers. "I slept till about eight. Strangest thing-I must have eaten something at Barney's that didn't agree with me, because in the middle of the night I got up and vomited, but then went right back to sleep. No more problems after that."

"Just the one time?" I press. If it was food poisoning, it would have gone on all night, and Mom would feel miserable now.

"Just once," she affirms. "After that I felt fine and slept

like a rock until this morning."

"That's weird," I comment. "Has that ever happened to you before?" I find myself wondering if it has, and she's just forgotten.

"Oh, now and then at Rob and Colette's," she answers, somewhat dismissively. "Usually when Col gave me leftovers, and probably something was spoiled."

This is the first I've heard of this, although, come to think of it, I do recall her mentioning being sick now and then at Rob's. I had never given it much thought until now.

"Did you have a French dip last night at Barney's?" I ask, trying to think back on what she ate.

"Yes, that's almost always what I get there," she answers.

"Any heartburn before you vomited?" I ask her, wondering if she could be developing acid reflux.

"No, that's something I never have," she assents. "And I feel perfectly fine now."

Her appetite does speak for itself as we eat a late breakfast. I make us blueberry pancakes and she devours three of them. She fills me in on her Easter with Craig and Loire, and it's interesting to compare her version to what Craig has already shared with me. He and Loire had told Mom they'd come down on Easter, pick her up for church, and Craig had made reservations at one of Mom's favorite restaurants for brunch afterwards. They had left Dayton early to be sure they had enough time to pick Mom up and get to Good Shepherd, but Mom wasn't here when they reached her place. Her car was gone as well. Craig had pounded on the door for good measure, looked in the front window, and finally knocked on the door of her neighbor Marie. She told him she'd seen Mom "all dressed up for Easter" and that she'd left about 30 minutes ago. Craig could only assume that Mom had gone to church on her own and forgotten they were going to pick her up. They sped over to Good Shepherd, and, true to Craig's hunch, there sat Mom in a pew saved for them, waiting as if nothing had happened. (And, in her mind, nothing HAD.) According to Craig, she had no recollection of them ever having discussed him picking her up. Ouch... Shades of no Chili Time. Craig and I are seeing more and more of this and it's continuing to raise questions about the wisdom of Mom being behind the wheel. I probably need to have her drive with me riding shotgun so I can check out what she's like behind the wheel.

As we eat, we hatch our plans for the day. It's another warm, sunny day, so we decide to go to Preston Park to walk part of the trail around the lake. Then we'll do our Kroger-ing and I suggest to Mom that we go to visit Dad's gravesite. We can pick up a bouquet of flowers at Kroger to take with us. I know she likes to do this, but doesn't trust herself to go alone, because getting to his grave involves walking over bumpy, uneven ground. If I'm with her, she can hold on to me, and it gives her much more confidence.

It ends up being a beautiful day with Mom. There's something about its very ordinariness that is comforting, and I revel in the two of us being together, so easy with each other. I am loving these opportunities to "do life" with Mom when I come up here, and the times when it's just the two of us are so special. Our walk down at Preston Lake doesn't take us very far-maybe ¾ of a mile, but it's a clear, sunny day, and it feels good just to be outside. We head to Kroger after that, and it's a slow, measured trip. From there we drive to the cemetery.

Greendale Memorial Gardens is an old cemetery, and Mom and Dad had bought four plots for a ridiculously low sum early in the 1960's, even though they were still in their late 30's at that point. Mom always said it was too good of a deal to pass up. (Dad would add, tongue in cheek, that "people were dying for a deal just like it.") For Mom's lack of short-term memory sometimes, she has an uncanny ability to direct me right to Dad's headstone, which never ceases to amaze me. We've been here countless times over the past six years, and her precision is unerring every time, guiding me along the labyrinthine paths effortlessly.

As I pull the Jeep to the side of the drive and park, she remarks, "It should be in that second row over there, about six or seven headstones down."

"How you remember this is beyond me," I comment. "There's no way I could ever find this on my own."

And she's exactly right; it's six headstones down the second row. We walk slowly down the grassy path, stepping carefully over a couple of headstones, and she's hanging on to me for dear life. Her feet barely clear the ground, and once she stumbles, grabbing my arm with more strength than I would have thought possible. No matter how many times I do this, I never get over the jolt I feel when I see Dad's name on the headstone. It's modest, no statues or gargoyles; just a bronze plaque set in the ground, but it means the world to me, and to Mom as well. In large gold letters in the middle of the stone, 'Bradshaw', and at the top right, 'William Callan, M.D.', then his birth and death dates of 'September 10, 1924 to November 2, 2003'. Under Dad's name is the symbol of an eagle holding an olive branch, which many veterans of World War II chose to have put on their graves.

I think of that fearless 21-year-old medic, with two years of college under his belt when he enlisted. Dad never liked to talk about the war, and even when we asked him questions, his answers were brief and to the point-nothing like our usual conversations with him. I know that Luxembourg had been his favorite country to visit; he talked about how beautiful it was, but that's about all we could get out of him. It was years before we discovered he'd been awarded a bronze star for driving back across enemy lines in the dark to pick up one of the injured in their company who had been left behind. I remember when I was 12 or 13 and fully grasped what 'enemy lines' meant, asking Dad if he'd been afraid when he did it.

"Oh, sure," he had told me. "Mostly because at any time we could have driven over a mine. It was dark, and I couldn't see where I was going. But we had to go back for him. There was no choice to be made. I'm just thankful we found him alive and got him out."

That was all. I take the flowers out of their wrapping now, a colorful arrangement of hydrangeas, irises, and Gerber daisies, and then unscrew the vase from its inverted position in the headstone.

"Will you be okay while I walk down to the spigot and get water?" I ask Mom. The water source is at the very end of the row, about 200 yards away and I return with the vase two thirds full, sit down cross legged on the ground, and arrange the flowers in the vase, fluffing them until they look the way I want them to. Gently setting the vase into the vacated ring it came out of in the headstone; I get up and come to stand beside Mom. The grass is just starting to green up around the grave sites, and the red and orange of the daisies look cheerful against this backdrop. Words aren't even necessary between us, both of us comfortable in the other's silence. Momentarily I feel like I'm with both of my parents instead of just one and the peace it gives me is vast, even if it's completely irrational. It's as if, because Mom and I are here together, both honoring Dad's memory, that he's in both of our hearts at the same time.

"You never stop loving, do you?" I ask Mom, speaking for both of us. "That part never changes."

"No," answers Mom quietly. "It certainly doesn't."

"I feel like he's been gone for so long," I say. "I miss hearing him sing."

"I do, too, Bet," Mom responds. "I never stop missing him."

"He's so proud of you, Mom," I tell her. "He probably had a thing or two to say to The Big Guy about getting you in to Beecher."

Mom smiles. "That would make him happy, I'm sure."

We stand quietly for a while longer, listening to the birds and feeling the warm sunshine on us. I could stay here for hours and be perfectly happy. I look at Mom's half of the headstone-her name is at the top left, with her birthdate of August 4, 1927 inscribed, with a vacant space for her death date. Underneath those dates is inscribed, 'Wife, Mother, Grandmother'. Yup, she's definitely all of those things, and I hope that space above those words stays vacant for a long, long time.

By the time we get back to Beecher, it's almost 5:00, and I convince Mom to let me make grilled cheese sandwiches and tomato soup for dinner, so we don't have to go back out. She needs to relax. We watch '60 Minutes' after dinner, and then I pack my lunch and we end up watching the movie 'Ordinary People'. My mind drifts as I'm watching it; I'm doing a sort of mental sum-up of the weekend. Mom has seemed less forgetful to me this time, and I haven't noticed any major memory slips or lapses. One thing that does make me wonder is that she hasn't said anything today about her clothes. Her thought processes seem fairly lucid, and I wonder if her settling in and getting some of the transition behind her has made a difference. I've noticed that she doesn't seem to have trouble finding things, and she's doing her own laundry and keeping a running grocery list on her kitchen counter. The only thing I really haven't been able to monitor is her driving, because I kept forgetting to ask her to drive anywhere. 10:00 rolls around, and I know I need to get to bed. I hate this last night, knowing I leave in the morning.

"Thanks for another wonderful weekend," Mom tells me as I kiss her goodnight and head into bed. "You've been so good to me. I'm right behind you. I just want to watch the first part of the news."

4:45 AM comes way too early and I so wish I could call in sick and stay another day, then head back leisurely this afternoon. Instead, I haul myself out of bed, fix my first cup of coffee, and let the shower blast me awake. Thank goodness I know how to work it now. I do the full Monty with my makeup today, dry my hair, and I see Mom wave good morning in my mirror. I wish she could sleep through all of this. I lug my stuff out to the Jeep, come back in for my lunch and purse, give Mom a big hug and kiss, and am on my way at 5:30 sharp. Her last instructions are, "Call me when you get to work."

It's still pitch black when I back the Jeep out of the parking area, and I hate the idea of stopping for the three bags of clothes in the dark. What if I just left them? But I can't take that chance. I turn out of the parking lot and pull down the road several hundred yards, slowly easing off to the side. My heart is pounding, and I feel like a criminal as I dart over to the pine trees, and there, big as life, is the first bag. I hoist it up, carry it to the Jeep, and put it in the trunk, leaving the hatch open for the other two boxes. Back and forth with the second box, now the third…slowly I'm aware of being watched, although I can't put my finger on what alerted me to this. I've got the third load in my arms, carrying it to the Jeep, and as I shut the trunk as quietly as possible, I look over to Breck's parking lot and notice one of Beecher's security cars parked in the space by the garbage dumpster.

Ohhhh, no. This is not good for business. Clearly, the guy on patrol has been watching every trip I made to recover those bags. His lights are on now, so there's obviously someone in the cruiser. I don't remember seeing his lights on when I pulled the Jeep over. I probably didn't notice because my own headlights were already on. So now he's probably sitting in his cruiser wondering what could be worth hiding and retrieving at 5:30 in the morning, which means he'll stop me for sure. Never in a million years is he going to buy the truth, and he'll go through all the boxes just to prove me wrong.

This is all running through my head as I walk with Jello-y legs to the driver's side of my Jeep, get in, and close the door. I bet he'll let me head down this street so I'm in front of him; then turn his light on and pull me over. I ease the Jeep into drive and draw a ragged breath. Oh my gosh, what if he takes me back to Mom's cottage for her to identify me, given my story? Then she'll know exactly what happened, and that I hid her clothes out there…I'm sick to my stomach.

I'm passing his cruiser now…no movement on his part

yet. He probably just wants me to think I'm home free and then he'll pull me over. I continue down the road, going under the speed limit so at least he can't say I was speeding; still no sign of him in my rearview mirror. By the time I reach the main road that passes in front of Beecher Springs, I'm thinking I might be okay. I make sure to put my left turn signal on as I pull out of Beecher. Still nothing. At the first intersection I make a right onto Brampton Road, and I feel my stomach unclench a little. Five minutes later as I turn left onto the park road, using it as my shortcut to Preston Road, I know I'm free and clear. Hallelujah. The clothes thief with the unbelievable true alibi has stayed under the radar.

I stop at the Treadwell's on Preston Road to reward myself with two large coffees, and rifle through my lunch bag to get a Granola bar out. Now, my drive begins in earnest. As I navigate my way down to I-75, I can feel myself slipping into that early morning autopilot. Once I'm on I-75, I join the hushed stream of early morning traffic headed across the bridge and up the cut in the hill into northern Kentucky. The coffee is delicious, and by the time I pick up I-71, the first streaks of dawn are appearing in the sky. I pop Five For Fighting's 'Two Lights' in the CD player…I've listened to this CD so many times that I know all the words by heart. I love the thoughtful lyrics, and the unique arranging. It's one of those CD's that grows on me every time I listen to it.

"Took a flag to a pawnshop for a broken guitar", I sing lustily as dawn washes over the hills of I-71. "Took a flag to a pawnshop/how much is that guitar? /took a flag to a pawnshop/I bought me that guitar/What's a flag in a pawnshop to me?"

I've got all his vocal inflections down perfectly, and it pleases me. And, as I pass through Verona, I sing my personal favorite, 'History Starts Now' that was mildly popular the year Kerry graduated from high school. I always associate it with her for that reason, and her senior class; a very special group of kids. "What kind of world do you want/

Think anything/Let's start at the start/Build a masterpiece/ Be careful what you wish for/History starts now."

Nothing like music to make my spirits soar, and I witness a beautiful spring sunrise. It's a gift to begin my week this way. I don't quite feel the same way about the message on my machine when I get home from work. I've just dropped Mom's clothes off at Goodwill. She'd been fine when I called her from work this morning to let her know I made it safely, but this message tells me otherwise. It's clear she's been stewing all day.

"Betsy," (she always uses my full name when she wants to emphasize something) she begins, "I'm very disappointed about my clothes. And I'm especially upset about my navy pants. The only ones you left me with (as if she'd had no say in the pairs she kept) are the thin ones, and the cold air goes right through them. I wish I had those heavy pairs back."

That's the end of the message. I know that out of the four pairs in her closet, ONE of them must be made of decently heavy fabric, especially if it's part of a coordinate ensemble. I can tell she's upset. Looks like I'll be back at Goodwill tomorrow, doing my best to salvage some navy pants. I call her and tell her I'll do my best to replace them, and leave it at that, at the same time warring with myself for not telling her the truth about bringing them down here to Goodwill. It would just upset her more.

Tuesday on my lunch hour, I high tail it to Goodwill, hoping the boxes are still at this center, and that I can locate them. There's an older man wearing out the one employee I see, so while I'm waiting, I walk over to a piano that's in the middle of the room and quietly start playing it, mainly to see how in tune it is. Immediately the employee ends the discussion with the angry man and walks over to me.

"You play really well," she comments.

"Just this one song," I tell her, and grin. It's "Corner of the Sky", from 'Pippin', one of my all-time favorite musicales.

I taught myself the accompaniment when I was in high school when our varsity ensemble sang it.

"You need a piano?" she asks me, gesturing towards the Wurlitzer I'm playing.

"No, I've got one already," I reply. "This was a beauty back in the day. It just needs to be tuned. Actually, I need your help with something else-and you may or may not be able to help me."

I lower my voice, as if I'm sharing some gem of personal information, and I'm amused at myself for doing this.

"I brought two boxes and a white garbage bag full of clothes from my mom's closet here last night-I dropped them off about 5:30. When I got home, there was a message on my machine from my Mom. She's really unhappy with me for giving away too many pairs of her navy pants. So, what I'd like to do if the boxes are still here is to pull out three or four of the pairs and take them back to her."

The girl is looking at me, and I can tell she's amused by the story. Somehow her amusement makes me feel better; like I'm a little more understood. "Guess I went overboard," I confide. "I would have thought four pairs of navy pants would be enough of a fashion base."

Now she laughs out loud. "You're not the first person who's ever done that," she assents.

She leads me across the room to a corner near the entrance where boxes and bags are piled into several of their large bins on wheels. "I'm pretty sure this is all of our intake from yesterday," she explains. "We had a lot of drop-offs and haven't had a chance to go through any of it yet. Do you want to start looking through this stuff first to see if it's here? I'm positive nothing from yesterday has been taken to any of our other locations yet."

"Yeah, thanks," I reply gratefully. I see the grumpy man leave with a package, which pleases me; he needed to leave the girl alone. I start digging into the cart. After I've lifted several bags out, I actually spot the corner of one of my packing boxes, down at the very bottom.

"Here they are!" I exclaim to no one in particular, although I know the girl heard me, because she comes back over and starts helping me lift boxes and bags out to allow me to get to the packing box. Finally, I've cleared enough to lift my boxes, and I set them down on the floor, riffling through them to try to find the navy pants without disturbing the rest of the clothes. I know they're close to the bottom of the box. Blouses...sweater...sweater...bingo. Here they are. I pull out three pairs in a row. I check fabric content. These definitely feel 'heavy' to me.

"Well, there you have it," the girl tells me. "I'm glad it was that easy!"

"Me, too," I breathe. "This whole closet cleaning thing was a real challenge."

"These Depression Era kids," she comments, which surprises me to hear from a 20-something. She must be parroting that from someone she works with who is much older than herself. I re-pile the boxes in the bin and thank her for her help.

"Hope your piano sells," I tell her.

I'll take these up to Mom next time I go. There's another message on our machine Tuesday night, and I brace myself for more scolding, but this time, Mom's message has a much different tack.

"Bet, I just wanted to call you to tell you I was sorry about how angry I was yesterday. I was thinking about all of this when I did my devotion this morning. The theme of it was letting go of things and moving on in peace, and I realized I needed to do that. Being upset about those pants was very petty, I know. I just wanted to thank you for taking the time to clean out my closet at all. And whatever happened to the clothes is fine, too."

I listen somewhat incredulously, and I'm so glad she's found some middle ground. I call her back, and all I say is, "You don't need to apologize, Mom. You've been through change after change lately, and it's been hard. We're good… always."

We talk awhile longer. She and the Knoll girls went to a movie today, and the April birthday party at the Manor House is on Thursday of this week. Later, when Mike and I are eating dinner, I relay the story to him. Sometimes I'm too long-winded, and he'll humorously tell me, "Cliff Notes," meaning, 'cut to the chase'. But this time, not. He listens intently, and I can tell he's all in on the narrative. He loves the comment Mom made about my being able to wear scrubs, but her need for an extensive wardrobe because 'people see her every day.'

"That is so your Mom when I first met your family," he remarks.

And it was. When I tell him about the Goodwill pants retrieval, he looks at me in the way only Mike can, high fives me, and says, "Oh, Betsy. You really get the award."

Life goes on, and hopefully a pair of navy pants was worn to the April birthday party at the Manor House.

Joan, On Her Own

Chapter Six

DIVERSIONS
(May 2010-August 2010)

Flu season has dwindled to almost nothing by mid-March at Highbridge, and the late nights of our sick waiting room packed full of feverish, congested patients have dissipated along with it. Allergy related illnesses, with their attendant secondary infections, are the order of the day, but that's a much smaller percentage of our patient base, and we're winding down earlier and earlier. Spring break has come and gone, and, as April gains traction, at least one of us at the front desk is able to leave by mid-afternoon. This trend continues into May, and it's an unexpected perk for me. To be home by 4:00 some days is heavenly. It makes the evenings seem so much longer.

From childhood on, I've loved being outside, spending hours of every day growing up either in the woods that surrounded our neighborhood or riding my blue Schwinn two-wheeler. Spring takes me back to those years when I'd clamor off the school bus, race home, throw on play clothes, and disappear outside until dinnertime, then heading right back out until it was dark. These bonus afternoons of early dismissal from work give me the perfect opportunity to start working in the yard. There's nothing like getting dirt under your fingernails, and it's a sure sign of spring. The only downside to these early evenings is that no matter how much extra time I'm given at home, I continue to want more. Finding that equilibrium between work and time off can be a challenge.

There are things I would like to be priorities; there are things that must be priorities. Between the two, there is always tension-a pull that can rightfully be described as work/life balance. When it's a good, or even a decent, balance, I feel like what I do in my free time fills me up and allows me to be more effective at the things I have to do; i.e., my job. I'm still coming to terms with this balancing act even at 53. There are times when I sail through weeks of work in an extremely positive state of mind, using great problem-solving and interpersonal skills, and it's those times I feel like I'm really making a difference in the environment of Eastbridge.

Then there are other times, when, seemingly for no reason, I'm exhausted, can't get enough sleep at night, and feel that work is sucking me dry. At those points, I can't pull myself out of the ditch, either...I just go through the motions, am patient with myself, and know that God is journeying with me until the fog lifts. My prayer life is a huge asset, and, as frustrating as that wait can be sometimes, I always learn a lot about who God is AS I wait. As much as I'm enjoying this position, and making it my own, it's an incredible energy drain. There are countless interruptions every day in just about any task completion scenario, and, based on how our work area is configured, there is zero privacy, with an inherently loud volume level to the office. It's a force to be reckoned with, and this is probably the biggest challenge of my summer.

Having lived in Louisville for 25 years, there's a flow

to our seasons; Thunder and Derby always signifying true spring to me, no matter the weather. For the uninitiated, Thunder Over Louisville is an incredible event that takes place on the Saturday two weeks prior to the Kentucky Derby. It kicks off with an outstanding military air show along the Ohio River in the afternoon, concluding that evening with a spectacular fireworks display. This year is no exception. For the past six or seven years, one of Mike's best customers (the one who affirmed my newly painted kitchen and dining room to Mike, so I'm forever in his debt!) has sponsored a guest tent right down on the river, inviting all of Mike's branch, along with other customers and vendors. Over time, it's turned into the equivalent of a family reunion, with people arriving throughout the afternoon, and then hanging out together the rest of the day. Mike's company has a large branch in Cincinnati as well, and good friends of ours, the Dreyers, always come down for this event.

Whether you participate in Derby activities or not, there's a festiveness to the two weeks leading up to the event itself that is unmistakable. The city looks freshly scrubbed and pristine, flowers are blooming everywhere, and Derby hats are as necessary as comfortable shoes for race days. Each year the event seems to grow a little larger in proportion, with more media attention attached to it. What used to be a one-day event has now turned into at least two, and Oaks Day, the Friday before the Derby, has become a prequel to the big race. So have all the Friday night parties leading into Derby Day, when news coverage is rampant, and the most heavily star-studded parties showcase their attendees. Based on this influx of crowds on Oaks Day, the Louisville natives have begun to prefer going to the track on Thursday of Derby week in recent years, nicknaming the day 'Thurby'. Mike and I have only been to one Derby, in 1995, and to one Oaks; both so much fun.

Our Derbies are usually spent at the home of Chris and Janna Strong, who throw a big Derby party for all the people who work at Stephenson, along with their own friends and family. Chris is the operations manager for their company, and Mike and he have become very close over the years. This group of people is near and dear to my heart, and I know them well, as Mike has worked with most of them for the past 20 years. I've grown as close to Janna as Mike has to Chris, and I feel like I'm with family whenever the group of us is together. There's a unique and special bond between all of us, and this is beyond a doubt my favorite party of the year.

Oaks Friday dawns fair, warm and clear, and Mike is up and out of the house early, playing in a yearly golf scramble with customers. I get up ahead of my alarm and take my cup of coffee out on the deck for a while, savoring the beautiful morning. I'm excited because we only work a half day today, and my hair dryer is going when I hear the phone ring. It's Callie, and immediately I can tell she's crying. My heart stands still. Andy has had a tough winter, and it's impacted her as well. Shortly after Christmas, his parents had decided to divorce, presenting it to Andy and his sister as a decision they'd made without consulting either of the kids. It had wrecked Andy, leaving him reeling and angry over their lack of consideration for he and Sydney, especially in terms of the way they had handled it as a done deal. After the fact, Callie had filled in the blanks for me, explaining that Luther and Karen had two completely lives from one another and had wanted to do this for a long time.

Since their divorce, Andy's dad has moved into his own place, and contact with Karen, Andy's mom, has been sporadic for all of them. Callie tells me that no one had been able to reach her this week, and by last night, there was some concern on the part of Andy, his sister, and his Uncle Ben. With Andy's dad being out of town in Florida temporarily, Ben had finally decided to drive over to Karen's house to make sure everything was all right. Andy and Sydney had gone with him. The house was closed and locked up, but Ben finally managed to get in, and had found Karen crumpled on the living room floor, unable to speak, the product of a massive stroke. At that point EMS transported her to the nearest hospital, fearing she might not even make it there.

Ben, Andy, Callie and Sydney have been at the hospital since 9 PM last night, keeping vigil in the intensive care unit. As Callie relays all this, I feel the sting of tears in my eyes-for all of them, and for the hopelessness and pain they must feel. It rips my heart out to think of all of them having to go through this, let alone what may lie ahead in terms of the damage this has probably done to Karen's brain and vital organs if she even pulls through.

I talk quietly to Callie, sensing that she's calming down as she's pouring the details out to me. I try to offer comfort without platitudes; simple words don't seem to get it at a time like this, but I know Callie understands. The best words I can think of are the most natural ones-to tell her that I love her and Andy, and that I'll be praying for all of them. Andy and Sydney should not have to be witnessing their mother going through this, and it sickens me for them. I tell her that, too, and that I'll check in with her once I finish at work, and we hang up. I drive in to work utterly reeling, feeling that this beautiful spring morning has almost become a mockery.

As is my wont in situations where deep personal emotion is involved, I can't bring myself to talk about it to anyone at work. It's too raw; way too painful. Jeannie would be my one exception, but the appointment line is busy in back, and I can't take her away from what she needs to do. I just compartmentalize, power through the morning, and am thankful we're busy. I call Callie around 1:30 once I'm home, and miraculously, Karen is semi-responsive at that point. They had contacted Luther late last night, once she had made it to the hospital, and he'd immediately left Florida and headed back. Callie tells me he is extremely upset and emotional, and rightfully so. Luther had asked Karen, as he quietly sat beside her bed and held her hand, if she knew who he was, and she had nodded. Asking her to blink twice if she was tired, she had done that as well, which, to me, is very encouraging. This is all good news, yet, here are Callie and Andy, in what should be one of the happiest periods of their lives, forced to deal with all of this, and the ongoing ramifications it will have. I feel like they've been robbed;

first by the divorce, and the impact it's had on Andy, now this. He deserves none of it, and it makes me crazy. Then I think of Callie-her strength, her loyalty, her incredible generosity of spirit, and I know what a heavy load this is for her to shoulder. She wants nothing more than to be beside Andy, helping him through this, and pouring strength into him.

I verbalize these feelings to her as we talk, because I want her to know how I feel, and her response is simple.

"Thanks, Mom. I totally agree. But you play with the cards you've been given, and there have sure been a lot of two's and three's lately. Hopefully it'll get them out of the way early on."

Her attitude and her response to life in general, amazes me so often. That ushers our spring in.

May progresses from there...Karen's recovery is slow, but nothing short of miraculous. She's on dialysis for about a month, but eventually comes off when her kidneys resume full function. She's stable enough by Memorial Day that Callie and Andy come to Louisville, and the four of us drive up to Dayton to spend the weekend with Craig and Loire. I've shared the situation with them, and they are extremely sensitive to what Andy and Callie have experienced.

"I won't bring it up unless Andy does," Craig tells me a few days before we drive up. "It sounds to me like they just need to get away, have some fun, relax, and feel normal. That's a lot to deal with-at anybody's age. I don't want him to feel like he has to explain everything, for Pete's sake, it's the first time we've ever met the guy."

I'm looking forward to being with family, and to seeing Vivie and Emmy. I don't get to do that nearly as much as I'd like. Craig, too, could probably use an extra dose of support. I think the ugliness of these past five months have exacted a silent toll on him, in ways I probably can't even imagine. I still wake up at night sometimes and think back on everything that's happened, the weirdness of Rob and

Colette, and how they chose to handle the situation with Mom. I struggle with huge resentment toward them at this point in time, and my ongoing prayer is that God can take that away, leaving instead a sense of peace and acceptance in me.

I realize Craig and Colette's last conversation was extremely volatile, but Craig has done everything she asked him to do where Mom is concerned; at this point, without any help from their family. Yet he's the one I feel like they somehow 'blame'-for what, I don't know, and I think Craig has internalized a lot of that. It's so unfair to him. Life seems to be full of unfairness recently. Mike and I both want to show Craig our support and being together should be good for that.

We have a wonderful time with them, and I treasure my time with their girls. Vivie, at eight, is much more front and center, with a little bit of a 'princess' mentality; Emmy is quieter, does more processing from a distance, enjoys her solitude, and seems to live a lot more in her imagination. Being with them reminds me so much of those precious years with Callie and Kerry as they were growing up, and I realize how different my life has become as they've reached their adult and pre-adult years. I've adapted to that time and space without them and shifted the energy of parenting to other areas; namely work and my Mom. Still, there's a big part of my heart that misses all of us filling up the same place and sharing life on an everyday basis. That's limited to their trips home now. I'm learning to nurture long distance, I guess. So, it does my heart good to be able to love on Vivie and Emmy, and they're happy to soak it in.

We completely relax once we get to their place, Andy included, and maybe most of all. He seems to be his usual self-talkative, upbeat, and genuine. Craig has set a tee time for them to golf, and the three of them head out shortly after we get there early Saturday afternoon. Loire, Callie, the girls and I head up to their swim club. It's a beautiful day, and I end up being in the water with Viv and Em almost the whole time, goofing around and doing silly pose dives off the diving board while Callie and Loire catch up. Both girls are very good swimmers for their ages, and comfortable in the water, even if they can't touch the bottom.

After the guys get home from golfing, Craig grills out for us, and we sit around talking, helping Loire get dinner together and drinking rum punch. Loire is an amazing sister in law to have, and I grow more thankful each year for her. She is genuinely interested in everything Callie and Kerry do, and has been ever since she and Craig met. Both were much older and well established in their careers when their paths crossed at a get-together of a mutual friend, and he was 38 when they married; Loire 33. Their girls followed just a couple of years later. Loire has worked for years as an executive account manager for Barton & Stone, a financial consulting firm, travelling both nationally and internationally. She loves seeing Callie out in the world doing her thing and has a million questions for her about life in Nashville, her position in the agency she works for, and about the advertising industry in general. They rarely get to see one another, and I love listening to their interchange back and forth.

There is surprisingly little talk about Rob and Colette at all, and I'm grateful for that. Loire is not one to stir up dissension, and is very emotionally intuitive, so we had quietly talked a little about it while we were sitting out at the club. She loves Mom dearly and would do anything in the world for her, so she is completely behind her move to Beecher. There's also deep concern on her part for what is happening in our family. I think she wants to see where I stand with everything, since she and I really haven't had a chance to discuss it in any detail. I'm honest with her, but not vindictive.

"I just hate to see this happening in your family," she told me, and I know she means it. "Craig and Rob were so close when I first met your brother, and for so long before that. He was so proud of your family back when we were dating and would tell me about all of you. I feel like now that this has happened, their relationship will never be the same."

"Probably not," I agreed. "Rob is someone I truly don't know any more," I had added. "The fact that he would even remotely consider Craig capable of messing around with Mom's finances is absurd, let alone the fact that he's never expressed any interest in sitting down with Craig to discuss any of it. Then, out of nowhere, these accusations about Craig changing Mom's trust start getting thrown around like they're valid facts. And there's so much more behind the scenes stuff, Loire. I really don't get where Rob and Colette are coming from."

"Well, I'll tell you one thing, Bet," Loire had said fervently, her dark eyes flashing, "Your support through all of this has meant the world to him. I don't know what would have happened if you hadn't been here for him. There are nights where he wakes up and just paces the floor. I can hear him walking through the house in the middle of the night. This situation kills him."

"I'm sure," I had assented. "I know he and Colette had words, but he delivered on everything she asked him to do. We got Mom out of there. Still, somehow, he ended up being the bad guy in the situation, while Rob didn't lift a finger to help us in the search. Loire, I'm not even sure Colette told him we were looking for a place for Mom until she and Craig had toured the cottages at Beecher, and we had decided that was the only option for her. THEN Rob complains about Beecher being too expensive and wants us to look other places. Honestly, as much as I would have liked there to be a consensus about where Mom ended up, I'm almost glad it worked out the way it did. It's kind of sidelined Rob having a say in anything unless it's medical."

Loire just shook her head and stared out at the pool for several moments. "Why didn't he just call Craig and talk to him about it, Bet?" she asked me. "Even if they disagree, at least they've heard each other out."

"I guess that's not Rob's style of communication," I had

answered. "Mike and I both had really hoped that he would call Craig, and that it would clear the air between them. But I think anything that brooks conflict, Rob runs from. If he felt Beecher was too expensive, I wish he would have been up front about it from the beginning and helped more when we were looking."

That had been all. Mike hadn't brought anything up with Craig, either. After a delicious dinner, we sit around the kitchen table and play 'Apples To Apples', while Viv and Emmy watch 'The Little Mermaid'. Even after they go to bed, we continue to play, occasionally getting raunchy, and with constant laughter.

"You deserve their silence," Loire laughingly apologizes to Andy, because the girls hadn't left him alone the entire evening, tickling him, hanging on him, and calling him 'honey bunny'. Andy had been a great sport about it, and Callie had thought it was hilarious. We finally go to bed around midnight and sleep in on Sunday morning. After lazy coffee, Loire takes us for a drive around Dayton, showing us a lot of the historic homes, and their artsy downtown district. It's an old, but growing city, surrounded by the farmland of Ohio, with a distinct juxtaposition of new to old.

We meet the guys at the club for brunch and leave to head back to Louisville in the early afternoon. It's almost exactly a three-hour drive, and then Callie and Andy are driving back to Nashville, so they have all of tomorrow to relax and spend some time with Karen, who is making slow but steady progress. Andy seems to be rolling pretty well with all of that, and I haven't pressed. Other than a few questions and letting him know I'm continuing to pray for his family, I've not pushed for details. He'll talk if he needs to. Hopefully this trip was a breath of fresh air for both Callie and him, and I'm glad Craig and Loire have had the opportunity to meet him. At separate points in our visit, they both told me how much they like him, which I appreciate. It helps me to know Mom, Craig and Loire have all met him now. It's like I'm slowly building that frame of reference, and I need my family to help me do it.

Mom seems to be holding the line, and I feel guilty that I haven't been back up to Cincinnati since my April closet cleaning trip. Partly I haven't made it a priority, but my justification is also that she's settled in so well there's no pressing reason TO go. Our phone conversations are frequent; at least every other night, and they vary in length, depending on what she has going on. I've learned the names of all her new 'Knoll Girl' friends; what they're like and who her favorites are. I've also acquired a pretty good feel for her social schedule and what events occur when. Mom's accounts of day to day life continue to amuse me, both because of her childlike candor, but also because it's obvious she's enjoying herself. The only cloud on the horizon is her driving, and that's becoming a troublesome issue…one that's going to require a decision soon.

Craig often drives down on Saturdays to go through Mom's bills and pay them for her, sometimes taking her out to lunch. On one of these Saturdays in early June, after he's written out some bills and gone through her mail, he asks her if she needs any gas in her Accord. She tells him she does, and they drive to the nearest gas station, about five minutes from Beecher. He has planned on driving, but Mom insists she wants to, and Craig is appalled at how much her driving has deteriorated. Like me, it's been quite a while since he's driven with her behind the wheel.

"Betsy, she was drifting all over the road," he states, as he relays the story that following Sunday. "She's not aware of anything peripherally anymore, and when she pulled up to the pump, I figured we'd bought the farm. She about mowed the damn thing down."

I can't help myself. I laugh, mostly because of the way Craig tells the story, even though I know it really isn't funny. It's not funny at all, and Mom could kill somebody, or herself.

"Oh, Craig," I sigh. "This is our next big hurdle…Just when she's settling in and having some fun. I hate it."

"I know," he responds, more calmly. "What would you think of one of us talking to her about it, but then telling her she could set the date that she gives up the car? Within reason, of course…but that way she'd at least have some hand in it. It's time, though…actually, it's way past time. She couldn't even remember how to put gas in the car, Betsy. I got out with her, of course planning to do it myself, and she shooed me away from the pump, telling me she'd done it for years. Okay, so I just sort of hover and watch her…it was painful. She had the gas hose in her hand but couldn't find the little door to open to put the hose in the gas tank. Finally, I opened it for her and said, 'Here you go, Mom.' Then she acted like she knew it was there the whole time."

Craig has leased Mom's Honda Accord through his friend Mark Spencer for the past three years, and the lease is on a month to month basis. I know Mark will agree to anything to help Mom out, so that's not a concern.

"Her picking a date seems reasonable," I answer. "Of course, nothing is going to seem reasonable about this plan to Mom. She's going to be devastated. That car is her ticket to freedom and independence. But it needs to happen, and probably the sooner the better."

"I think we ought to shoot for the end of the summer," Craig reflects. "It's June now, and that gives her the rest of this month, all of July, and all of August. That's a good block of time for her to get used to the idea."

"And target the end of August?" I reiterate. "Yeah, that does give us some time. That sounds about right. But I think she needs to hear it from both of us, rather than just one of us. That way she knows we're a united front. The irony of this whole situation is that she was so worried about passing her driving test last summer, which she did with flying colors. That's kind of scary when you think back on it. Now here we are, even though the state deemed her fit to drive, telling her we don't think she is."

Craig chuckles. "They don't see her ploughing into gas pumps," he states, and starts laughing. "So, we'll start working on her now, and hopefully she'll be more used to the idea by the end of the summer."

That's probably wishful thinking on our part, but at least we have a plan going forward. And, it will give her time to continue a lot of her involvement at Good Shepherd without having to rely on other friends for a ride at least through the rest of the summer. She's mentioned wanting to help with Vacation Bible School, which she has done for years, and having her own wheels will be helpful for that; it usually takes place in mid to late July.

On one of my days off in June, I do something I haven't done in forever-three years, to be exact-I meet my friend Mary Claire, who still lives in Cincinnati, at General Butler State Park for the day, a location midway between Cincinnati and Louisville. It's scary how fast time has gone by, and I can't believe it's been three years since we've seen each other. We talk frequently on the phone and sometimes even write letters (we're both of that era), but there's nothing better than catching up face to face. Life has gotten in the way of that recently, and it's time to rectify the situation. Mary Claire and I have been best friends since we were randomly assigned the same locker by our 8th grade homeroom teacher, and other than possibly Mike, she knows me better than anyone else in the world.

There's no replacement for a friend who grows up with you, and Mary Claire knows all my quirks, vanities, and bad habits. She also knows my entire family, and the dynamics of our growing up years. We spent hours in one another's bedrooms from middle school into early adulthood, and I could describe her room in minute detail to a stranger, as she could mine. Letting a friend read your diary was one of the ultimate acts of trust when we were growing up, and Mary Claire was one of the few people I allowed to ever read mine-usually during our sleepovers. She, too, loved music and was an excellent flautist in our high school band. We coached each other through auditions; hers for first chair flute; mine for Varsity Vocal Ensemble our senior year.

We tried on each other's clothes, shoes, makeup, glasses, fragrances, and shopped together incessantly, borrowing items back and forth as need arose.

Both of us had other friends, and of course there was an ebb and flow to the seasons of our friendship, but it's my belief that God kept us friends for a reason. Our faith in Him would bind us together in an even more powerful way in adulthood. Graduation from high school took us to different colleges; Mary Claire to Muskingum and Miami University, me to Hanover College and Eastern Kentucky, and through those years we were voracious letter writers. Each summer we returned home to Cincinnati to work, and following graduation from college, we came home for good (or so I thought at the time)-she in the purchasing department of Stevenson, where she met Mike, me to teach elementary music in inner city Hamilton, Ohio, about 30 minutes north of Cincinnati.

Mary Claire introduced me to Mike at a party we all attended the spring I lived at home, and I have her to thank for all that came after. Two years later, after Mike and I had married, and Callie was born, it was Mary Claire who would show up on her lunch hour at our apartment, bag of lunch in hand. After spending a fleeting 40 minutes with baby Callie, she'd tear back to work. It would be Mary Claire again in 1985, following Mike's transfer to Louisville with Stevenson, who would make the trip to visit us, sleeping on the couch in our cramped two-story town house because we didn't have a spare bed.

Despite the 110-mile stretch of interstate between us, we raised our kids together; two apiece. Clayton and Maren were born four years apart, Mary Claire becoming a single parent when Clayton was six and Maren four. Marrying Kevin was self-admittedly not a wise choice for her, and as his violent temper became more and more of an issue, she cut her losses and moved out. That had been a difficult time in her life, and one we shared deeply. Living briefly with her parents until she got on her feet, she moved into an older town house near them a few months later, in the community that we had grown up in. We continued to get together whenever I was in Cincinnati visiting my parents, and several times a year we would converge on Butler State Park for long, lazy picnics, or to rent a cabin and spend the weekend with the kids.

Those times were memorable. We trekked around the park, did crafts, and devised indoor treasure hunts. As Callie and Clayton got older, they began creating treasure hunts for Mary Claire and me. To this day, we joke about one of Clayton's clues when he was eight or nine. It read: 'The wiener rises at dawn.' Clayton has always been wicked smart, with a very dry sense of humor, and we knew exactly what he was alluding to; however, we also knew that the next clue would most likely be taped to the package of hotdogs in the cabin refrigerator. (And it was.) There was another trip to Red River Gorge when our brood was a little older-a carefree stretch of four days with few showers, campfires, roasting marshmallows, and board games, and the feeling of time being frozen and magical.

Those years segued into the time I have always considered the "full court press years" of parenting-those that extracted every ounce of grit, patience, and resilience from my poor body and brain; that is, high school. My level of communication with Mary Claire flagged, but we hung on for dear life, squeezing in cards and phone calls between events, college visits, and graduations. It was during this time that Mary Claire met Dan. They were both at a mutual neighbor's cook-out one summer evening, and Dan ended up walking her home. They clicked in a big way, and in May of 1999 they were married. This began what I have always felt to be the best chapter in Mary Claire's life. Dan is the opposite of Kevin in every possible way, and he worships the ground Mary Claire walks on. Thoughtful and forward thinking, with a heart the size of Montana, it was obvious he loved Clayton and Maren, and he loved the Lord as well. Following their wedding, Mary Claire and the kids moved into Dan's home in Southwoods, bidding their townhouse goodbye. It's this dwelling that has become my second home over the years.

Our day at Butler is a gift…we sit out at a picnic table, soak up the sunshine, and eat the lunch we've jointly brought, talking endlessly and interrupting each other constantly. Mary Claire is a wonderful listener, but she can also tell great stories, some of which are extremely humorous, and I listen intently. It's very evident to me as she talks that her faith in God has grown exponentially since I've last seen her, and it encourages me. She and Dan are headed to West Virginia next week for their vacation-to do mission work. There's a community that they've become involved with there, Eolia, that is part of Appalachia, and they work in Eolia's service center that oversees a myriad of community needs. Dan works on a lot of construction and mechanical projects while he's there, as part of a larger team. Mary Claire helps with the cooking and preparation of all the meals for the various teams of workers that are involved with the community. While they're there, they stay in simple, rough cut bunk houses with all the other team members. That's their on-site work.

When they're not in Eolia, they're stockpiling supplies for weeks and months in advance that they transport there to either distribute to those in need, or to sell at a hugely discounted price at the community center. Items range, and it's just about anything they can get their hands on; cooking supplies, skillets, utensils, lamps, blankets, dishes, mixers, appliances; you name it. Mary Claire tells me in her calm, understated way that they've collected so much they need a second couple to help them transport all the supplies. I can't wait to hear about everything once they return from their trip. Just listening to her talk about it gets my blood flowing. This is a venture I'd kill to go on. More and more I find myself leaning in this direction in terms of how I want the rest of my life to look. We leave Butler with the agreement that we're going to try to meet here every few months, and I drive back to Louisville thanking God that this friendship of my childhood has endured.

The heat and humidity roll in as June progresses, and my plants start taking off. June 6th is Mike's 50th birthday, and we've decided to do a casino getaway, just for something different. There are several in Indiana that are within an hour of us, and we've invited his family to join us. As big as Mike's family is, you never know who will show up, but everyone is included. Kerry, who is staying in Lexington for the summer to do an unpaid internship as assistant event planner at one of the larger Lexington country clubs, Twin Oaks, has moved heaven and earth to get that Sunday off so she can join us. She desperately needs this time, as she's working six and seven days a week and I can't wait to see her.

We have a great time at the casino. Mike's older cousin Scott, and his wife, Marlene joins us, too. They're two of Kerry's favorite people, and it does my heart good to see her relax and enjoy their company. Mike's family has truly become my own over the years and being with them always recharges me. Talk flies, people yell over each other, and there's usually a haze of cigarette smoke, courtesy of Michelle, Marlene, and Steve, but it's the comfort of family, to me. All of Mike's siblings are very big-hearted, and they're so much more connected than my fragile family at this point. Having Kerry there to share it with is icing on the cake.

As June steams into July, Jeannie and I grow closer at work, going out for Mexican on Saturdays that we work together, and I spend a Saturday with them at their swim club, hanging out with Lynsey and her son, and Jeannie's husband. Mike and I meet them for dinner one night, and it's nice to have taken it to the 'couple's level'. Work moves along, lots of summer well-checks and school physicals, and we have an employee lunch cookout in mid-July, on a cool 96-degree Friday. That's one of the few times I stay on site to eat lunch…more and more recently, I find myself walking down to a church that's about an eighth of a mile from the practice, and, weather permitting, sitting out at one of the picnic tables the church has placed at various spots on their property. One table is directly under a huge hundred-year-old sycamore tree, which offers great shade and a beautiful view up into its branches, and that's usually my go-to spot. The relative silence and outdoors restores me after the noise level of the office, and it helps my state of mind just to be still and not to have to converse with anyone for that hour. I've started bringing whatever book I'm reading, or a couple of Time magazines; being able to read takes me somewhere else, too.

Vacation rolls around in mid-July-destination Florida, and this year we've invited the Dreyers, our friends from Cincinnati, to join us for part of the week. They'll be coming for the four final days we'll be there. As much as I love it being just the four of us at the beginning of our week, it is fun when they arrive. Paul, Mike's close friend, has a great sense of humor, and Callie and Kerry really enjoy them. This is one aspect I love about the ages our girls are now, because they're fully adults interacting with other adults. There's no real parenting left for me to do, and I can sit back and truly enjoy everything about Callie and Kerry being with us. They both are so comfortable and welcoming to Paul and Kristi, and especially to Tony, their youngest son.

Tony has multiple learning disabilities and his speech is difficult to understand. It's no indication of his IQ or overall cognitive function; he has a mind like a steel trap, a quasi-photographic memory, and an extremely well-developed sense of humor. His brain just relays information differently, and reading is a challenge for him. Like Paul, Tony works for Stephenson, in their Cincinnati warehouse, and Paul expects him to be held to the standards of any other employee. Possessing Paul's maniacal work ethic, he owns his own Jeep and has enjoyed tricking it out with updates and improvements over the years. Paul and Kristi joke about him being 'the millionaire next door' based on his legendary saving habits.

Callie and Kerry love him, and they're perfectly willing to engage him in conversation, treating him as a peer (he's three years younger than Kerry), and constantly joking with him. He's a great listener, following all conversations, especially when Mike and Paul talk sports, often interjecting a comment of his own. By the end of the four days, we're able to understand Tony; maybe not everything but a good bit. Nor are we afraid to ask him to repeat himself if we don't catch it the first time. One of the best moments of the trip occurs on our pontoon boat when we head out into the bay, letting Tony drive. He does so for most of the trip, which gives Mike and Paul the opportunity to relax. At one point, Tony cuts across a good-sized swell from another boat at just the right angle, sending a wall of water crashing over the side directly onto Paul and Kristi. Tony acts completely surprised by what happens, but Cal and Kerry are certain he does it intentionally to get them wet.

Cal and I take our usual long walks, talking about everything under the sun. She's had a tough summer, starting with Luther and Karen's divorce, compounded by Karen's stroke and multiple complications, and her work situation has become very demanding. She's putting in longer and longer hours, more and more responsibilities are being added by her clients and superiors, and she's been doing a fair amount of travel. Add to that an employee who is a perfectionist, but still young enough and new enough that she doesn't feel she has the leverage to say no to anything, and you have a slow cooked recipe for stress. She does have a good working relationship with her boss, and she finally spoke up, but this was only when she had reached the end of her rope, instead of asking for help or an assistant before she reached her breaking point. Grumpy and irritable from lack of sleep (she doesn't sleep when she's stressed out; I don't know many people who do), and with Andy struggling to come to terms with his mother's stroke and parents' divorce, Cal is in the thick of it.

Their joint issues with life have erupted on each other, but Callie also feels that a lot of Andy's anger is displaced, and that she's an easy target for it, instead of him owning the true causes of it. In late June, about three weeks ago, they had talked, and she had suggested they break up for a while, tired of Andy 'not letting her in', and frustrated by the anger she was seeing. She had also mentioned him seeing a counselor, to help him work through some of these issues. He agreed, and has been seeing a therapist, which is a great first step. But even as the counseling is progressing, he's very closed off from Callie in terms of sharing any of his feelings about things.

"You know, Mom, I don't expect a blow by blow from him," she tells me as we walk one of our mornings, "but we're a team in dealing with everything that he's been through, and even if he just talked to me about it in generalities, it would help me. I think it would help BOTH of us. I get that he needs time to process all of it, and make sense of it, but I wish he'd be a little more open and vulnerable. It's like he doesn't want me to know anything…almost like it'll give me the upper hand emotionally somehow if he opens up."

These words are hard for me to hear. Already I'm sensing some issues that go deep. Their relationship should not be this difficult so early on. I'm no queen of fairy tales, or even a 'girlie-mom'; growing up with three brothers has made me pretty much of a realist when it comes to male/female stuff, but I hate seeing Callie and Andy struggle. This should be the fun chapter of their relationship…the falling in love part. But based on 'the hand they've been dealt' (Cal's own phrase), I feel like they're staggering under the load. Deep down, I also wonder if Andy's seeking this counseling reluctantly, afraid he'll lose Callie if he chooses not to continue it.

I know her well enough to trust she'll draw her own lines in terms of what's acceptable, and that if she senses there's no productive, healthy way forward for them, that she'll choose to end the relationship, and I tell her this.

"But," I also caution her, "YOU are not responsible for Andy's mental and emotional well-being. Sure, you contribute to it, but he's responsible for fixing his own 'stuff', and he's got to want to do that. And Cal, that displaced anger is a cheap fix instead of working it through on his own and staring it down. It's critical that he do that, and that's not easy for anybody."

The more Cal and I talk, the more I feel like they have some huge hurdles to overcome if they are to have a healthy relationship. But I also know how much she cares about him, and how willing she is to meet him more than halfway.

"I will cheer you on as long as you have the energy to invest in this relationship," I state, wiping sweat off my forehead as we reach our halfway point and turn around. "Just don't invest at expense to yourself."

I'm blessed to have this open of a relationship with Callie, and I don't take her confidences lightly. I feel like she's painted a genuine enough picture for me to offer her sound insight when she needs it, as well as to know how to pray for Andy. Only Cal can ultimately make the decision to pull the plug on this relationship, and I sense that there's enough strength and love between them that for now, she's just going to give it some time. Something else that has helped her, in a somewhat unrelated way, has been seeing her company step up to support her since her talk with her boss in late June. Last week, she had spoken with one of her supervisors, and had been promoted to Account Executive for the Honda National Team, along with being given a significant raise. All of this had come as a complete surprise, but obviously, her boss had listened to her and taken it to the appropriate people, who had evaluated her concerns. In addition, they are allocating corporate funds for her to hire an assistant, so she can be training and delegating as she moves into this new role. Knowing they've given such consideration to her concerns is very affirming, and her company's way of acknowledging her commitment to them. Any thoughts she'd entertained about looking elsewhere for a position in the industry are gone. Extrapolated into a 'life lesson,' it has reinforced for Callie the value of asking for help when she needs it, and the importance of communicating with regularity, rather than letting it bottle up until it becomes toxic. I hope it gives her more assurance in moving ahead with Andy as well.

Later in the week, she and Mike go out to lunch, just

the two of them. I feel like Callie will benefit from hearing Mike's perspective on the situation with Andy instead of mine alone. Mike's very rational, but also grounded and less emotional, and I think it will do Cal a lot of good to talk with him. They enjoy themselves. In Mike's typical manner, he listens without judging, and suggests giving the situation 'some time and space to breathe'.

As always, coming off vacation is hard for me. I miss the girls a lot, and it takes me a few days to get back in my work routine…after that, it's pretty much autopilot. In early August, following my first ever bone density scan, a call comes through to me at Eastbridge from Dr. Black, my ob/gyn who did the scan. This, the most un-private of places, is hardly where I'd choose to have any conversation with any doctor, but I don't have a choice. So, with my whole team eavesdropping (to be fair, it's kind of hard NOT to) Dr. Black relays the results of my scan to me. It shows that I am in full blown osteoporosis. WHAT? I'm literally in shock. It's something I've given zero thought to; EVER. I've always eaten lots of calcium-rich products, especially yogurt; I even took calcium tablets for years, because it was the one thing that took the edge off my PMS, believe it or not. (Mike had come across a medical article online touting it, had given it to me to read, and in desperation I had tried it. The difference was amazing.) So, I'm stunned by this news.

My mental picture of osteoporosis is of frail little 80-year-old women tottering around like gently curved C's, moving timidly and looking up from the floor to speak to you. Not only is it in my spine, Dr. Black informs me, but also in the 'pelvic girdle', my hips, pelvic bones, etc.

She explains, "As much as it's no comfort at all, Betsy, you fit all the high-risk criteria for it. You're Caucasian, you're small boned and thin, and you're post-menopausal. That's your statistical trifecta. I'm really glad we went ahead and did this when we did."

Well, that's just special. I'm so comforted to be a statistic. That makes everything more real and much easier. Pardon my sarcasm. "So, what do we do?" I ask her.

Already I can feel myself starting to detach, and I desperately want to get off the phone before I say something I'll regret. I feel far too exposed having this conversation at work, even though I know Dr. Black wanted me to have the information as quickly as possible, and that's why she called me here. I've not been on any long-term medication EVER, and I realize that will be changing. This isn't something that will clear up and go away. Dr. Black walks me through trying Boniva for a year...the drug Sally Fields says is miraculous...I've seen the commercials, and always dismissed it as being for elderly people. I guess I'm part of that club now. Welcome, Bet. Here's your walker.

Dr. Black explains how the pill is taken once a month, how I am not to eat or drink anything after taking it for at least one hour, and tells me she'll call in the prescription so I can get started; we'll do another scan next year to see where I stand.

Okay. Well. Let's get rolling on those wonderful pills. I remember my manners, thank Dr. Black for calling me, and hang up. I'm slowly beginning to process all of this, and I look out the window into the sick waiting room and shake my head. Part of my brain is telling me not to overreact. Tons of people deal with this every year, and it's not life-threatening. It's just that...well...it makes me feel old, and suddenly vulnerable, especially because I've felt nothing as the condition developed. I feel blindsided big on this. But we also caught it early. That's a good thing. I hadn't realized a condition like this could deteriorate so quickly following menopause. Heck, I've only been finished for barely two years. That's crazy. And that's also some big damage to my bones. I know Mom has it, and she's taken Fosamax for a long time. I just didn't see this coming at all. I randomly look over at LaDonna, who's sitting on the well side. She's not checking anybody in right now.

"Well, guess what?" I say to her, in mock cheeriness.

She swivels in her chair so she's looking directly at me.

"What?" she asks, and I can tell there's genuine concern in her voice.

Marcy, too, who is the biggest eavesdropper in the world, echoes LaDonna.

"What?" she echoes, from behind me where she does posting and scheduling. Good grief. No conversation can ever be one on one, either. LaDonna rolls her eyes in disgust at Marcy, in a silent 'I know you want this conversation to be just the two of us,' which amuses me to no end. I know they have both heard my entire side of the conversation.

"I have full blown osteoporosis," I tell LaDonna, in a very clinical, detached fashion. (I know she loves me confiding in her-her body language exudes her thrill of being in the know. She's leaning in, eyes widened and trained on me, and without realizing it, she's turned her body to block Marcy-so funny!) "Knock me over with a feather," I continue. "I can't believe it."

LaDonna shakes her large head.

"That's crazy, Betsy," she replies. "I knew you had your bone scan a few weeks ago-I remember you went on your off day. I just figured everything was fine since you hadn't said anything. What are you supposed to do?"

"She wants me to try Boniva," I answer, "and then do another scan next year. She told me I'm high risk for fractures, too, based on how severe it is. 'Way to plant fear."

LaDonna shakes her head again. It's just a head-shaking kind of day. "You'd be the last person in the world I'd expect to have osteoporosis," she states loyally. "You sure don't look like you do. You have wonderful posture."

For some reason, hearing what is tantamount to a pep talk issuing from LaDonna's negative lips cheers me greatly.

"You know," I say slowly, "it could be a lot worse. And I'm thankful they caught it early. Hopefully we can reverse it a little."

We discuss it for a few more minutes, then I have a

patient come in, and the flow of the day resumes. I tell Mom about it that night, and she's very sympathetic.

"I hate hearing that," is her comment. She doesn't try to rationalize it, or tell me it's not a big deal, which I also appreciate. "Hopefully you'll see some improvement once you get on the Boniva," she offers. "The Fosamax has held me pretty steady over time. It's just no fun to get old, is it?" she asks me.

I laugh. Already I feel better about all of it. I think it was more the shock of it than anything else…Having Mom to tell makes it all seem okay.

The next several days at work, I have some fun with it, asking Marcy and LaDonna to reach things that are higher up in our cupboards because I'm afraid of fracturing my back. Since they're both easily three inches shorter than I am, they find great humor in this. I purposely drop a fee ticket near LaDonna, start to reach over, and then grab my back.

"What am I thinking?" I exclaim. "I can't reach down to get that. It's way too risky with my back so fragile."

LaDonna starts laughing, which in turn makes me laugh. "Anything to keep that back in one piece," she answers, flopping the fee ticket I 'faux dropped' on the counter.

Marcy, too, gets in on the action. "Would it be better if we just got a wheelchair or at least a back brace for you?" she asks jokingly. "You're becoming a liability, Betsy."

With each of them being a year older than I am, and having chronic health issues of their own, I do appreciate their empathy on this. I wish they could be more like this all the time. A week later, I take my first Boniva. It's torture for me to have to wait to drink my coffee, and my head is pounding by the time I am 'safe' to drink it at 8:30 that Wednesday morning at work. I literally run downstairs, find the biggest coffee mug there, and feel much happier in the next 30 minutes as I pour it into my bloodstream. Already this has become a part of my 'life fabric', and I'm forging ahead with it. I've done a lot more research over the course of the week, and there are a lot of options available. Let's just hope Sally Fields knows what she's talking about with this wonderful product of hers.

During that same week, Craig calls me with a driving update on Mom, and it confirms the necessity of getting her off the road as soon as possible. Since our conversation earlier in the summer, I've eased into the discussion several times when we've talked on the phone, suggesting that she probably needs to start giving some serious thought to not driving anymore, and to settle on a date to end the lease on her car. And, as I had mentioned to Craig, her passing her driver's test last summer is her leverage with me to continue driving. I can tell she feels like Craig is really backing her into a corner on this, and I don't like that for either one of them.

"I'm just not ready to give it up, Betsy," she tells me with significant ire one night. "I don't want to have to depend on other people to take me everywhere, nor have I had any accidents."

"We'll keep talking about it, Mom," I had told her calmly, "but maybe, like Craig suggested, target a date, say, the end of August, and get yourself ready for that transition."

"He needs to stop badgering me about it," Mom snaps back. "I'm tired of talking about it with him."

Tired or not, the most recent account of Mom's questionable driving comes from the Theisses, her friends from Good Shepherd who have recently left and joined another congregation. Since his college years, Craig has been close to Paul Theiss, a dear friend of my Dad's, and continues to stay in touch with him. Recently, when Craig had been in Cincinnati on business, he and Paul met for lunch. They were discussing Mom's transition to Beecher when Paul brought up her driving. Apparently, he and Jackie, his wife, had recently followed Mom somewhere from a central meeting point when all of them were going out to dinner, and Paul expressed some serious concerns about Mom's lack of awareness behind the wheel. He told Craig she had run two red lights, as well as having run up on a curb on a main thoroughfare. All this, coming from an objective source, is extremely concerning. So, our clock is ticking. We agree to wait to talk to Mom about it until after her birthday, which is August 4th. Our two families are going to meet at Mom's place the weekend following and take her out to dinner to celebrate. No need to put a damper on things.

"We'll just talk up the end of August," I tell Craig. "We need to get this done."

We drive up for her birthday celebration on Saturday, and I've already made up my mind I'm coming back for a long weekend at the end of August. Today will be a short visit, and with the car situation pending, I want to spend some longer one on one time with her. This will be a difficult month for Mom. Our birthday trip is also the perfect opportunity for me to return those four pairs of navy pants that I rescued and rejoin them with their thinner fabric-ed compatriots. They've had to wait far too long for this reunion.

I've picked out what I think is a very pretty birthday outfit for Mom, and I hope she likes it. It's a pair of white slacks (elastic waistband in back for extra good fit and comfort!) with a black jacket. There are red and white flowers appliquéd on the front, with thick white edge-stitching all around the jacket. Because of the black and white, I feel like she'll be able to wear it just about any time of the year, especially as fall begins. With temps currently soaring into the 100's still, we may be awhile off on that.

Craig, Loire, Mike and I meet at Mom's place around 3:00 that Saturday afternoon, and Vivie looks like she's grown two more inches since Memorial Day weekend. Emmy is completely gap toothed in front; having lost her two front teeth on the top, and you can see the jagged edges of her permanent teeth starting to descend. She can't wait to show me this, telling me, "There are four more teeth that are so loose they could come out any day. I might have to be on all liquids if I lose them all at once!"

Craig looks at me and rolls his eyes. "Obviously her mother talking," he remarks drily, winking at Emmy.

Mom looks good. Her hair is freshly done, and she has one of my favorite pants sets on-a sage green pair of pants with a collared floral print top. While everyone is talking when we first arrive, I quietly slip the bag of navy pants back to Mom's bedroom, find hangers for them, and pop them into the closet. I don't plan on saying anything to her about it, and wonder if she'll even realize she has four extra pairs now. The important thing to me is that they're THERE. I slide back out to the living room, where Viv is telling Mom about the tennis lessons she's been taking. I hear Emmy say to Mom, "But Grammy, Vivie needs lots of practice. She can't play in the lines," at which I start laughing.

"Emmy, you don't even know," Vivie reproves her defensively. "You don't take lessons yet."

"I will soon," Emmy responds, undaunted. "But I can see you hitting your balls outside the lines all the time. Plus, you miss a lot of them."

Mom comes to Viv's rescue. "I would love to see you play," she tells her. "Tennis is a hard game to learn. You have to be quick."

"And Vivie isn't quick," Emmy interjects. She's not going to let this go. Mike is suppressing a smile.

"Emmy," Loire says to her, "that's enough. There are things you're learning to do that you're not really good at right now, like your passing in soccer. Sometimes things take practice. When you try new things for the first time, most people aren't very good at them right away."

"I know," Emmy says, nodding, as if in complete agreement. And then, "Vivie's a really good example of that."

Mike, Mom, Craig and I can't help ourselves…all of us laugh out loud. I'd forgotten about this age-appropriate sibling rivalry.

As we're laughing, Mom's phone rings. She answers, and from her end of the conversation, I can tell it's Colette.

"Yes," Mom tells her, "and I really appreciate it. You can never have too many pairs of navy pants."

Oh, my gosh, I'm thinking. *Did Colette give Mom navy pants for her birthday? Was the sad saga of not enough navy pants shared after I cleaned out her closet?* I continue to listen, wondering if Mom will tell her that all of us are here. I have a feeling she won't. It's as if she doesn't want her to know, and for some reason that really irritates me. I move over closer to Mom, touch her arm, and say, "Tell Colette we all said hello," and smile brightly.

Now Mom has no choice. I'm standing right there. "Betsy says to tell you hello," she says into the phone. Then, "Yes, they're here to celebrate my birthday with Craig and Loire and their girls. No, just Vivie and Emmy." (I'm assuming Col asked if Callie and Kerry were with us.)

Shortly after that, their conversation ends. "How are they all doing?" I ask Mom, honestly wanting to know.

"They're fine," Mom answers. "Just getting ready for school to start, and the boys have ball games."

It's weird after eight months to have had even this slight amount of contact with Colette, and I realize how distant their family now seems. It makes me sad in one way; in another way I just feel a sense of resolution in knowing they chose to make the decisions they did. It's never again come up with Mom. I think she's forgotten about her concerns as she's settled in here, and I don't think she has any idea that Rob and Col no longer communicate with any of us. It would kill her if she knew.

Our dinner is fun. We've made reservations at one of Mom's favorite restaurants near Beecher called 'C'est Fini'. It's been in operation for at least 30 years, with delicious crepes and desserts, and Mom puts away her entire entrée, along with a Grasshopper, her favorite 1960's crème de menthe drink. She really seems to enjoy herself, even though she's on the quiet side, mostly listening to our conversations.

Our waiter brings her a birthday cake after we eat, alight with candles, and we sing to her, Viv and Emmy helping her blow them out. The waiter is nice enough to take pictures of us, and he gets some good ones. Happy 83, Mom... and many more. Whoever made the statement, 'The only constant in life is change' about nailed it. Our next big challenge is making the Honda Accord go away.

Chapter Seven

EQUINOX
(Late August – September 2010)

"Hey, Mom," I ease in once we're seated at 'C'est Fini', for the second time in a month. We've ordered our entrees, and we're here because I thought it might be easier, and more pleasant for Mom, to have The Car Discussion in the warm, familiar environment of her favorite restaurant. She may never want to eat here again.

"Let's talk about letting go of your car. I know you feel like Craig's been on your back about it, but he and I both think it's time to end your lease. Both of us know it won't be easy for you, but we think it's the wisest thing to do."

I have promised Craig that I would have this in-depth discussion with Mom while I was here this weekend and get some solid closure on it for all of us. He's been uncharacteristically blunt about letting me know he wants me to do the heavy lifting on this.

"You've got far more patience with Mom than I do," he told me, "and she already thinks I'm the villain in this."

The other smaller consideration was that neither of us (me from a purely defensive posture towards what Craig has already had to endure) wanted Rob or Colette thinking that Craig had made this decision solely on his own, especially since Mom's car is leased through Mark Spencer, his friend. I know it'll go down better for everyone involved if I'm front and center on this. Having talked a lot to both Mike and Mary Claire, I'm pretty fatalistic about getting it done promptly. I know it's the only way to go, and we've given Mom the entire summer to get used to the idea. She takes a long sip of her Grasshopper as if to ward off whatever is coming.

"But there's nothing wrong with my driving," she states stubbornly. "And now that I'm not on the interstate anymore, I don't have to worry about making quick moves from lane to lane, or even passing other people."

"Well, that part's true," I agree, sipping my glass of wine. "But here's the thing, Mom-your reflexes are slowing way down, which is normal for your age. It's not you, so much, that I worry about." (I can stretch the truth a little on this point.) "It's that other person who could be driving stupidly and not paying attention, and you might not be able to react in time. If you were in a situation like that, and something happened to you, I couldn't live with myself. And, if YOU caused an accident because you couldn't react fast enough, YOU'D never forgive yourself. That's a lot to live with."

I look directly at her across the table, and, unbidden, tears fill my eyes. "Mom," I continue, "this is so hard for me. I know this will be a life changer for you, and I don't want you to think I'm doing it lightly. I just can't see taking the risk of something happening to you, or someone else. That's where Craig and I are coming from, and we're trying to prevent that from ever happening. That's not saying it would, but it COULD."

I pause, and just wait. This is such a hard conversation to be having, but it is a foregone conclusion, based on what Craig has witnessed, and what Paul Theiss shared with him.

That was back in June, and Mom's had two more full months to get used to the idea. She was also able to help with Good Shepherd's Vacation Bible School, as she'd wanted to, and I know she thoroughly enjoyed that week, save probably for her encounters with Pastor Morehouse. So, knowing we've been planting seeds for the past three months, I'm far more direct in my addressing the inevitable. Still, I'll give it as much love and patience as I can. I want the idea of our concern for her first and foremost in her mind.

"With you being at Beecher now, it's going to be a lot easier than you think," I muse, "because of the transportation shuttles they offer, and because you're close to so many of your friends. If you were still over at Rob and Colette's, it would be a whole different situation, Mom. But at Beecher, you'll have access to their services every day that can take you to Kroger, the malls or Walgreen's…wherever you need to go. And, if you ever wanted to use them, Beecher can provide a private driver for you; very similar to what Craig and I were talking to you about when you were still at Rob's and concerned you might not pass your driver's test. You don't have to utilize that option, but my point is, you've GOT options. The weekends I come up, we can run errands constantly, if it's what you want to do."

Mom just looks deflated, more than angry or upset. "I just hate depending on other people, Bet," she says quietly.

I look at her and nod. "I know," I acknowledge. "That'd be hard for me, too. But Mom, people like it that you feel like you can ask them to help. They enjoy being able to do that for you."

Mom looks at me skeptically. "Maybe for a few times, but not on an ongoing basis," she replies. "That'll get old fast. And without Nancy at Good Shepherd anymore, or the Theisses, that really limits my choices of who I can call."

"We'll figure it out," I assure her. "Beatrice Odell is here at Beecher, and she goes to church pretty regularly, doesn't she? You could always ask the Castilles, too. I know it seems undoable right now, but I think you'll be amazed. I know you probably don't want to hear this right now, but God's way ahead of us on this, Mom, and He'll be opening doors. And, this probably doesn't matter either, but you'll be saving the monthly stipend you're paying for the lease."

"Yes, Craig has pointed that out to me every time we've had this discussion," Mom responds, somewhat sardonically.

We both just lapse into silence for a few minutes, and then Mom speaks up. "I guess I really don't have a choice in this, do I? It probably is time, and I know you and Craig are doing this out of concern. I do appreciate that. It's just so hard to be told you have no choice in something; that you have to give up something you've been doing your entire life that gave you independence. But I guess that's where I am now."

I smile sadly at her. "It's not easy, Mom-for you or for us. But I think Dad would have wanted us to shoot straight with you on this, and I feel like we're doing the best we can. Thanks for at least trying to see it through our eyes, too. You're being an awfully good sport about it."

And that's pretty much the end of our discussion. I sense that she knows it's a done deal, and she tells me she'd just like to keep the Accord for a couple more weeks. I will relay all of this to Craig, and hopefully it will be easier for him moving forward.

We talk about other things after that and continue to eat; Mom doesn't seem to have lost her appetite, which relieves me. I really haven't had the chance to talk to her in depth about Bible School, and I'm curious to hear her take on it, especially in terms of Pastor Morehouse's involvement with it.

"Oh, he was smack dab in the middle of it," Mom tells me with disdain. "This year's theme was nautical; we were supposed to be travelling on a cruise ship with the Apostle Paul, visiting all the churches he planted, and learning about some of the things he experienced through his life as a missionary. The whole title of VBS was 'Adventures At Sea', and the last day, the elementary kids went on a paddlewheel boat trip around Preston Lake. It was high jinks for them, and they talked about some of the things Paul encountered on his travels at sea, like being shipwrecked, and when they had to throw cargo overboard to lighten one of the ships during a huge storm."

She reels these facts off proudly, as if she just finished learning them this past week herself. I know better. Still, it's amazing to me she can recall what transpired on a day to day basis. I can tell how much she enjoyed it, and obviously she remembers a good bit, even though it was roughly six weeks ago. I guarantee she was the oldest volunteer there, and it makes me so happy for her that she was able to be a part of it.

"Every day," she continues, "all the teachers, helpers, and the refreshment crew (I like how she still uses the word 'refreshments' instead of 'snacks') had to wear these red T-shirts that had a ship's wheel on the front, with the VBS logo that said 'Paul's Adventure Cruise' under it. And then, on the back of the shirt, since we were supposed to be part of the crew, it just said, 'MATE' in big capital letters."

I erupt in laughter-this is too much. Mom painting this picture is priceless, especially that she's talking so enthusiastically about it, and given the discussion about her car that has just preceded this.

"Wow," I state, giggling. "That's a lot of red running around Good Shepherd."

Mom nods. "And of course, Morehouse wore his red T-shirt every day, except his said 'Captain' on the back, not 'mate'. And, to make it feel more like a real cruise, every time we saw him or passed him during Bible School, we were supposed to salute and call him Captain Tim, and he'd call us 'Mate Joan', or 'Mate Lucy.'"

I'm laughing again, hard this time. "Oh, Mom," I breathe, "I cannot picture you doing this! Never in a million years!"

I can tell she's getting wound up and really owning the story as she's divulging its details.

"He's not my captain!" She declares emphatically. "Nor did I ever salute him. Instead, I would just say, 'Hello, Tim', if I passed him. I don't think he cared much for that."

"Sounds like you were fostering mutiny, mate," I choke out, still laughing. "And I bet you weren't the only one. At least you were there. Who else taught and helped out?"

Mom ticks through the list of women and men in the congregation who assisted, and it runs the gambit-from young mothers with infants in the nursery to retirees with grandchildren in the program, or people like Mom, who just wanted to show up and lend a hand, as she's been doing for the past 60 years of her life. She mentions two of my longtime friends, Lucy and Cathy, who I met for lunch today on my way to Beecher. We've remained close from the time Mike and I were newly married and still in Cincinnati attending Good Shepherd. There were four of us on the VBS 'Refreshment Committee' in 1984; Lucy Allgeier, Cathy Hunter, Lesley Knight, and me. It was the first time all four of us had met one another, and we became fast friends. Crazy to think of that through-line 26 years later, and the strength of those friendships now.

"Do you still have your T-shirt?" I ask Mom. "I want to see it when we get back to your place."

"Oh, yes," Mom answers. "They didn't order enough 'small's', so I took a 'medium', just to be nice, and gave someone else my 'small'. It fit me like a dress-came down to almost my knees. I'll show it to you. You could probably sleep in it."

She does pull it out once we get home, and it furthers the picture of that entire week. I'm so thankful she had the chance to be a part of that week-to see all the little guys, to hear the older ones singing each day, and to see them present their music that Sunday as part of worship. It makes my heart happy to know she felt like she contributed, and clearly, she enjoyed it. I hope not having her car won't detract from future opportunities like that.

Our weekend flies, but it's a good one, and great to be back with Mom for that longer stretch of time. We attend the usual Saturday night service at Good Shepherd, but at Mom's request, we go back again on Sunday morning. A special farewell reception is being held for their pastoral intern who worked with them this past summer, and Mom adores him. The son of one of the congregation members I grew up with, he's currently finishing seminary. From all Mom's accounts, Adam has been an incredible resource and encouragement to the congregation in his preaching, youth work, and his teaching of Mom's weekly Bible study. I think it's very exciting for their congregation to witness 'one of their own' accepting that call to ministry, then seeing him pour out his gifts within that framework. Mom raved about him all summer, telling me what a great speaker he was, what a gentle demeanor he had, and what an outstanding job he'd done across the board.

"I wish they could just give him Good Shepherd, and move Morehouse somewhere else," she'd told me several times.

I know her being there to thank Adam and to express her gratitude is important to her, and I'm looking forward to seeing him as a full-blown adult after remembering him as the active little kid that crawled under the pews during the service. It's a beautiful reception, and a great time for me to see people I don't normally cross paths with at the Saturday night service. I keep an eye on Mom, but she seems very comfortable mixing and mingling on her own, working her way to a seat at one of the tables they have set up in the fellowship hall. Lucy and Cathy are both there with their husbands, and Nancy Rhodes has even come back to show her support for Adam, although she's made the decision to leave Good Shepherd permanently, which I know is hard for Mom.

The Reinholds spot us and come over to talk, then move on to find a seat; the Castilles sit near us and Sherry asks me how Mom is doing. I put a bug in her ear about Mom giving up her car soon and explain how reluctant she'll be to ask for rides.

"Call her and offer," I suggest to Sherry, knowing she will. "And spread the word-this will be a big adjustment for Mom, and you know how she is about imposing on other people."

Sherry assures me she will. "I don't see that as a problem for anyone," she states resolutely. "But I'll definitely talk it up. Anybody that lives over near Beecher would be more than happy to pick your Mom up."

Once everyone has mingled, and has been through the brunch line, (they have a huge spread laid out, complete with a large bakery sheet cake with the message 'Go and Bless-We'll Miss You!' in huge script on it), the president of Good Shepherd's congregation, Don Wickmann, steps forward to speak. He's informal, but his words are heartfelt, and he begins by thanking Adam for all he's done this summer.

"It's a rare person who can come into a congregation, especially one where most of us remember you as an eight year old, or a thirteen year old, and assume the role of humble leadership that you have in just three short months," Don addresses Adam, who is sitting near the front of the gathering with a group of the high school kids.

"It's an even rarer individual who has the servant's heart that you do, and the humility you exhibit," Don continues. "Adam, you are wise beyond your years, and we're recipients of that gift. Thank you for giving so much of yourself to us. You've really spoiled us, and there will be a definite void when you're back at seminary."

He finishes up by saying Good Shepherd's congregation would welcome him back with open arms once Adam graduates from seminary, and is sure God has amazing plans for him. Everyone in the fellowship hall bursts into applause, some of the senior high boys whooping. Adam stands up and comes forward to speak, and immediately there's absolute silence. The respect for him is palpable.

He thanks Don for his 'words of love and kindness', and then begins by saying that this internship "has been a dream come true for me", stating that it gave him "the perfect opportunity to repay a debt of gratitude. All of you," he continues, looking around slowly at the seated faces before him, and smiling, "are the reason I'm in seminary at all. I had the joy of growing up in this family of believers and watching you serve each other through the years. This was a group of people who cared about each other deeply-not just on Sundays, but every day of the week. It was the way you surrounded my mom when she and my dad divorced; it was what you did for my grandparents when my aunt was so sick, and after she died. You never forgot to remember. You always took care of each other and went out of the way to lift each other up. People throw the expression 'church home' around today, and, to me, those two words are interchangeable-this church WAS the same as my home. I thank each one of you in this room for your contribution to making this 'our home'. Wherever I'm placed following my graduation from seminary, this place, your love, and Christ in your hearts, will be a part of me, too. It's been a blessing and a privilege to be here serving you this summer…more than I can ever put into words. God bless each of you and thank you-everyone."

I couldn't have said it better. What incredible words for this congregation. He verbalized exactly how I feel about this church, and it's wonderful to hear it expressed from someone else who is no longer a member here but believes so strongly in how God uses this group of people. I'm glad Mom got to hear these words. She and my dad have been a huge part of this church through the years. Again, huge applause, and in one solid wave of movement, everyone stands. Wow. I love witnessing this. What a gift this young man must have been. Renee, his mom, has tears streaming down her face, and her parents (Adam's grandparents) are beaming.

Pastor Morehouse closes the presentation, and his words are equally potent. He has nothing but praise for

Adam, noting how there were responsibilities he gave him that he knew were far and above what he might have asked of 'any normal intern'.

"But it was a no-brainer for me," he tells us. "This was no 'normal intern'! This is the person any senior minister prays to have on their staff; this is the pastoral candidate any search committee prays to come across and call. We as a congregation are going to have the distinct privilege of saying, 'I knew him when', because God has big plans for this man."

Lastly, he presents Adam with a farewell gift from Good Shepherd's entire congregation.

"And, Adam, I want you to know I was completely in the dark on this," he states. "When I asked, several weeks ago, about doing something special for you as a going away gift, Don told me that this was already in the pipeline, being handled by the congregation at large. So, I want Don to be the one to present it to you. Don, if you'd come up here, and all the elders, I'd like to offer a prayer, and then, Adam, we've got a little something for you."

They all come forward, surrounding Adam and each placing a hand on him as Pastor Morehouse begins his prayer. What a beautiful visual. His prayer is genuine and meaningful, and I wonder what lens of perspective Mom is viewing him in as she hears him pray.

When he finishes, each of the elders hugs Adam, Pastor Morehouse waiting until last, with a warm embrace and huge smiles between them. Adam has a slight reserve to him, but also an unmistakable warmth-much like his mother and grandparents.

Now Don Wickmann steps forward, and says, simply, "Adam, we are so grateful for you, and we wanted you to have something you could really use; something that would always remind you of us. Hopefully this will do just that."

It's a square box, not too large, and elegantly gift-wrapped. I'm guessing it's an inscribed watch, from the size of the box. There's a total hush in the place as he unwraps it, and Don offers to hold the ribbon and wrapping. Adam lifts the lid off the box, and Don looks a little pale. Sure enough, it looks like a jeweler's case, and Adam very solemnly lifts the lid of the case. I can't quite see from where I'm sitting- all I see is a rolled-up scroll of pale green paper tied with a small white ribbon that looks like it fills up most of the case. Adam looks at Don, and I can tell he's a little perplexed.

"Maybe see what's on the paper," Don instructs Adam. I glance over at Pastor Morehouse. He, too, looks like a little kid waiting to see a Christmas gift unwrapped. It occurs to me that he might not even know what the gift is.

Adam hands Don the case to hold, and somewhat awkwardly unties the ribbon, handing it to Don as well, and then unrolls the scroll. He studies it for several seconds, and then looks at Don in utter shock, out at everyone waiting in rapt silence, then back to Don. Shaking his head slightly, he looks at the paper a second time, and I see his mouth quiver.

Don looks directly at Adam, smiles, and says, "Hopefully this will make your next semester a little easier. We're cheering you on, Adam."

Now Adam's eyes fill, and mine right along with his. I know the generosity of this congregation too well. I look to my left at Mom, seated beside me, and she's wiping her eyes, too.

He looks at us, then at his mother and grandparents, and says, as his voice cracks, "There aren't words…but thank you…so very, very much. You have no idea how much this will help me out."

He wipes his hand over his mouth. "Wow. Hopefully my shock tells you what I can't find the words for. This is some staggering generosity."

We stay for about a half hour longer following the presentation, and both Mom and I make our way over to talk to Adam. I'm amazed at how comfortable Mom is as she speaks with him. It's as if she's talking to one of my brothers or nephews.

"We are surely going to miss you," she tells him as she hugs him, which, in and of itself surprises me. "You made our Bible class so interesting, and you're a very good teacher."

"Thank you, Joan," he answers quietly. "Your group of women is very special, that's for sure. I learned a lot from listening to all of you."

We leave right as the 11:00 service is getting under way, and I can hear music pouring out of the sanctuary, heavy with percussion. It's a praise chorus we often do at Broadfield, called '*Come, Now Is The Time To Worship*', by Phillips, Craig and Dean. Regardless of this being my old church, it seems perfectly natural to be hearing this semi-contemporary song here, and a part of me wishes I could go in and sing instead of leaving. Instead, we stop at Kroger for Mom, and then take some flowers over to Dad's gravesite. I want to do this as often as possible before the weather makes it too difficult. On the way there, we talk about Adam's reception.

"What a great gift!" I comment. "I could tell how touched he was."

"He deserved every penny of that and more," Mom declares. "But at least that will put him a semester ahead and take some pressure off him."

"Wait…" I interject. "The congregation gave him a check for an entire semester's tuition?"

"That's my understanding," Mom responds. "I'm not sure that was the plan going in, but I think everyone was so generous that it turned out to be at least that much."

"That's incredible," is my comment.

And it is. The example of their generosity is fresh in my mind when we eat at Stiver's for a late lunch after we've been at the cemetery. Mom seems to be holding up well, even after being up early this morning, and more than holding up her end of the conversation, when we see a military family come in. It looks to be a father, maybe on leave, with his wife and kids. I note where they're seated and lean across the table to Mom as we're eating.

"What do you think?" I ask her. "Should we anonymously pick up the bill for the military family that just came in?"

I've never done it before, but it would certainly be easy enough to do, and they'd never know who took care of it, especially because Mom and I will probably leave the restaurant before they do. She swivels her head in the direction of where they're seated, locates them at their table, and then turns back to me, as if she had to see them first in order to make her decision.

"That's a nice idea," she answers. "But let me help you out with it."

"No, you gave to Adam," I tell her, "and I didn't get to. This is on me. All of you inspired me."

So, we confer with our waitress, who appears visibly touched that we're doing this, and about 10 minutes later she brings us their bill. I go ahead and pay it when Mom and I leave, including a tip for the other waitress as well. Pay it forward, baby.

Sunday evening they're featuring a cook-out at Beecher's Manor House, and a group of the Knoll Girls are going. I'm invited, of course, and I can't wait to meet these ladies for the first time. We meet at 5:30 in the parking lot and walk up to the Manor House together. Mom introduces me to Kay, who lives in the row of cottages to the right of her and is a dark-complexioned brunette. Marie, her next-door neighbor to her left, is bigger boned and big haired, with a warm laugh and the innate gift of being able to make good conversation. Something about her reminds me of an older version of Bette Midler. I can tell they really like Mom, and they talk non-stop all the way to the Manor House.

The cook-out is fun. All the tables are covered with red and white checkered paper tablecloths, and the food is served buffet style, which I love, because I can load up my plate. They've grilled hamburgers, hotdogs, and brats, with all kinds of fixings, along with potato salad, baked beans, and even devilled eggs. I eat way too much, but this is high up on my list of favorite dinner fare. Marie seems to know all the goings on of the various residents, but not in a gossipy way-just more of an interested manner. She's telling us about one of the men who just lost his wife, and what a hard time he's having.

"I'm glad to see him here tonight; it takes courage to come to something like this when that grief is so fresh," she remarks.

She enjoys filling Mom and Kay in on everything, which amuses me. Kay will occasionally interject a comment that usually begins with, 'Don't quote me on this, Marie, but that's not what I heard', and then relate her version. Hmmm...I'm beginning to feel like I'm at Eastbridge. I can tell Mom is following the conversation, but she contributes very little. She's never been anything close to a gossip, and I realize how much that has impacted me through the years. Probably for that reason, I loathe it as well. Mom does start talking when we somehow segue into talking about World War II-probably because Kay mentions the new Patton movie, and they start comparing notes on the war. Mom is very out front in telling them about Dad's service in Germany, as well as two of my uncles, one of whom (Uncle Henry) was in the Pacific Theater, the other fighting under the real Patton in France. Kay and Marie listen attentively as Mom talks, nodding along, asking questions, and obviously savoring this information. Kay's older brother also fought in the South Pacific, and they discuss that for a while, Marie chiming in that her brother's heart had been damaged by scarlet fever as a child, and that had precluded his enlistment.

"He was so discouraged-all his friends in college were enlisting, and he felt like he was such a lightweight," Marie recounts.

"Did he finish college?" Mom asks, which surprises me.

"Oh, yes, and went on to get his doctorate in psychiatry, which made my parents very proud," Marie answers. "It trumped my degree as a dietician all to hell."

Kay looks aggrieved, and Mom actually chuckles. "So much for that," she offers Marie. "Our career options back then were so much more limited. It occurred to very few of us that we could be psychiatrists if we chose to."

I'm amazed to hear Mom say this, and I remain quiet, because I want to see how Marie and Kay respond. I certainly can't own the generation they grew up in.

"Joan, that's so true," Kay concurs. "I remember my father telling me to consider being a teacher, nurse, or secretary, because anything else would make a potential husband uncomfortable. Can you imagine that?"

Mom raises her eyebrows. "We had to play it safe, didn't we? I remember really enjoying the seven years of school I taught to help put Bill through med school; I was the breadwinner for those years, and it made me feel important."

Kay pats Mom's arm with her brown hand. "It's wonderful that you did that for him," she remarks. "I hope he appreciated it."

I swallow, wondering if Mom will get emotional. But her response is sweet. "Oh, of course he did," she says. "He lost both of his parents before he was even a teenager, and since he was the baby of his family, all of his brothers and his sister had families by the time he started med school. There was no way any of them were able to help him, other than letting us live with them for a little while right after we were married. I was happy to do it. We always said those years of being on such a tight budget were some of the best we had. It made you appreciate the simple things."

Marie smiles, "Sometimes you just have to do what's in front of you and know it's the right thing, don't you?"

This interchange is fascinating to me; especially their honesty. We stay a good while before we walk back to the cottages, and I tell Kay and Marie I hope I get to see them again. Each one of them hugs me goodbye. This has been a full visit, but one I wouldn't trade for the world. Hopefully I can be very faithful about getting up here at least one weekend a month through the fall. My drive back to Louisville Monday morning is fragrant with coffee, but otherwise uneventful.

September begins hot, but after the first week, the true heat, and especially the humidity, end. It's more in the upper 70's and low 80's during the day, which makes for some delightful outdoor lunches during my workweeks. The leaves of the sycamore tree I sit under are already dropping in dry, crackly profusion, and I love the sound they make as the breeze brings them down to the ground. They always land like they're skidding to a stop-with a brittle whisper.

Lesley and Zack Knight, our friends in Cincinnati that we met at Good Shepherd years ago, come down to see Crosby, Stills, and Nash with us in med-September. The concert is at The Palace-a small, ornate hall in downtown Louisville with a very intimate feel, and superior acoustics. It's the perfect venue to hear one of my all-time favorite rock groups. To this day, I credit them with developing my ear both in detecting and singing harmony, because no one can intertwine melodic lines the way they do, nor with their nuance and intonation. I used to sing along with them for hours through my high school years as I sewed in our basement-their song 'Wooden Ships' has always been my favorite. Lesley and Zack, being the music junkies they are, appreciate their music as much as Mike and I do. They come to our place before the concert, and while the guys watch golf, Lesley and I sit out on the deck, have a few drinks, and catch up. I don't get to see nearly enough of her, and it's wonderful to have this time.

It's a good concert, although it's evident to me that their voices are aging and lack the suppleness they used to have. Still, they bring the house down with all their oldies; 'Suite Judy Blue Eyes', 'Southern Cross', 'Love The One You're With', and "Teach Your Children'. Les and I are up dancing and yelling, having a blast. It's so much fun to share a night like this with people you know so well, and even though Mike and Zack are more sedate, they have an equally good time.

Zack and Les spend the night with us and leave after a big breakfast on Sunday. I hate to see them go.

I've talked to Craig in depth about my conversation with Mom regarding her car, and we're both focusing on the end of September; we'll finish her lease out for that month, and that'll be all she wrote. In the meantime, however, two events take place to alter our plan. First, Craig runs out of gas in Mom's car as he's taking it to fill up one of the Saturdays that he's in Cincinnati helping her with bills. He routinely asks her if she needs gas-this time she told him 'no', but he thought better of it and checked anyway. When he looked, he noticed the needle was on 'E', and as he was driving to the gas station, it sputtered and died, leaving him to walk the rest of the way to secure a gas can, put it in the tank, and then drive her car to the station to fill it up. Luckily, he only had about a mile to walk each way, but it raised some definite red flags for both of us.

The greater irony of the whole incident was that Mom was supremely irritated with Craig when he finally made it back to her cottage, telling him she'd 'been worried sick about him'. The thought of Mom being the one in the car when it died is not a pretty one; in fact, it's a borderline dangerous situation.

"If she's too forgetful to even check her gas gauge occasionally, then she has no business being behind the wheel," is Craig's blunt assessment.

Sadly, I agree.

The second event solves the problem for us, even as it is another pointed reminder of Mom's increasing forgetfulness. (As if we needed one.) Shortly after the concert with Zack and Lesley, Craig calls me to tell me 'the car is officially gone'.

"What happened?" I ask, somewhat breathlessly. I fear the worst now. Plus, Craig sounds very…over it.

"Well, for starters, Mom called me at work today," Craig begins, "to tell me her car wouldn't start. Okay, so I'm thinking maybe her battery is dead; maybe the starter is shot…but I can't get down there right then to check it out, so I call Mark to see if maybe he can send one of his guys over to take a look at it. You'll love this, Betsy…the battery is deader than a doornail, but her driver's side door was open. Not just unlocked-open. Which means it's been open ever since she drove her car last. So, at this point, I'm really inclined to just have Mark tow the car back to his lot and be done with all of this. There's no point in replacing the battery just to let her drive two more weeks. The way things are going, she could leave her door open again, and run out of gas again…I just don't trust her to be aware of this stuff anymore."

And yet again, I agree with him. "What have you said to Mom?" I ask.

"Well, nothing, yet, because I wanted to talk to you about it first," is his answer. "Mark's guys did come and tow the car, so he's got it, but what I was thinking was to tell Mom that the car ended up having some major electrical problems when they checked it over, and that it would be very expensive to fix, especially for just two more weeks of being able to drive it. Rather than doing that, we'll end the lease early, since we're so close anyway. That way, too, we don't even need to address her leaving the car door open or draw any attention to why the battery died."

I nod, even though Craig can't see me do it. "That sounds about right to me," I state. "I think we'd be foolish to do anything else."

So, we're finished with the car. Yet another chapter closed; another boundary shrinking. Craig relays this information to Mom, and she isn't happy about it, but truly, it's a worry off both of our shoulders. We've only been postponing the inevitable. I talk to her a few nights later; mentioning that Craig had told me her car had some major electrical problems.

"That's what he told me," she retorts, with heavy emphasis on the word 'told'. "I think it was just a convenient way to take the car early."

"But you couldn't start it, right?" I ask her bluntly. Although I know I probably shouldn't bring it up, especially because Craig had planned on taking the high road here, "And your driver's door wasn't shut all the way, which probably ran the battery down. That's a lot of investment just to drive two more weeks, Mom."

I stop at referencing the empty gas tank episode, but I'm tired of her always acting like Craig is the villain. He's done way too much for her to deserve this attitude, even though I know she feels like the rug is being pulled out from underneath her.

"I guess," Mom replies resignedly. "But I'm not happy about it."

"No, and you don't have to be," I state. "It makes me almost as sad as it does you. But we'll make it work as best we can, and I'll be up in two more weekends to be your wheels for Saturday and Sunday. We can drive wherever you want to go," I offer lamely. This almost feels like adding insult to injury. There's nothing else I can say.

"I'll look forward to that," is Mom's generous reply.

Cooking and baking always seems to figure in to the complexion of fall, Mary Claire and I joking that it's a throwback to the 'Hunter/Gatherer' of the past in our DNA, and that sense of pending winter when food needed to be stored away. It has a lot to do with Mom, too, I've come to realize. August and early September were when our apples ripened. We had four or five trees in our backyard growing up, and Mom made good use of their abundance. She'd invest hours peeling and quartering them, baking either pies or making delicious applesauce. Many of her pies were frozen in our downstairs freezer, to be brought out at random times over the course of the next nine months. She'd found a wonderful recipe for 'Apple Crumb Pie' in the Cincinnati Interlocutor one summer, and to this day, it's the only pie recipe I use. It seems right I carry on this tradition of fall, and on one of my Wednesdays off, I dive in on my pie making. Two are made, one for Mike and me, the other to take up to Mom. Her pie making days are over, but I know how much she loved doing it, and I want to see her devour a piece.

Lasagna seems like another fall staple to me, and it's so fun to make and freeze, knowing you can pull it out any time to use. It's also a great treat on a work night. So, another evening I make two batches of lasagna, one for us, and, again, one for Mom. Donny has yet to come over to see Mom's place, and I thought if Mom could just heat up lasagna and not go to any trouble, she could invite Donny and his girls over for dinner; an invitation that would be harder for them to decline since food was involved... Anything to get them over. Eight months...they live in the same city, fifteen minutes at the most from Mom, and they can't make the effort to stop by. It defies belief. Meanwhile, Craig drives an hour each way nearly every Saturday to pay her bills and take her out to lunch. Go figure.

I know she still sees Rob and Colette occasionally, and Colette has brought all three of the boys over without Rob at least a couple of times to take Mom out to dinner, which I'm thankful for. I know she misses seeing them a lot after living with them for the past eight years and being with them daily.

Work is work, but I'm doing a decent job balancing life, detaching once I leave the office at night. I enjoy most of the people I work with, especially the medical assistants. Part of it, for me, is the age difference. Most of them fall somewhere between Callie and Kerry's ages, and they're a good, if very diverse group, of girls. All of them are very open with me, (sometimes TOO open!) but the more I learn about each of them, the deeper a place they have in my heart. Some of them have very difficult lives, and a few of them really have trouble making ends meet. In my humble opinion, they don't make nearly enough for the responsibility they have. I know their health coverage through our practice is expensive, too, because even though we're a large practice, our total number of employees is small, versus being a huge medical corporation. Liz and Lynsey have both shared openly with me about how much comes out of their paychecks for healthcare, and it's almost one entire paycheck each month (we're paid bi-weekly) for them. That's a big chunk out, with not a lot left over.

The Saturday I'm going up to see Mom is also a Saturday I work, so I pack the Jeep before work, and I'll leave for Cincinnati from Eastbridge. Most of our Saturdays in the fall are crazy-it's usually when our number of sick visits start climbing, and once we get our flu vaccines in, families bring their kids in droves on Saturdays. Add in the allergy shots we give on Saturdays as well, and it can be stupid busy. This Saturday is no exception. We're slammed. Marcy and I are scheduled together, which makes me happy. Increasingly, I like working Saturdays with her, and it's given me an opportunity to get to know her better, because it's just the two of us. I've discovered that she has a killer sense of humor, though she hides it well, and we've been able to have some good laughs. She's also much more talkative when it's just the two of us. Laid back in her approach to just about everything, it makes for a nice morning.

We've started bringing in food on Saturdays, as our treat...Marcy knows I love donuts, so she brings in a mini box of them from Gas N' Go, and they are delicious. She always does a trio of them; a glazed, a cinnamon twist, and a chocolate crème filled, which I always eat last, because it's my favorite. (Deferred gratification.) McDonald's is Marcy's true love; so I get her a bacon and egg biscuit with hash browns, and usually throw in a cinnamon bun for good measure. We call it our brain food, and even though I never eat breakfast during the week, I do enjoy it on the Saturdays I work. All these small acts of kindness back and forth between various people I work with are building relationships, albeit in some very quiet, understated ways, and I love being a part of that. As stressful as this environment can be, we need to know we're surrounded by people who genuinely care about us, and it's worth it to me to take the time to do this.

This Saturday happens to be a donut morning (we

alternate between), which puts me in a happy place as Marcy bustles in with our Gas N' Go boxes. We get our morning underway, and she's just come back upstairs from her break when one of our medical assistants quietly walks up to me and asks, without any fanfare, if she can borrow five dollars for gas. She needs just enough to get her to her mom's house, and then her mom is loaning her some money. Tori is a train wreck, but I love her. She's a little termite of a girl; maybe 100 pounds soaking wet, and in her early 20's. She loves her eye makeup, and works two jobs; at Eastbridge, and then a few nights and weekends at a Gas N' Go. Deathly ill for the past two months, I wouldn't be surprised at all if she has chronic bronchitis. Despite being on heavy antibiotics, she's had a wracking cough she can't lose, and wears a surgical mask for that reason.

About a month ago when she was trying to scrounge up some money to buy lunch at the end of a pay period, I had told her that if she was ever in a bind, to ask me to float her some cash. Yeah, I know a lot of people would call me a sucker for making that offer. But here's the thing, I'm in no position to confirm any judgment. My thought process is this: if someone I work with is truly in need, I'd much rather have them ask me for help than think I'd judge them and not ask out of fear or embarrassment. Then the argument of being taken advantage of comes up. That's fair. If someone does start taking advantage of me, then I make the call of telling them the well is dry. Just because you're willing to give doesn't mean you're a fool. Discretion enters in and I trust myself well enough to balance the two. Who hasn't been in that cash-strapped position of a near empty gas tank? Mom, for starters. And, if it's not FOR gas, I'm still okay to give her the money. This is the first time Tori's ever asked me, and I'm going to trust her on this.

I tell her I don't have cash on me, but can write her a check and I double the amount she's asked for. Still, I'm worried she'll be able to make it to a bank with Saturday hours to cash it. None the less, she thanks me profusely, and I can tell it made her very nervous to ask. She turns to walk out of our work area, and even more quietly than Tori asking me for the five dollars, Marcy leans towards her as Tori passes her, grabs her hand, and stuffs a wad of cash into it.

"That's in case you can't find a bank to cash Bet's check," she tells her in a low voice.

Tori's eyes fill up. "Thanks, Marcy," she says simply. She turns to look back at me. "I love you guys," she says, and heads back to the lab.

Marcy, ever understated, turns to me, nods as she winks at me, and that's all we ever say about it. Still, it warms my heart that Marcy, too, cares deeply about these girls. I'm glad for the opportunity to have experienced this.

I'm on the interstate by 12:45, with a fresh warm-up of coffee in my travel mug and munching on my last donut. Placed squarely in the small of my back is my new 'support cushion' that I've fashioned for myself after reading a lot of online articles about osteoporosis. One of the things I've come to realize is that my lower back aches probably have a lot to do with my back muscles working overtime to compensate for a weakened, less than solid, spine. It referenced sitting being much harder on these muscles than standing, as well as driving being a source of muscle strain. The tip offered was to take a large beach towel and to roll it up, placing it in the small of the back, and then leaning back into it, thus filling the space, and giving the muscles of the lower back additional support. Since my back had been bothering me intermittently through the summer, I decided to give it a try, and it really does help.

I'm planning to meet Mary Claire, Dan, and their granddaughter, Hallie (Clayton's little girl) for a late lunch at Barney's around 2:00. I make fantastic time up 71 and am ahead of schedule when I hit I-75. I debate stopping to use the bathroom ("relieve myself", as Dad would say) at the rest area off the Richwood exit, but as I glance over at it on my right, there are semis literally lined up along the entrance to it, on both sides of the road. I decide not to deal with all that congestion, and don't get off. As I get to the Florence-Union exit, traffic is slowing down, although it's still moving. I-75 can get really congested through this stretch on weekends, especially as it leads up to the I-275 interchange, so I settle in behind a semi and cruise along, not able to detect what's causing the slowdown. Fifteen minutes goes by and I've only come five or six more miles. This isn't looking good. And all this wonderful coffee is catching up with my small bladder.

By the time I make it to the 275 Interchange, traffic is virtually stopped. Now we move roughly 10 feet every few minutes; stop/start, stop/start.

Houston, we have a problem...A big problem. Along with that, I can clearly see the cause of the delay now. It's down to two lanes way, way up in front of me, and it looks like they're re-surfacing. Oh, joy. This could continue all the way down through the cut in the hill to the Cincinnati Bridge. I decide I'd better call Mary Claire to give her an update. It's already 1:35, and there's no way I'll make it by 2:00.

"I'll be at least an hour late," I tell her, explaining what's going on. "If you guys don't want to wait that long to eat, or even don't want to go at all, I totally understand. I didn't bargain on running into this."

"No, no...don't worry about it," Mary Claire reassures me. "We'll just leave for Barney's a little later, that's all. We'll grab a table and take some toys to keep Hallie occupied...I wish I'd thought to have warned you about the construction; we've been hearing about these gridlocks all week on the news. Just take your time and be safe. Call me when you're close."

I decide not to call Mom yet, even though I know this will back up my ETA to her place as well. I'll get a better feel for time first, and try to at least be across the bridge, maybe even to Barney's, before I touch base with her. In the meantime, my body seems to have made its decision...one I must concur with as I sit at a dead standstill. I suppose that what happens in my Jeep stays in my Jeep, but I see no other alternative.

Finally, I am across the Brent Spence and the Ohio state line. Now the lanes open, traffic fans out, and I accelerate. I roar up Preston Road once I exit 75 on Mitchell Ave.

"Hey!" I greet the restaurant's host after parking the Jeep and hurrying into Barney's, a change of clothes tucked under one arm. "I'm actually meeting some friends here, a couple about my age with…" but before I even finish he's leading me back to their table.

"There you are!" Mary Claire greets me, jumping up to hug me. Hallie looks at me with great interest, and then bangs both hands palms down on her highchair tray.

I return Mary Claire's hug, and then excuse myself to escape to the restroom.

"So…how was the drive?" Mary Claire prompts.

"Rest area full of people and trucks…no stop. Bumper to bumper traffic. Bladder full of coffee. You connect the dots." Dan and Mary Claire both roar, and Hallie, observing this, shrieks with glee to mirror their laughter.

Toward the end of our time there Hallie gets fidgety, so Dan lifts her out of the highchair, and since there's no one sitting close to us, lets her play around our table.

It's good to see all of them, and we talk a good bit about some of their upcoming plans for Eolia. They're also very curious about how the car situation went down with Mom, so I fill them in on the events that led up to it being towed back to Mark's leasing lot.

"Oh, that's going to kill her to not have her car," Mary Claire laments. "But maybe, in a weird way, it was a relief to her to have you and Craig just pretty much say, 'It's time'. And you did give her the freedom to set her own date on when she'd end the lease and let her prepare for it mentally."

"Yeah," Dan chimes in, "I'm not sure there's any easy way to make somebody give up their car. That's just tough all the way around."

We linger for a good hour, and, as always, I wish we had double the time we do. After hugs in the parking lot, I drive to Beecher. Mom is watching TV when I arrive but seems chipper and alert. I can tell she's lost weight when I hug her; her shoulder blades are right there under my hands.

We decide to go to Good Shepherd's 5:30 service, and on a whim, I ask Mom if she'd like me to call Donny to see if he and his girls want to meet us there and then go out to dinner afterwards; anything to get them to spend time with Mom.

"You can try," Mom says, "but don't get your hopes up. He probably won't even answer his phone."

But he does answer, and, as always, is pleasant. "Hey, Bet, how are you?" he asks me, as casually as if we talk every day. I explain I'm staying at Mom's for the weekend, framing up church and dinner afterwards.

"Church I'll have to pass on," he answers immediately. "The girls are knee deep in homework; you know how that goes in high school. My rule is that we do it all on Saturday, so Sunday can be more relaxed and that way nothing gets put off. But we could definitely meet you for dinner. Where are you thinking about?"

We decide on Chili Time (the one that wasn't there); it's easy for both of us to get to. I bite my tongue to keep from saying that it wouldn't kill Donny to knock off the studying an hour early and to meet us at church. But at least Mom will get to see them, all except Mackenzie, Donny's oldest, who is at her mother's for the weekend. I'm glad that at least the twins, Stephanie and Suzanne, would rather be with Donny. They rarely spend a weekend with their mom.

I put the apple pie and lasagna in the freezer before we leave for church, with Mom exclaiming, "You don't need to do all this for me!"

"I was doing it anyway, for Mike and me, Mom," I tell her, smiling. "I can't make one of these without thinking of you," indicating the pie. "Remember making these by the dozens?"

"I certainly do," Mom replies, "sitting at the kitchen

counter, literally peeling hundreds of apples. But there was nothing better than seeing that freezer stocked full of apple pies and applesauce. I loved it. That was one of the few desserts all of you liked, so there was never any arguing."

I explain my lasagna premise as I load it into the freezer. "This is a meal you could invite Donny and his girls over for," I tell her, lifting the foil off the aluminum pan so she can see what's on the inside. "Or Rob and Colette and the boys," I add hastily. "The baking instructions are right here," (I've taped them to the foil) and you can freeze this and then thaw it out later."

"That's very thoughtful, Bet," Mom says. "I could even invite the girls over one night."

By 'the girls' I know she means 'The Knoll Girls', and that hadn't even occurred to me.

"Absolutely," I answer. "Whatever you want it for. Put it to good use."

After church, we drive to Chili Time and Donny is already there waiting for us, with Stephanie and Suzanne. They're fraternal twins; Suz taller, bigger, blue eyed and fair haired; Steph fair but freckled, with dark, almost black hair, and brown eyes. He stands up to hug each of us and helps Mom to get seated. Both the twins have always been on the quiet side, observing much more than they interact. Mackenzie, their older sister, is more of a talker, and very bossy. They're sweet girls, though, and I've always really liked them both. Like Donny, there's not a mean bone in their bodies. I ask them about school, and they start talking more freely. They speak quietly, but they're very appropriate, and they express themselves well. Each has a part-time job, which I applaud Donny for, even though I know it can't make his life any easier.

I ask him about his lawn care business, and he tells me it's thriving. He's done a great job getting and keeping contracts for a number of school districts in Cincinnati, along with numerous churches and businesses. Inevitably, when he talks about his jobs, it leads into various tidbits about people we went to high school with that are 'at large' in Cincinnati now. It's amazing the people he runs into based on his business contacts. As he talks, and slips into his "Betsy, you'll never guess who I ran into..." I can't help but smile.

In some ways, Donny has changed the least of my three brothers from childhood to adulthood. I'm not sure if that's good or bad...I just know he soldiers on, content in what he does, seems satisfied with everything he has (and doesn't have) and holds little bitterness towards anyone. For everything he's been through in his life, even though he's made some poor choices, it still seems like he 'travels lighter' than Rob or Craig, and I like seeing that in him.

Now that he's got my attention, he seems to forget about Mom, and isn't good about drawing her into the conversation. I find myself purposely turning towards her as Donny and I talk, asking her if she remembers who he's talking about, but I get the feeling she's checked out. I wish Steph and Suz would strike up a conversation with her, but they don't. At the end of Donny's 'litany of people', I look at them and say, "Sorry about all these high school stories. We're finally finished."

"Dad's always like this," Suz, who is the more outspoken of the two, states. "We're used to it."

She and Steph exchange knowing looks. Steph adds, "That'll probably be us someday," to which Suz throws her a dark look and quickly fires backs, "No it won't."

I do make it a point to tell them that Mom would love for them to come over for dinner some night, so they can see her place at Beecher. I feel like I'm practically begging, but I'm shameless.

"It's the cutest set-up," I offer. "You'll love it," and I hit some of the high points.

"Do you stay there overnight?" Suz asks me.

"I do," I nod. "It's my vacation time away from Louisville. Mom and I always party together."

How can Steph and Suz not want to spend time with Mom? It's beyond me. They ask me about Callie and Kerry, and I give them all the dirt. They're extremely interested in Callie being in Nashville and what I tell them about the city. Maybe they're trying on college there for size. We wrap up dinner, and Mom seems tired and withdrawn. Donny picks up the bill for all of us, which I hadn't expected, and I thank him.

"Thanks for meeting us," I tell him as we head to our cars.

"We need to do this again," he tells me.

"We do," I agree. "It was great to see all of you."

As Mom moves around to her side of my Jeep, I say to him in a low voice, "Please try to get over to see Mom, Donny. It doesn't have to be a long visit, even just for half an hour. She's been in her new place eight months already, and you haven't even seen it. She'd love to see more of you."

"I'll try," he says. "I'm just so busy with my business, and the girls, and their schedules…"

I look directly in his eyes and purse my lips.

"Please try to make the time," I reiterate. That's as far as I'll push.

"Donny seems like he's doing really well with his business," I comment to Mom as we drive home.

"That makes me happy," Mom replies. "He's sure worked hard enough to get there."

Sunday is a quiet day for us, lazy and relaxing. After a big breakfast, we decide to go for a walk around the grounds. It's a pretty morning, with a cool breeze, and both of us wear jackets. Fall is much more evident up here than in Louisville. Being two hours north makes a big difference, and a lot of the maples have already begun to turn peach and scarlet.

We walk across the parking lot, turning right onto the residential road that leads back to the rear of Beecher's acreage.

"Are you still going to the fitness center to exercise your three days a week?" I ask Mom as we stroll along the road. She hasn't mentioned it much recently.

"Oh, probably not three times a week anymore," she answers. "Maybe just two. Sometimes I just don't feel like getting up in the morning and making myself go over. And then, once I get my day started, I don't think about it again."

"Well, two days a week is better than nothing," I answer. "I'm glad that at least you're still going. Your walking pace is good."

I wouldn't say we're walking briskly, but for an 83-year old woman, Mom has a nice, determined pace; very even and steady. Her stride just isn't the length of mine. A couple of cars pass us, and both times the residents in them wave. We basically walk a huge oval around the back half of Beecher's property, past various condominiums and town homes with a variety of floor plans, way back behind the Manor House, and then loop back past their park and picnic area, where there are tables, grills, and a sheltered area to eat in. There's also a great play area for little guys; presumably grandkids.

"This is beautiful," I remark. "I don't think I've ever been back this far. You and I could pack a lunch and come up here to eat."

"We could," Mom responds. "I think they bring the kids that are in their daycare program up here to play sometimes."

We end up walking for over an hour, which is a lot of ground for Mom to have covered.

"Did I wear you out?" I ask her as we trudge through her parking lot, returning to her cottage. "We probably walked well over two miles."

"Well, I'm a little tired, but it felt good to get out and get some fresh air. I probably need to make myself do that more often. It's just not as much fun when you're not here."

"Of course, it isn't," I agree, and start laughing. "Would Kay or Marie ever walk with you? Or Beatrice? Kay seems like she'd be a walker."

"I should ask her," Mom reflects. "Boy, do I have some pressure in my abdomen from walking."

"What do you mean?" I ask her. "Like you have to go to the bathroom?"

Mom shakes her head. "No, not like that. More like… it's sore. Like sore muscles. Kind of crampy."

"Like period crampy?" I ask her.

"Sort of," she says. "It just feels heavy."

"Well, sit down on the couch and get your feet up," I suggest. "We probably overdid it walking, and maybe you strained some muscles. Do you want me to get your heating pad?"

"No, no," Mom defers. "It's not that bad. I'll just rest a little bit, and I'm sure it'll go away. It usually does."

"What do you mean it USUALLY does?" I ask Mom, suddenly suspicious. "Have you been having this feeling for awhile?"

She sighs. "Oh, not a lot, but now and then. It always goes away, though."

"How long have you been feeling this?" I ask her, knowing she probably won't give me a straight answer.

"Bet, really, it's not a big deal," she states. "Just every now and then it feels…crampy."

"Since before or after you stopped driving?" I ask her, thinking maybe that will help her with a frame of reference.

"Ohhhh," she hesitates, "maybe before."

"Back as far as Vacation Bible School?" I ask her. I know she was on her feet a lot that week.

Now she looks confused. "Oh, I don't think that far back. I just really don't remember."

I sit down on the couch at her feet, and gently jiggle her ankle. "Know what I think?" I ask softly.

"What?" she returns.

"I think you should probably see your physician and get this checked out," I tell her. "It's probably nothing, but it would sure give me some peace of mind. If you're feeling discomfort every so often, it could be something that needs attention."

"You worry too much," Mom tells me. "It's just my body getting old. If it really hurt, I'd see my doctor. If it continues, then I will. But it's nothing."

I can tell she's not going to budge on this, so I leave it alone. It's something I'll keep an eye on myself, but it makes me uneasy. Two other issues I've wondered about are how Mom is handling her hair appointments and getting to Good Shepherd each week, now that her car is gone. When I ask her, she tells me she's started using the beauty shop at Beecher.

"I miss Pam, but there's really no other way to slice it," she explains. "I'd have to hire a driver to take me to my appointments, and I can't see doing that. And really, it's pretty convenient just to walk over to the main building and have it done right there."

This intrigues me. In all our phone conversations, she hasn't mentioned this once. "Is it hard to get an appointment?" I ask her.

I know Mom's not the only car-less resident at Beecher-they have an entire assisted living facility right behind her cottage, plus their skilled memory care facility and rehab center in a building called Buckman. That's a lot of people with hair.

"Doesn't seem to be so far," Mom answers. "And the lady that does my hair, Ginny, is so sweet. I have a standing appointment on Thursday mornings, at 11:00, and it seems to be working out well so far. My only concern will be when I'm due for my next permanent. Pam did such a good job with those, and she always gave the solution extra time, because my hair is so thick."

"We can always go back to Pam for your perms," I state. "We can schedule them on the Saturdays I'll be up here, and I can drive you. That's no problem."

"Well, that might be a good plan," Mom remarks amiably.

"Or, even if you don't want a perm, but just want Pam to give you a cut, or a wash and set," I add. "That way, you can at least get to her once a month. I don't want you to have to give her up completely. You've been with her for years."

I feel horrible that I hadn't even thought about this collateral fallout before Mom gave up her car, and yet she's forged ahead with a Plan B that I wasn't even aware of. I'm humbled by how flexible she's already been.

"What about you getting to Good Shepherd?" I continue. I've scooted back to the opposite end of the couch from where Mom is laying, so we're feet to feet.

"It depends on the week," Mom replies, "because it's kind of a group effort. Sherry and Lew Castille come to get me the first and third Saturdays of the month, and then Carl and Dorothy Reinhold do the second and fourth Saturdays. I just told the Reinholds you'd be here, and that they didn't need to stop by last night. It seems like way too much for them to do that week after week, but Sherry told me that they have it all worked out, and that she wanted no protesting from me. So, I'm not," she finishes.

I laugh. "Yeah, I can hear her saying that to you," I grin. "You're surrounded by good people, Mom."

"Yes, I sure am," she concurs. "One of them is here on my couch. And for Wednesday Bible study, Beatrice Odell drives me, since she goes to the same study."

"Oh, that's great," I answer, because I know Beatrice is just a building over from Mom in a two bedroom apartment.

Mom has a funny look on her face and I'm thinking she's going to tell me something that transpired in their study, when she admits, "I felt so stupid the other day. I never like to keep Beatrice waiting on Bible study days, so I usually walk over to her apartment early and just wait outside her apartment for her, and there are chairs in the hallway where I sit. Well, anyway, last week I went over, sat and sat waiting for her, but she never came out of her apartment. I knocked on her door just to check and make sure she was alright, but still no answer. So, I came back home and about halfway through the day, I realized that I had the wrong day; it was Tuesday, not Wednesday! Oh, I felt so dumb!"

"Whoops," I say, because I can't think of anything else TO say. I have this strong visual of Mom, all dressed and with her makeup on, making sure she's early so she doesn't impose on Beatrice, walking over to her apartment, then patiently sitting outside it keeping vigil. Knowing Mom, she probably waited the better part of an hour, only to be waiting on the wrong day completely. The fact of the matter is, any one of us can screw up a date or a time. We have parents do it at Eastbridge constantly. But because Mom has done it so often lately, it hurts me for her.

"We have parents do that at work all the time; they'll mix up a day or a time for an appointment," I say, echoing my thoughts. "Just curious-did you go back on Wednesday?"

"I did," Mom affirms. "What I didn't tell Beatrice was that I'd been there Tuesday, too."

"No harm done, I guess," I reply.

Yes, we took the car at the right time. We make a Kroger forage in the afternoon, then come home and sit out on Mom's back porch and play Gin Rummy. I brought a bottle of wine up with me, and I open it and pour us each a glass while we play. It's a perfect afternoon to be out here-clear and sunny, with that special fall clarity to the light as the sun is closer to the horizon. I arrange our two chairs close to each other, putting her glass table between them for our cards and wine glasses. We settle in our chairs, and I deal the first hand.

"This is the life," I remark, kicking my flip-flops off, and taking a sip of my wine. It's peaceful out here, and you can hear the lazy thrumming of crickets.

"It is nice," Mom agrees, arranging her hand and looking around. "We've sure had a beautiful weekend. I wish your Dad could see this place. He'd be out here on this porch all the time if he were here."

"He *would* be out here all the time, wouldn't he?" I grin. "As soon as the paper came every day, he'd disappear out here, and you wouldn't see him until he'd finished it."

We play for quite a while, the shadows lengthening and a cooler breeze picking up. I beat Mom three consecutive hands, and I don't like it. That never used to happen.

"I just can't think quickly anymore," she remarks. "And I'm really indecisive about what cards to hang on to."

"That's me every hand," I state. "Plus, I always have 'discard remorse.'"

We play one more hand, and while I'm deciding what to discard, Mom scrutinizes the garden beds. "I really need to get those weeded and looking presentable," she says, as if it's just occurred to her. "I don't know why I haven't tackled them sooner."

Initially I'm stunned; the thought of Mom working in these beds is ridiculous, for starters. She can barely bend over anymore, let alone kneel or sit on the ground. Surely, she realizes this about her own physical limitations? She frames it up more as a task she just chose to neglect this summer. Or, is she acting like she ran out of time, but knows full well she can't do yard work? My heart hurts again for her. The gardens she had on Willowbend growing up were beautiful, and she treasured her time working in them.

"We'll have to start on those early next spring," I suggest. "That'll be a fun project for us. What do you picture putting in them?"

"Well," she says, somewhat hesitantly, "I'd have to give it some thought. Maybe some day lilies, like on Willowbend, and some tall hollyhocks along the back…Zinnias always grow like wildfire and are hardy. We probably want to plant perennials that will come back, I'd think."

"We can map it out," I say. "And next year you'll be one of the stops on Cincinnati's 'Home and Garden Tour.'"

"Fat chance of that," Mom laughs.

After she finally beats me our fourth hand (by hording the Ace's), I tell her I'm surprising her and taking her out to dinner.

"No, we don't need to eat out again," she protests. "You save your money."

"Yeah, we do," I retort. "Humor me. Eating out is the best way I can think off to kick off my work week."

Mom looks at me and rolls her eyes. "Well, if it's going to help your work week, who am I to hold you back?" she responds. "Just please tell me I don't need to change clothes. I'm feeling too lazy to go and do that."

"No change of attire required," I confirm. "Just a healthy appetite."

I take us to C'est Fini, and as we pull into their parking lot, Mom exclaims, "Oh, Bet, no! You're spoiling me! We've been here so often lately!"

"I'm hooked," I tell her solemnly. "Plus, everywhere else was full tonight; I called around for reservations to at least a dozen other places!"

"You did not," she challenges me, but I can tell she's pleased.

We have a wonderful dinner. Mostly, this is just sacred time with her. The car situation is behind us, and she seems to be adjusting to it very easily, which again reinforces to me that perhaps, deep down, she knew it was time. We were able to see Donny and his girls last night, and though I don't hold out much hope that he'll make any effort to get over to see Mom, at least we got to share a meal with them. And, Mom seems to be happy and holding the line in most ways.

She's just slowing down noticeably. She's in a good place, and has settled into Beecher exceedingly well-better than I would have even anticipated. So, in my heart, tonight's a celebration of sorts-of blessings that have been worth waiting for.

We talk about everything under the sun-Eastbridge, Mike's family (Mom knows all of them well from get-togethers years ago), Kerry and Callie, Good Shepherd, Barack Obama, you name it. It always amazes me how conversant Mom can be when it's just the two of us. At one point, she's smiling into the distance as I finish up an Eastbridge story, and she looks the happiest I've seen her in forever. She has the most beautiful smile. It looks to me like she's going to pick up the thread of our conversation, but she's still dreamily gazing into the distance. I put my hand lightly over her hand and pat her.

"What is it?" I ask her. "Why are you smiling?"

She turns to me, and says with utter peace in her voice, "Oh, no reason. This is just so pleasant."

Make my weekend. And it IS so pleasant. This is a good chapter. And on Monday morning, my driver's seat is mostly dry when I pull out of Mom's parking lot at 5:40 AM. I stuff my osteo towel under me for additional protection and limit my coffee intake until I hit I-71. As the faintest hint of light creeps into the dawn sky, I hear Zeppelin's 'Ramblin' On'…one of my all-time favorites. 'The autumn moon lights my way' seems eerily appropriate as I roll past Sparta and Warsaw. This week is off to a good start.

Chapter Eight

THE GREAT PUMPKIN
(October 2010)

Sadly, the creative portions of my brain work most effectively during the middle of the night. Many good things have been born during these hours of occasional insomnia between 3 AM to 5 AM. Thus, it is no real surprise that the idea for decorating my Halloween pumpkin occurs over a period of several nights in this exact time frame. I heavily credit the Robitussin DM that I am currently taking nightly in copious amounts for these random, yet detailed visuals. I am in the final chapter of my once yearly sinus infection, and the cough that always comes with it.

This idea has been tugging at the corners of my mind for several weeks, and I have tried not to think about it during waking hours, because it makes me anxious. Every year, Highbridge has a pumpkin decorating contest, with first, second, and third place prizes awarded. The pumpkins are then displayed along the counters of our front desk check-out area, and it gives the office a festive, lighthearted feel.

In addition, it is supposed to engender spirit and a sense of camaraderie among the employees that I have yet to see develop.

Instead, it emphasizes the 'haves' and the 'have-nots' in terms of craftiness and artistry, neither of which define me. Still, as much as I'd like NOT to participate in this show of harvest, my pride refuses to NOT let me. My anxieties about this run along several lines: thinking of organizing and buying supplies overwhelms me; then, what if I screw up the implementation and ruin the pumpkin? The obvious through line here is fear of failure…I'm fully aware of this. There is much to be said about knowing yourself well at 53.

So, when these nebulous ideas begin presenting themselves to me during the wee hours, my initial skepticism becomes medicinally induced enthusiasm. The first morning I wake up following my vision, I pretty much dismiss it, thinking that I'll forget a lot of the details, but surprisingly, they stay with me. It's a very simple design, but also somewhat unique, especially based on the materials I will use. A large, round pumpkin will be my first order of business.

Stars and crescent moons of various sizes will be carved into the pumpkin's surface in a freeform pattern. All told, there may be seven to eight cutouts of these shapes. This is where I get excited. Each cutout will then be covered from the inside of the pumpkin with gold or silver fabric; something gauzy and see-through, like mesh or lame. The outside will be decorated with gold and silver sweatshirt paint, outlining the cutout shapes with different patterns of application, like dots, zigzags, and 'X's.

The final touch will be some decorative metallic stickers to sprinkle amongst the cutouts, giving it a little more "pop". Once I've really thought this through, I can see it's totally doable, and my creative juices start flowing in earnest. Implementation is never my issue; it's the devising of the plan, so now I'm "turbines to speed". (I'm a child of the 60's who watched 'Batman' until Mom and Dad decided it was too violent and redirected our TV viewing.)

I'm also amused because scoring one of the prizes is the farthest thing from my mind. I'm more excited about seeing my project come to fruition. Thank you, sinus infection. All our pumpkins are "due" at Highbridge no later than Monday, October 26th, so this becomes my target date. Since I'll be at mom's the weekend prior to the 26th, my completion date for everything will be Friday night of the 23rd. Mr. Pumpkin will then journey with me to the Queen City for my visit. I find a great packing box at work to put him in, so he won't get jostled around, and set it aside for my trip. Mom will enjoy seeing this work of art. She and my Dad always had such fun with the holidays, Halloween included. Dad was extremely creative, and a pro at pumpkin carving. He usually did one for each of the four of us, and we lined them up on the broad slate windowsill in our living room. Our responsibility was providing him with a freehand drawing of the face we wanted carved on our pumpkin, and he would do his best to replicate it. He had also designed a base of wood that housed a light bulb, and that was placed inside each work of art for illumination. As soon as it was dusk each night, mom would "plug in the pumpkins" and they were a sight to behold.

Craig, Rob, Donny and I would walk down our driveway to the street, admiring how ghoulish and awesome they looked lit up and glowing from our living room window. I find myself wondering now if part of my enthusiasm in tackling this project isn't a subconscious nod to my parents for all the thought they put into making our holidays special. Sort of a payback-a *Look, I'm carrying on the tradition* kind of thing. I, too, will have a cool pumpkin.

So, I plot and plan over the next week. Somewhat ironically, I'm reminded of Dad again, because I'm becoming more and more like him as I age. The organizing, the getting my supplies together, the breaking down of the project into its various stages, are all so much his style of working. I take a couple of Macy's boxes and trace my various size moons and stars onto them, doing a small, medium, and large version for each shape. These will be taped to my pumpkin until I'm satisfied with the placement of all of them, then I'll trace them onto the pumpkin's surface. Mike comes into play here as the pumpkin surgeon. He seems oddly enthusiastic about the project; probably because he is far more competitive than I am and thinks I have a shot at first place.

Monday I am the early person on the team, so I leave the office right at 4:30, intent on purchasing my pumpkin. The weather has been glorious and my rides into and home from work have been a gift. The light is much lower on the horizon now and I love the drive in the mornings, especially on my early days, with mist blanketing the fields and the sun just beginning to traverse the tree line. We are in full blown autumn, and there's that sense of 'quickening' as the month leans into November. Ever since I was a little girl, the months of October, November, and December have always been my favorites. They just seemed more exciting than the rest of the year. Maybe it was a combination of the change in the seasons…green leaves to golds, oranges, and reds…the crispness in the air…then, too, maybe it had to do with the fact that my family spent a lot of time together during those months. I always loved being at home with my brothers, mom and dad-there was a security and a coziness to it that was comforting to me, especially as a teenager, when the outside world seemed to be much more of a challenge to navigate.

Today, as I head out Route 34 on my way home, the woods on either side are a peach-infused haze. Each day slightly different hues are prominent depending on the foliage that is peaking or ebbing in color. God is amazing in His artistry. I pull into St. Andrew's Episcopal Church a mile from home. Their youth group sells pumpkins and gourds as a fund raiser for their mission trip each year, and I love supporting them. Huge piles of orange glow and beckon, and I find what I have in mind. I pick out two more for our front steps at home, and another hefty one for the porch of Mom's cottage. Money well-spent, I feel.

I don't bother to change out of my scrubs when I get home. Instead I open the kitchen storm door to let the evening breeze blow through the screen and fire up a couple of candles. This time of evening solitude is so precious, especially after being in our noisy office all day. The only sounds are the hushed rustling of the leaves outside and the occasional jangle of my wind chime. Waves of leaves are floating down on the invisible pulses of the wind and I feel my world center itself. I can't imagine not being calmed by nature.

I wash the pumpkin, towel it dry, grab my cutout shapes and start fiddling, taping loosely until I've got the configuration of shapes spaced exactly the way I want it. Outside the sun has dropped below the horizon, bathing the kitchen in evening afterglow, but I'm oblivious. Mike pulls in, and I meet him at the door, grinning. "Check it out... first place in the making," I state.

"Lights might help first place," Mike comments, flipping on our overhead kitchen lights, and giving me a kiss. He walks over to the counter, carefully inspecting my work thus far. I really haven't explained much of the detail to him, other than to ask him to cut out the shapes for me.

"Are these what I'm cutting out?" he asks, fingering one on the un-taped edge.

"Yeah," I nod. "Now that I've figured out the placement, I'm tracing these in black marker, and then you can just chop on the lines."

"Mmmm," Mike affirms. "Trace 'em now, and I'll cut after we eat."

Nothing like a team approach.

Tuesday night I stop at Dee's Crafts with my list assembled. Mike has the pumpkin carved, and from here on it is entirely my baby. Dee's has a great variety of silver and gold fabrics, so I buy four different types, each with a different texture. Next comes my sweatshirt paint, and I even buy two thick Sharpie's, a gold and silver, in case I decide to outline with these as well. Two packets of star and planet stickers complete my purchase, and I'm pumped to get started. My plan is to tackle the fabric coverings tonight and then do all the external outlining Thursday and Friday nights once I get home from work.

* * * * *

Saturday morning…I'm loading up the car for Cincinnati…A grey, misty day. I always put off packing until the last minute, because I've come to loathe it over the years. Mr. Pumpkin is comfortably ensconced in his box, looking very one of a kind and stunning, if I do say so myself. My mental picture has translated well, and I'm happy with how it turned out, especially the texture that the 'recessed' fabric on the inside of the pumpkin provides. My original idea of cutting squares of the fabric and then pinning it tightly to the flesh inside the pumpkin worked like a charm, and it almost gives it an ethereal effect with the netting and the gauze.

I've got some lasagna cut up into squares in refrigerator dishes and frozen for mom, so she can take them out of the freezer one at a time and just heat and eat; I'm starting to worry more about her eating habits as she's getting frailer. I know from my own experience how unappealing it is to cook for just one person if Mike's not home and I also know Mom has always snacked more than she's eaten 'three squares a day'. Another nagging thought is whether she'll even remember that she HAS these in her freezer to use. Hopefully these will be less intimidating than the big batch I made her my last visit in case she wanted to invite Donny or Rob over.

Scrubs for Monday are packed, ugly purple travel bag is in the back seat, I kiss Mike goodbye, and I'm off. Over the course of the years, I have really come to enjoy these two plus hours of solitude, where I'm accountable to no one.

Craig calls it 'windshield time', and that's aptly put. I pray out loud for the first half hour as the farms roll by on 34, and I feel myself unwind inwardly. No matter the stresses of the work week, no matter the level of fatigue, I am always happy to make this trip and spend time with mom. It's a gift I'm giving myself. My plan is to stop at Mary Claire's for lunch, just a quick visit, but way too good to pass up. Two hours later I pull off I-75 onto Mitchell Avenue and begin the trek to Southwoods and my second home, Dan and Mary Claire's.

Built in the 1960's when Southwoods was busting at the seams with young families, she and Dan have done a lot to make it their own, with lots of warm, inviting touches. I'm greeted by their two dogs upon arrival, friendly and bumbling, and I give Mary Claire a big hug in greeting. She's working on lunch for us…taco salads, and sucking down a diet Mountain Dew, her version of coffee. I help myself to a Dew as well, and we head out to their back porch. It's a screened in summer room that Dan has erected in various stages over the years, filled to overflowing with potted plants and flowers. Carrying our salads out to a small table covered in oilcloth, we dive into conversation immediately. One of the gifts of Mary Claire is being able to pick up wherever we left off regardless of the length of time between visits. There's never any "easing in" that needs to happen. Years of familiarity allow us to jump in with both feet. We discuss our weeks, where our tolerance levels are with our respective jobs, and Mary Claire fills me in on their mission work in Eolia. She asks about my recent trip to Nashville to visit Callie, and I describe my time there, as well as how Cal's relationship with Andy is progressing. We bounce from topic to topic, in our usual marathon fashion. Time flies, and around 2:30 I reluctantly announce that I'd better head for Beecher, knowing Mom's waiting for me.

We pile our dishes up, and as we're carrying them to the sink, I exclaim, "Oh, wait! There's something you've got to see! I'm really proud of this."

I lead Mary Claire out to my Jeep, pop the hatch, and

there, resplendent in his box, sits Mr. Pumpkin, gleaming quietly. "Martha Stewart I'm not, but look at this work of art," I direct.

"Oh, my gosh, Bet," Mary Claire says. "Can you lift it out of the box for me?"

I gingerly heft it out and, holding it, revolve slowly in a circle so she can view it from all angles.

"Bet, that is beautiful," Mary Claire remarks, peering closely at the fabric coverings. "How are these anchored?"

"Pins…Home Ec 101," I respond, winking. "It was so easy."

"You outdid yourself, doll," Mary Claire grins. "I guarantee you you'll place."

"Right?" I answer. "Maybe the prize will offset what I spent on supplies…but honestly, this was fun to do."

"You go, girl," Mary Claire giggles. We hug goodbye, hard, and her parting words to me are, "Let me know how your mom is doing."

Beecher Springs is only eight minutes from Mary Claire's, and I cruise past the luxurious new condos at the front of the development to mom's area of more modest cottages. Parking, I lug my first batch of stuff up to her door. Her heavy door is ajar, and I can tell she's opened it to wait for me. Peering inside, I see her asleep on the couch, and I knock and do a trilly "Yooooohoooo, Joan!" She starts, realizes it's me, and rises unsteadily, shuffling over to the door. I swear she looks more diminished every time I see her. It's always a shock after having been away for a few weeks. For a brief second my eyes fill. You'd think I'd be past this by now…it's not like I expect her to spring up from the couch and bound over to the door, but her frailty still has the power to broadside me. All of us have taken her wellspring of energy for granted too long. Now each visit seems to bring noticeable decline.

Her face lights up as she reaches the door. "Come in,

come in," she welcomes me, fumbling with the lock on the screen door. She attempts to hold the door open and doesn't quite manage.

"Hi, Mommy," I gush. "Let me hold the door…I don't want you to lose your balance." As she relinquishes the door, I bring my travel bag and scrubs in, placing them deliberately in a corner where I know she won't stumble over them. Walking back to her, I open my arms wide. "Give us a hug, Pooh bear," I say, and she walks into my embrace, literally skin and bones.

"Did you have a good nap while you were waiting for me?" I ask her as I start unpacking.

"It's all I do, Bet," she replies, almost apologetically. "If I lay down, I'm out like a light. There's so much I should be doing around here to get organized." The expression 'doing around here to get organized' is one of her pat expressions that she has employed for years. Housework, laundry, and cooking all got lumped into that phrase, and it functioned as a catch-all for 'life happening'. 'I need to get organized' was her way of saying that life was out of control at that moment, which it mostly was with four children. It's amusing to me that, 45 years later, Mom is still using this phrase as she is settling into this new chapter of her life.

"Not to worry," I reassure her. "You've earned the right to nap whenever you want to…there's nothing you ever HAVE to do." I am constantly reiterating this to her, because I think she sometimes feels guilty about things not being more organized and ship shape when I come. I could care less, because that's not how I'm wired up; let alone the fact that she was such a conscientious housekeeper for years that it's the last thing she should be worrying about now. Besides, she has her wonderful Sandy, who comes every Wednesday to tidy up.

After unpacking, I put mom's big pumpkin in one corner of her porch where it's most visible to passersby. "Why is that out there?" Mom asks, peering at the pumpkin through the screen door.

"Halloween is just around the corner," I answer, "and you should probably give it some homage. Wait till I show you what else I have."

Mom looks vaguely confused, but gamely says, "Well, I guess I should get out my Halloween decorations. I'm not even sure where they are at this point."

"We'll dig and find 'em," I offer. "They're probably in one of the big boxes in the garage." Over the course of the past eight months, I have cleaned, sorted, and reorganized all her closets and cabinets inside the cottage, giving Mary Claire and Dan boxes and bags full of things mom doesn't use any more for their mission thrift shop. I've yet to get to the big boxes Craig has stored out in the garage, but I know he's marked everything in his usual organized way. It'll just be a matter of looking for his box marked 'Decorations'. Now that mom is no longer driving, it'll be easy enough just to pull the boxes into the center of the empty garage and take out what she needs. I make a final trip to the Jeep, elbowing the cottage door open and bringing in my pumpkin.

Carrying the box to the eating area, I set it down on the table and turn to mom. "OK, so I told you about our pumpkin decorating contest at work, right?" I begin.

She nods, and prompts," The one you didn't want to have to deal with, right?"

I grin. "Yeah, that one. But that was before I had this wonderful, award winning, Robitussin-induced idea. Close your eyes."

Mom raises her eyebrows dramatically, clasps her hands together, and closes her eyes. I know she can tell I'm taking the pumpkin out of the box, and I intone, "Open, sesame."

Her eyes fluttering open, she focuses on the pumpkin in front of her. "Well, this is certainly attractive," she says, as her eyes move from side to side, taking it in. "This fabric covering is interesting." She indicates the sweatshirt paint surrounding the cutout shapes. "Did you do all of this, too?"

"That was the fun part," I answer, "that, and putting the stickers on."

"Did you cut out all these shapes, too?" she inquires. "I was never a good cutter-outer."

"No," I answer. "Mike did that part for me."

Mom nods her head, as if quietly expressing relief that Mike took this odious task off my hands.

"Let's leave it on the table to admire," she suggests, and starts to remove the salt and pepper shakers from the lazy susan in the middle so my pumpkin can sit on it. After I put it there in its place of honor, Mom awkwardly steps back, still gazing at it.

"I would never have thought to do any of that," she says quietly, as if to herself. And then, directly to me, "That's a first-place pumpkin if I have anything to say about it."

The weekend is a slow, quiet one. Over its course I am shocked by the amount of deterioration I see in mom compared to barely four weeks ago in September. I find myself watching and observing her very closely to try to pinpoint anything I may have overlooked before. One of the first things I'm aware of is the strong odor of urine on mom's person. It's unmistakable, and this is the first time I've ever noticed it. I know she wears Depends undergarments at night, because I've seen them in the bathroom cabinet under her sink, but I'm not sure about her daytime use of them. Mom has always been a very private, self-contained person when it comes to any discussions regarding bodily functions and female issues, and I have never 'gone there' with her. This is based more on the respect I have for her, and the desire to preserve her dignity, than it is out of any discomfort I have with these topics myself, but I find myself wondering now if maybe I need to ask a few questions in a very matter-of-fact way. This smell is bad, and I hate to think of Mom being around other people that might notice it in a social setting.

I decide on a plan of action that will be very benign, and

I go to check her supply of Depends. Is it possible she's run out? I peek under her sink, and there is the better part of a large opened package there, so I know supply is not the issue. *Could she be forgetting to change them?* I wonder. Especially if she's using them all the time now, maybe she's just not changing them frequently enough. Or, worst case scenario, maybe it's easier not to use the toilet at all, based on the physical up's and down's it requires, and the readjustment of panties, and slacks. Could Mom be relying completely on the Depends now, to take care of all urinary function?

Just mulling all this over makes me sad. Mom was always such a stickler about personal appearance and 'looking our best' when we were growing up. It hurts me to think of her letting her own hygiene slip either because she's too tired to invest in it OR because she's cognitively not aware of it, or both. We sit and talk for a while on the couch, and it's warm enough to open the windows. In that scant time, I notice that she has dozed off, sitting upright but with her head canted way back, her mouth open. I gently touch her arm and rub it.

"Hey, sleepyhead," I murmur, "let's get you comfy for a real nap. How about stretching out so your legs are up?" She doesn't argue, but nods gratefully, and I get her positioned on her back, tucking an afghan around her. "Did you still want to go to church?"

"If you do," she deflects, and closes her eyes again.

"I'll wake you up at 4:45 and we'll see how you feel," I say, smiling down at her.

"I won't sleep that long," she retorts, and then, apropos of nothing, "What are you going to do while I sleep?"

Again, I smile, even more broadly. "Sit and stare at you," I say, straight faced. She grimaces and sticks her tongue out at me, which delights me.

"That's mature," I state. "And when I get tired of staring at you, I'm probably going to read this book that Andy's uncle gave me when I was I Nashville," I continue. "I'll be right down here," and I curl up in the L of the couch with my book.

Around 4:45 I get up and gently tap her shoulder. "Mom, it's 4:45," I say. "Do you want to go on napping?"

She looks at me almost in disbelief and I realize that she's slept so deeply she's forgotten I was here. "No, no," she defers. "Let's go to church, Bet. Can you drive?"

I'm momentarily dumbstruck by this, as mom hasn't had her car for over three weeks now, but then I write it off to her being disoriented after her nap. I find myself wondering if she's ever walked into her garage thinking that her car was still out there when it isn't any more. (I don't want to picture this.) I help her sit upright, and ask if she needs to change her clothes, silently hoping she opts to wear what she has on, so we don't have to do an outfit change. She looks vaguely down at her polyester pants and the plaid collared shirt she has on. "No, I'm fine in these," she declares, and I help her stand, asking her if she needs to use the bathroom before we leave.

"I don't need to," she states, somewhat dismissively.

It's go time, I think.

"Do you have a Depends on?" I ask. "Do you want to put a fresh one on before you go to church?"

Now she looks at me like I have three heads. "The one I have on is fine," she says, somewhat haughtily.

Uh-oh, I'm on thin ice, I warn myself. What to say now? It pops out before I consciously even think it through. "Well," I suggest, "let's put a fresh pair on anyway, just to be on the safe side."

This time she's a little more emphatic, and a little more defensive. "Bet," she says, "those Depends are expensive. I can't change them every hour, you know."

I nod, as if this is a very rational discussion about the weather. "I know they are, mom, but I think it's been awhile since you changed it, and it smells kind of stale." (I deliberately refrain from using the words 'stinky', 'stench-y' or 'urine-y', all of which had been quick vocabulary options.)

"I don't smell anything," Mom declares.

By this time, I feel like I'm all in and stepping in it besides. "I know," I say gently. "It's always hardest for us to smell ourselves. But you really need to change it, Mom. If I were in your shoes, I would sure want someone to be honest with me. Plus, you don't want to walk around with all that wet and bacteria next to your skin. Fresh is better. Do you want me to help you? "

This is the first time I've ever asked to help mom with anything related to bodily function, but even though the line's been crossed, it somehow seems perfectly normal in the context of the discussion.

"No, Bet, I can do it on my own," Mom states firmly, and begins to move towards her bedroom. I pray that I haven't humiliated her; that it's just more of a 'let's do this' thing. I do make a mental note to check the discarded undergarment to see how much fluid it contains. I'm curious about the degree to which Mom is utilizing them. I probably need to go out tomorrow and buy her extra packs so she doesn't feel like she has to use them so sparingly. Up until right now it had never occurred to me that she was no longer able to run out and buy a pack if she was running low. All the residents have access to a van that takes them out to shop at various stores all over Cincinnati-Kroger, Walgreens, Target; but if I was mom, the last thing I'd want is to have to lug my big bag of Depends back on the van with all eyes on them. This will be something I can own for her.

We head to church with a fresh Depends on, no further discussion about it, and on the way, I find myself thinking about something else I purposely haven't brought up with Mom, because I wanted to see if she'd reference it on her own…the pressure in her abdomen she had mentioned last time. She's said nothing about it yet, but it's something I'm paying close attention to-that, and the random vomiting. No mention of that, either, but more and more, I wonder if it could be happening all the same, Mom just forgetting after it happens.

I drop her off at the entryway of church, to save her the walk from the parking lot, which has become standard protocol for us. As I'm walking in, I run into the Reinholds, so by the time I reach the vestibule, easily ten or more minutes have elapsed. I glance around. This service is always lightly attended, so there aren't a lot of people here, but I don't see Mom anywhere. Knowing Mom, I'm sure she just marched right into church, picked out a pew, and is sitting there ready to roll. I walk to the double door of the sanctuary and gaze in; knowing her shock of white hair will be easily visible. (As Craig refers to her hair, 'Einstein on crack') But there are no snowy heads in the sanctuary.

What the heck? Where is she? I scan the sanctuary more slowly…still no mom. Maybe the restroom? I look over my left shoulder to the rear of the vestibule, where they have a refreshment table set up with brownies, cookies, and drinks. And then I spot her. I freeze, watching in part horror, part amusement, and overwhelming sadness. She's standing in front of the table, all by herself, leaning way over the platter like a child, a large cookie in one hand, a brownie in the other, literally cramming them into her mouth as if she's afraid someone is going to catch her doing it and make her put them back.

As she shoves the brownie into her mouth, half goes in, but the other half breaks apart and crumbles into smithereens, bouncing down her chin and ricocheting onto her chest. Mom no more would have done this six months ago than 'fly to the moon', as she'd say. This is the strongest confirmation I've had of how much her cognitive awareness is slipping. For a woman whose social graces were always impeccable, this is a night and day aberration. Had any one of the four of us ever displayed this kind of behavior in public, there would have been on the spot retribution, and no desire on our part to ever repeat that social gaffe. But I already know in my heart that I won't be addressing this breach of manners. Instead, I want to cry. As I move toward the refreshment table, Sherry Castille walks over to talk to Mom, and I read Sherry's acknowledgment of the situation on her face. I know she's seen what I have. We both reach Mom at about the same time, and Sherry speaks to Mom as if she's seen nothing.

"Hi, Joan," she greets her. "How's your week been?"

Mom's mouth is crammed full of brownie, so she motions upward to her mouth and holds up her index finger to indicate that she needs a minute to chew. (I guess the social graces have momentarily kicked back in.) Sherry gives me a warm greeting and a big hug; I take the opportunity to whisper in her ear, "Someone is very hungry," and she winks at me. As Mom swallows her bale of sweets and begins to talk with Sherry, I surreptitiously dust the crumbs off her blouse. She doesn't seem remotely aware of my doing it. Then we head into the sanctuary, relatively crumb-free. As always, I enjoy the service. We visit with various members afterwards, then go to Barney's for dinner.

We're back at mom's cottage by 7:30, curled up on the couch to watch 'Andy of Mayberry' reruns, and talking intermittently. I decide to bring up the abdominal issue, mostly because I'm curious to see if mom remembers telling me from my previous visit in September. "How's your tummy been?" I ask conversationally, glancing over at her to see if there's any overt reaction. Without missing a beat, she responds.

"Really no different," is her answer. "It still just feels, well…heavy…there's just pressure. That's the only way I can describe it."

The fact that she describes it so readily confirms to me that it must be a pretty ongoing issue for her, and that concerns me. "Does it actually hurt?" I ask. "Is it painful?"

She considers this for a moment. "No, I wouldn't say painful, "she replies. "It's almost like being full all the time- like I've eaten too much."

I wait for a minute to see if anything else is forthcoming. Silence, and she's watching me. "You know, Mom, we probably ought to get this checked out," I suggest. "It's probably nothing, but you've also been doing some vomiting off and on, and they could be connected."

Mom looks puzzled. "The vomiting isn't that often, and it's when food doesn't agree with me," she says. "I don't think they're connected at all."

"Well, maybe not," I concur, "but you mentioned feeling this way last time I was here, too, and I think somebody qualified needs to check you out. Would you consider seeing one of the doctors that's here on staff, so you don't have to worry about setting up a driver to take you offsite? That way we'll know for sure."

"I just had my colonoscopy in August...Colette took me," she replies. "If there had been anything, they would have found it."

I'm frankly amazed, after what I've witnessed today, that Mom can possibly remember when her last colonoscopy was. This is the first that I've heard of it, but I'm appreciative that even though Col and I aren't communicating, she made the time to take mom to her appointment.

"That part's good," I state, "but things can change. It could be something very small, mom, like chronic gas, or maybe even a low grade UTI...or nothing. Do you want me to call one of the doctors here and see when we can get you in?"

"No, Bet, I can do that," she reassures me, but I feel like she's giving me lip service.

"But WILL you?" I persist. "I don't want you letting it go for another month thinking it'll just go away." This is where I struggle. I'm trying so hard to not make her feel like all the control of her life is being stripped away, especially after taking the car from her just three weeks ago. I'm trying to let her make as many of her decisions as she's capable of, but that's where the gray area is for me.

She reaches over and pats my hand, smiling. "I WILL remember," she says confidently, "and I won't put it off. I'll call their office here first thing on Monday and set up an appointment. It's probably time I got to know some of these doctors anyway, since I don't have my car anymore." She turns to me and raises her eyebrows in mock consternation. "Now are you happy?"

She's so good natured about this stuff, I think. *If it were me, I'd be such a grump.* I look at her and grin. "Yes," and I pat her hand back. "Now I am."

* * * * *

Sunday morning is grey, quiet, and cool. I open a few windows, fix a big pot of coffee for myself, throw a load of laundry in for mom, and fix us pancakes. Mom eats three large ones smothered in butter and syrup, and we have a long, lazy breakfast. She tends to be a social eater, and if there's someone else to eat with, she'll eat more than if she's alone. I'm the same way. After cleaning up, I ask her if she wants to take a walk with me. She seems reluctant, but I wheedle.

"Pleeeeease?" I ask. "You might feel better if you got some exercise." She finally agrees, but on the condition that we don't go nearly as far as we have before, which has been close to two miles. "No, we won't," I agree. "And, if you get tired, just tell me, and we'll turn around."

The grounds are very quiet as we head out, and we make our way slowly up a gradual hill toward the Manor House and another group of condos. We've been walking for about 30 minutes when Mom says flatly, "Bet, I need to turn around. I just can't go any farther."

I know not to push, and I immediately respond, "Sure, that's fine. I wish I could carry you home piggyback."

She laughs. "I wish you could, too," she says, and

something in her tone of voice makes me realize how exhausted she is, and that she did this only because she knows how much I like to walk and didn't want to hold me back. I feel terrible for pushing her. We move slowly back to her cottage, and she collapses immediately on the couch. I get her a drink, cover her up, and that's pretty much the rest of her day. I curl up at the other end of the couch and read for hours, stretching out at one point and napping myself. Other times I stop reading and just look at mom sleeping.

I love her so much; this brave, understated woman who never asks for anything, and who is so grateful for the time I spend with her...what will it be like when she's not here anymore for me to hang out with? It's never what we do that matters to me. It's just the simple act of being together, and it fills me up in a way nothing else can. She is truly one of my best friends in the world, and she has taught me so much simply by being herself. I hate thinking about having to leave her tomorrow morning, because I know in my heart she feels better when I'm here with her. We're entering a tunnel where bit by bit, pieces of mom are falling off and beginning to be lost, and I can't see my way to the end of it. *God, be with us,* I silently pray, gazing at her sound asleep and lowering my book. *Don't let anything happen to her and keep her safe and healthy.*

Around 4 PM I decide to make a run to a nearby drugstore to pick up some extra Depends. I gently wake Mom and tell her where I'm going, and that I'll be right back. Mission accomplished. I stash them under her bathroom sink when I return. Then I quietly go out to the garage and find the Halloween decoration box. Digging through it, I pull out four items that I think will look good in the cottage, bringing them in and arranging them. One of them is a giant pumpkin in the shape of a teapot that Dad had given her years ago, and I set it on the lazy susan and move my pumpkin to a spot on the counter. She sleeps through the entire adventure but seems pleased with the decorations when she wakes up.

We eat an early dinner of grilled cheese and tomato soup, one of my childhood favorites. Again, her appetite is hearty. By 9:00, after Mary Tyler Moore re-runs, I can tell she's ready for bed, so I get ready, too, knowing I can read myself to sleep after she's tucked in. I sit in the quiet cottage after she's in bed asleep; such a role reversal from my childhood. I so wish I could stay to take her to the doctor's appointment she'd better remember to make. An hour later my eyes get heavy and I slip into bed quietly, listening to the solitary call of a nearby train as I drift off to sleep.

I'm up at 4:45 much against my will. This is the part I truly hate-the getting ready and getting on the road. It's only a shower, the makeup basics (moisturizer and eyeliner) and clean hair this morning. While I'm drying my hair, I see Mom's reflection in the mirror padding into my bedroom. 'It's so early for you to be up', I read her lips saying in the mirror. I shut the dryer off momentarily and retort, "It's so early for YOU to be up-go back to bed. I'll come in and kiss you goodbye when I leave."

Instead of going back to bed, she moves out into the living room and starts flipping on lights. This is so my Mom. She wants to be sure I'm sent off in the most hospitable way, nor would she dream of going back to bed until I'm gone. She comes back to the bathroom door to ask me, "Have you made your coffee already?"

I nod, and she asks me if I want her to pack a lunch for me. "Sure," I answer. "Just do some yogurt and fruit, and a few cookies or peanuts."

I finish my hair, throw my stuff in my duffel bag, and make a quick trip to my Jeep with all of it. As I am coming from checking the bedroom one last time to be sure I have everything, Mom is standing by the kitchen counter, and points to my pumpkin.

"Someone doesn't want to be forgotten," she says, nodding towards it.

And, I totally would have forgotten it had she not

reminded me. *Who's the forgetful one now?* I think to myself. I slide my pumpkin into its travel box, and then look at Mom.

"What would I do without you?" I ask her.

"What would I do without YOU?" she responds, opening her palms and shrugging her shoulders. "Thank you for spending your entire weekend with me when there were so many other things you should have been doing," she says, and hugs me. "I love you."

"I love you, too," I tell her, "and don't forget to call about your appointment today, because I'm going to ask you about it tonight when I get home from work."

She bats her eyes. "I won't, Bet."

We hug again, and I'm on my way in the predawn darkness. My Jeep clock reads 5:34. I pick up I-75 from Spring Grove Avenue, cruise across the Brent Spence, and am lost in somber thought.

Monday evening, I walk into our kitchen after work, glad to finally be home. Our message machine is blinking red, and I retrieve the one message there.

It's Mom: "Hello, Bet, it's Mom. Hope you had a good day at work. That was certainly a long day for you with your drive back. Let me know what everyone had to say about your first prize pumpkin. That really was one great pumpkin."

Joan, On Her Own

Chapter Nine

TURN AND FACE THE CHANGE
(Late October – Thanksgiving 2010)

Wednesday evening, October 28th, and I'm headed to church to rehearse, on the downhill side of my week. It's totally dark now for the drive in, and I embrace the feeling of impending cold and the year drawing down. It's been a routine work week. All our pumpkins are on display, and they do give the place an upbeat atmosphere. They run the gambit in terms of design and originality. Haley's is far and above the most creative in my book. She's one of our incredibly artistic medical assistants. Designed to look like a bag of popcorn, her pumpkin is painted white with red striping and lettering to function as the bag, then smaller 'mini-pumpkins' have been spray painted a soft butter color with wisps of cotton glued to them to act as the puffed corn kernels. It's adorable.

Another is decorated to be a gumball machine, complete with the black detailing and the silver chute where the balls roll out, with a variety of colored gumballs stamped all over the pumpkin by using a sponge cutout the exact size of a giant gumball. LaDonna made a clown out of hers, complete with a multi-colored wig and a red rubber nose. Marcy hasn't brought one in, and I seriously doubt that she will. I admire her ability to draw her personal line and say 'no' to this contest. I also know that Linda will give her a hard time about not contributing, which I don't feel is fair. It's just not everybody's gig, and it is a lot of extra work. Liz, my favorite MA, who is also very artsy, told me mine was "so cool; it looks like something you'd see at Pier One", so between that comment and Mom's pride in my work, I'm good to go, prize or no.

Speaking of mom, I'm concerned. Her deterioration seems to have accelerated, and I've talked to Mike and Craig about it at length. Craig and I are at a point where we talk at least two or three times a week now, and I slowly see us becoming one another's lifeline. It has struck me so often lately how difficult it would be to be going through this with Mom as an only child; trying to process it all without having any siblings to share ideas and feelings with. Craig and I are an unlikely pairing, with mom being one of our very few common denominators, but it's working for us, and I'm seeing our emotional reliance on one another grow. Our skill sets are diametrically opposed to one another, but that's where it's so helpful for each of us to be there for the other.

I so wish Rob and Donny were more present and engaged as well. The irony isn't lost on me that the two siblings who live in the same city as Mom are the two least involved, and it hurts my heart for her. She never says anything, but I'm sure she misses seeing more of them. For me, there's a certain amount of anger towards them. It's not that it's putting an extra burden on me (I just don't look at it that way), but because they don't seem to want to spend time with Mom. Why isn't that more important to them? I know there can be a big difference in a mother-daughter relationship compared to that of a mother-son, but I'm not even talking anything deep or extensive. I'm thinking more of them dropping by occasionally for lunch, bringing her dinner, popping in to sit with her for half an hour, or even just a daily phone call checking in, but any of these options seem completely beyond them.

The other more immediate concern that's weighing on me as I park at church is that I couldn't reach Mom tonight before I left for rehearsal. I've pretty much started checking in with her every day now, usually when I get home from work. When I called her Monday night, I asked her if she had scheduled her appointment, and she had. It's tomorrow morning at 10:40 on Beecher's campus. All she does is walk over to their office from her cottage. I wish I could be there to make sure she's telling the doctor everything, and I worry about her not retaining everything he'll tell her. Worst case scenario, I can always call him and follow up on the phone.

Last night I had gone out to dinner with Jeannie after work, and it had been too late to call when I got home. I guess it's possible, but not probable, that someone from church took her out to dinner...maybe Nancy Rhodes. Or, maybe she went to the Manor House with some of the Knoll Girls. Still, something doesn't feel quite right. I called Craig before I left for church to give him a heads-up and to ask him to keep trying to reach Mom, knowing he's as good as his word. Still, I hate bugging him. He's got so much on his plate anyway and has his girls at home, complete with all their activities. But he assured me he'll keep trying her.

I float through choir rehearsal, and it's always the favorite part of my Wednesday. Besides loving our director, Dave Rich, and having incredible respect for his direction and musicianship, this is my therapy after the stress of the workday, and the constant barrage of noise at the office. It's a luxury to focus on one task at a time, taking care to produce a specific vocal dynamic, or making sure not to breathe in the middle of a melodic line. This is how I'm wired up, and these are the pursuits that soothe and heal my frayed nerves after being in my 'hyper-response' mode all day.

I can feel my body unwinding, and my mind growing still, even as I'm singing. Dave has started our Christmas music, and there's a new piece, 'Sure On This Shining Night', by Lauridsen, that is stunning. I can tell everyone is enjoying the preparation. This is always the quickest hour and a half of my day, from 7:30-9:00, and too quickly I'm on my way back home in complete silence, thankful for the blessing of music in my life.

Immediately I see the glow of the message machine's red light blinking as I walk into the dark kitchen. An unwarranted surge of fear rises in me. I retrieve the message; it's Craig, with a simple 'Call me ASAP'. I dial his number with a tight chest, and he answers on the first ring.

"Betsy, you're not going to believe this," he says, and there is palpable fury in his shaking voice. "You probably want to be sitting down."

I absentmindedly pull out one of our kitchen chairs and sink heavily onto it. "Is it bad?" I ask in a small voice.

"Mom's okay, but there's quite a story behind this. I tried to reach her tonight from about, oh, six to eight, figuring she wouldn't be out much later than that even if she'd gone out to dinner with somebody. Most of her friends can't even drive after dark anymore. Well, when it got to be 8:30 and I still couldn't get her, I called Beecher's Security, thinking maybe she'd fallen in her cottage and couldn't get to the phone. Security was concerned, of course, and the man I spoke to said he'd check into it and call me right back. Okay, are you ready for this? Betsy, he calls me back five minutes later and tells me Mom's been hospitalized since early this morning. Apparently, she fell last night."

Craig pauses here, as much for a breath himself as to let me process what he's just told me. He continues, "Right...I'm beside myself, and I ask the guy, 'Why weren't we contacted?' He tells me, 'Mr. Bradshaw, we DID call you. You're Rob Bradshaw, correct?' I tell him no, that I'm one of Mrs. Bradshaw's other sons, and that I live out of town, that my name is Craig. He apologizes to me again, and says, 'Well, yes sir, we did contact your brother Rob. Did he not call you?'"

I exhale a shallow breath, and my entire body is going cold as the reality of Craig's words is sinking in. Craig continues, "I'm livid, Betsy. I cannot believe this really happened. I told the security man, 'Sir, I apologize for all the confusion. Our brother refuses to communicate with any of the three of his other siblings, and we had no idea this had even happened. I'm so sorry to have put you in the middle of all of this. It's a very unfortunate situation.' The man was very understanding. I think he was embarrassed for me and he said, 'Oh, Mr. Bradshaw, I've seen a lot of this over the years here. Nothing would surprise me. Communication in families can be very tricky, and I'm sorry you were kept in the dark. Apparently one of our residents saw your mom fall on Tuesday evening while she was out walking and called us right away. This same resident came out with a blanket and stayed with your mother until we could get an ambulance there, and we took her right over to Grace's emergency room, then notified your brother. He met her there, and then brought her back to her cottage after they cleaned her up."

I break in at this point. "What in the world was Mom doing out walking?" I ask incredulously. "And in the dark?" I'm starting to come unhinged. "She could have laid there all night, bleeding on the ground, or until a security patrol found her, if that resident hadn't seen her fall down! This is so messed up!"

"Sadly, Bet, it gets better," Craig continues. "I have no idea why she was outside Tuesday night. Didn't you tell me how tired she was on Sunday after you guys went for a walk? So, this doesn't figure. But here's the absolute best. According to security, Rob gets there and tells them he's going to spend the night with Mom, to make sure she's okay. I guess he figured she was fine the next morning, because he left, and went on into Holy Disciple. He probably would have left around 6:30 or 7:00…well, security tells me he came back at around 9:30 Wednesday morning, and took her to Holy Dis himself."

By now my stomach is in knots; both from an overwhelming helplessness as it relates to Mom, and from complete incomprehension of the situation. Why did Rob wait until Wednesday morning to take Mom to the hospital if he spent the whole night with her in her cottage? Did something in her medical condition change in status suddenly on Wednesday morning? Did Rob really think that we weren't going to be worried when we couldn't get Mom to answer her phone? Maybe it never even occurred to him that both Craig and I check in with Mom at least once every day?

"So, I guess Rob dealt with all of the paperwork signing her off campus at Beecher?" I ask, although it's a rhetorical question, since she's already in the hospital. He has medical power of attorney, and none of this would have been a problem for him. "Meanwhile, Mom's laying in her hospital bed, wondering why she hasn't heard from either of us," I say. "And I guess it's too late to get through to her room tonight, although we could call the nurses' station and explain what happened. Maybe if they know Rob hasn't communicated with us, they'd be willing to give us some info over the phone given the situation."

"That's a great idea," Craig agrees, "and rest assured I am ALL over this tomorrow. I'll be spending the day at Holy Dis, Bet. And, I'll tell you another thing. Rob may have medical power of attorney, but from now on, my name will be at the top of that call list so that this can never happen again. I cannot BELIEVE he thought he could pull this off and that we'd never find out it happened. This is going to blow up in his face tomorrow when he has to see me and answer for it at Holy Dis."

"I'm stunned that they thought it was okay to operate this way," I state, including Col in my assessment. "Talk about immature. They don't have to agree with us, or even choose to have family interaction, but a simple phone call of a few words, or a voice message? That would have sufficed. This is taking things to a whole new level of vitriol. Do you think Mom's asked either one of them if they've let us know?"

"Who knows," Craig answers. "But I do know one thing. They'll be squirming when they see me walk into that hospital room tomorrow and their little secret is up. This is going to be one long, sleepless night for me. Damn those two. I cannot believe they thought this was okay."

"I'm not sure they thought at all," I reflect, "or even care about the fallout. And, sadly, Craig, we've got to move forward in all this regardless of how they have chosen to handle it. Don't do or say anything you'll regret tomorrow. Remember, this is far more about Mom and her well-being than it is about their vindictiveness. The last thing Mom needs is to sense conflict between all of us right now. Her recovery takes precedence over all this. Try to remember that, okay? Rob and Colette have themselves to answer to, and karma's a bitch."

"Yeah, I know," Craig concurs. "It just blows my mind that they'd pull this stunt. And, on their own medical turf, too. Can you imagine the doctors' and nurses' shock tomorrow when I'm explaining to them that their colleague, my brother, didn't bother to let any of his siblings know that their mother had been hospitalized?"

"Be professional, and take the high road," I advise. "Build your case well." I ask him if he wants me to try to contact the nurses' station at Holy Dis, but he's loaded for bear, and wants to be the one to do it. I ask him to have the nurses convey to Mom that we're thinking about her, and that we'll talk to her tomorrow. We hang up, and I climb our stairs slowly, lost in thought. Mike glances at me from his desk in his study (the girls refer to it as his "lair") as I clear the top of the stairs, and in reading my face, he knows immediately something is badly wrong. Walking into the study, I give him a brief recap of my conversation with Craig. He listens without saying anything until I finish, then declares quietly, "That is way screwed up. Your poor Mom."

For me as well, sleep is long in coming this night.

I start work bleary-eyed on Thursday morning, but full of coffee and ready to pour myself into the day. I have become adept at being able to compartmentalize; some of it based on needing to be fully present to focus on the demands of the day. The other larger part of it stems from the realization that I am over two hours away from the situation with Mom. There is nothing productive I can do, other than pray, until I talk further with Craig tonight. I'm already very aware of the Lord mentally preparing me to go back up to be with her this weekend, and I'm trying to remain as calm and centered as possible until I have more specifics. And today, despite the initial slap of Rob and Col not letting us know about Mom, I'm very able to dismiss any emotion relating to them. Even though I have no idea what their motives were, and may never know, they had reasons for playing it the way they did. They are not accountable to me; they answer to God and to their own inner juries.

It's not a terribly late night for me at work, and I witness a flaming autumn sky on the ride home as the purple and violet streaks presage the night. As soon as I walk in, Mike yells down to me in greeting. He's also chomping at the bit to know what course of events today has brought. Coming to the top of the stairs, he yells down, "What have you found out about the traitors?"

I smile wryly. This is vintage Mike. Walking to the foot of the stairs, I look up at him and make a face. "Nothing, yet," I reply. "Let me call Craig and then I'm sure all ICBM's will be appropriately aimed."

I'm beginning to reach the point where I dread talking on the phone at night, because it always seems to come with a high emotional price tag. Depending on which one of us (Craig or me) has been in Cincy with Mom, there's always a debriefing involved; the person most recently with her giving the bystander an update so we're both on the same page. Shifting medical conditions, accelerating deterioration, and ongoing healthcare questions have all driven the necessity of these almost nightly phone conversations, yet I sometimes feel like I'm coming home to start my second job whenever I pick up the phone in the evening. I can only imagine how Craig must feel with both Viv and Emmy at home in addition to the travel his job demands.

A blinking red message light beckons me from the phone on the counter...no surprise. This is probably Craig's update from the day, so I retrieve the message before I call him back. As I hear it, I draw a sharp intake of breath. It's been well over a year since I've heard this voice at all, let alone on our answering machine. It's Colette, in her low, slightly breathy voice: "Betsy, it's Colette." (Not, as in the past, 'Bet, it's Col'.) "I wanted you to know that your Mom's been hospitalized, and she's here at Holy Dis. She had a fall at Beecher that needed some attending to. I had tried to call you earlier and leave a message, but I think I may have left it at the wrong number."

I instinctively save her message, and slowly place the phone back in its holder. "Curious-er and curious-er," I mutter, shaking my head in disbelief. There's something totally bogus in that message, but I can't put my finger on what it is. I go back and play it again, checking to see what time it was recorded. 9:33 this morning. Now my brain goes into overdrive. Colette probably knew at this point that Craig was either at Holy Disciple (possibly one of her co-workers had told her that either he was there or that he had called the nursing station last night?) or on his way there, and she was trying to cover her tracks.

The weird part is her feigned statement about leaving me an earlier message and realizing it was the wrong number, which is childishly see-through in its fallibility. I guess she wanted me to think she had called me much earlier, to make the whole situation look more credible. This must be a last-ditch attempt to try to cover up not having called on Wednesday, or even on Tuesday night, when Rob had been called by security. I shake my head again after re-playing it. This is almost laughable, if it wasn't so sad. Why try to save face now? I also wonder if, by Craig being at Holy Disciple today, the situation has already started to backfire on them.

Now I erase Col's message and go on to the second one, which is Craig's. "Give me a call…you're gonna love this."

I do, and he picks up immediately. "Hey," he greets me.

"Are you home already, or still at the hospital?" I ask him.

"No, I'm home now," he answers. "I left the hospital around 5:00. Bet, I'm telling you, those two defy belief."

"Start at the beginning," I direct. "What time did you get down there this morning?" I'm curious to pair his arrival time with the time of Col's message. It's roughly an hour's drive time from his home to Holy Disciple. "Also… did you end up calling the nurses' station last night to see if you could get any information?"

"I did," Craig answers. "I talked to one of the night nurses at the nursing station. Bet, she was incredulous. I explained to her that we had had no idea that Mom had been in the hospital for a day, and that it had taken the head of security at Beecher Springs to inform us that she'd fallen and been taken to Holy Disciple. Her response was classic. She says to me, 'Wait a minute. Is Mrs. Bradshaw your mother?' I tell her yes. 'And you're Dr. Bradshaw's brother?' I tell her yes. 'And Dr. Bradshaw never called anyone else in your family to let you know this happened?' 'That's right', I tell her. She says, 'I don't even know what to say,' and then there's just silence. Then she says, 'I'm really sorry about that.'"

"So, the word's out," I state. "Not sure they planned on this kind of fallout. So how was Mom, and how bad was the fall?"

"Well, when I spoke with the nurse last night over the phone, she just gave me the basics; Mom had ended up needing six stitches in the back of her head, but she was stable and resting comfortably. I asked the nurse to let Mom know that you and I were thinking about her if she was awake at any point during the night, and that I'd be coming down to see her tomorrow," Craig reports.

"Six stitches," I say. "It's amazing she didn't break

anything when she fell."

"Right?" Craig weighs in drily, "Nothing like a minor head injury at 83. So, I get down there this morning…" but I interrupt before he can get any farther.

"Wait, wait…I have to tell you this before you get into things," I blurt out. "When I got home tonight, I checked the messages, like always, knowing there'd be one from you. But, there was also one from Col from around 9:30 this morning, telling me that she'd tried to 'call me earlier' and thought she might have had the wrong number-just wanted me to know that Mom had fallen and was at Holy Dis and stable. Riddle me that, Batman."

"Well, we can piece that all together now, can't we?" Craig asks acidly. "I'm sure she knew that I was headed down there this morning, because I had called Mom's room around 9:15 when I was almost to the hospital and Colette happened to be right there in the room while Mom and I were having the conversation; Mom mentioned her being there to check on her. And I would bet you money that Colette also got hit full bore by the fact that I had called and talked to the night nurse, that we knew, and, in addition, that a lot of her co-workers knew how poorly she and Rob had handled the situation. Word like that spreads. No doubt she was trying to cover herself and make it look like she'd tried to contact you. How sorry is that?"

We continue to discuss his entire day at Holy Dis in depth. He had gone directly to Mom's room once he arrived and was fortunate enough to walk in right as the doctor who was treating her was talking to her in the room. Craig discussed the situation in detail with her and felt good about Mom's prognosis and probable discharge tomorrow.

Per Craig, Mom wasn't very happy about him bringing up the fact that Rob had never contacted us in front of both the doctor and another nurse who had entered the room, because after both of them had left the room, she had admonished Craig, "You don't need to keep bringing up the fact that Rob didn't call you or Betsy," to which Craig had responded, "Come on, Mom, really? You fell Tuesday night and we find out from Security 24 hours later because he refuses to communicate with us? You think that's ok?"

She had responded with an inept, "No, I guess not, I'm sure you were worried, but you're making him look very bad in front of his colleagues," as if that was of primary concern.

I suppose there will always be traces of characteristics from Mom's younger years that create a lot of ambivalence in me, and her need to control outward appearances has always been high on my list. This is a typical 'Mom comment', because it's important to her that Rob's medical reputation be protected. Anything that could potentially erode that, or cause it to be questioned, is a problem for her. The way I see it, it's unfortunate on two fronts: first, that Craig felt he had to draw attention to it in front of the medical staff. I wouldn't have brought it up, except to Mom herself, one on one, later. Secondly, it's unfortunate that Mom is still concerned with appearances, given where she is in her life. But, ironically, there's a common denominator here, and it's all about control-Craig not having it because Rob chose to cut him out of the loop; Mom not having it because she can't control what Craig is saying about Rob. Sometimes the apple doesn't fall far from the tree, I'm thinking.

After being with Mom for about an hour, with still no sign of either Rob or Colette, Craig stepped out to the family waiting area to make a few work calls. Suddenly Col appears, with a minimal greeting (I'm sure on the part of both parties) and tells Craig something to the effect of "We've got this under control, Craig," whatever message that was supposed to send. Per Craig, he had responded with something acerbic along the lines of, "Well, considering it took us an entire day to figure out that Mom had been hospitalized, don't tell me you've got anything under control."

Colette took it in stride, and was somewhat dismissive, stating that it really wasn't that big of a deal, just a head wound that needed a few stitches; as if that should eliminate the need for us to have been contacted. Given the fact that she and Craig have already had major words between them, I know it certainly could have been much worse. Craig volunteered no information to her about how he had found out, and their interchange was brief.

The only Rob sighting of the entire day had occurred right as Craig was getting off the elevator on Mom's floor. As the door of the elevator slid open, he saw Rob's back, opening the exit door to the stairs. Craig figured Rob had been in Mom's room, and when she told him Craig was headed to the hospital, he made sure he wasn't anywhere near Mom's room. Taking the exit via the steps insured that he wouldn't run into Craig getting off the elevator. No surprises there. I'm sure he steered clear of Craig intentionally. The last thing Rob would have wanted was an exchange of words between the two of them, especially one to be witnessed by his colleagues. And, perhaps on a more subconscious level, he had to know, by Craig's presence at Holy Dis, that we were clearly aware that he hadn't contacted us, and that more than likely, through Craig's dialogue with Mom's doctors and nurses, they were aware of what had taken place as well.

"Oh, the tangled web we weave," I find myself saying to Craig as he finishes his recounting of the day. "Were you ever able to ask Mom why she was out walking on Tuesday night? I'm so curious."

His response was 'no'. He said he'd been so angered by the exchange with Col that it had completely escaped his mind. But what he had remembered to ask her was why Rob had come back to take her to Holy Dis yesterday morning. According to Mom, after Rob had left to go to work, her head had started bleeding badly and she was very dizzy. When Sandy, Mom's housekeeper, had arrived at 8 AM, she didn't like the looks of Mom, and had called Beecher's medical staff to notify them. While Sandy was with her, Mom had vomited, and Sandy made the decision to stay with her until she knew other help was coming. In the meantime, they had contacted Rob with Sandy's update, causing him to come back for the second time.

"That's quite a story," I comment. "It surprises me that Rob left her knowing that she might be at risk, without asking any of the staff there to check in on her or to follow up. Thank God that Sandy came when she did. Can you imagine Mom alone in the cottage all day thinking she just needed to suck it up?" I'm seeing God written large all over this; both in the resident that saw Mom fall even in the failing twilight, and then again in Sandy's just happening to walk through Mom's door on her usual cleaning day. There are no coincidences, and I'm reminded again that God always has things covered even when our control is nil.

Craig had also decided to call Mom's financial planner of many years, Tom Peers, to see if her long term care insurance could be activated. This was a policy she and Dad had purchased back in the early 1960's, and by today's standards, it was ridiculously generous in its monthly payouts for what were dirt cheap premiums. Craig had spoken with both Tom and with representatives from DBM, the company Mom's policy is through, trying, as he puts it, "to get our ducks in a row." This is where Craig truly shines. He is so good at thinking about what might come into play and anticipating it far ahead of its necessity. I, on the other hand, get overwhelmed just HEARING the words 'long term care insurance'. After speaking to the representatives at DBM, Craig tells me there are two qualifiers for the plan to be activated. The first involves being hospitalized for at least three consecutive days, which has strong potential. The second involves Mom meeting at least six criteria of a list of decreased cognitive function benchmarks, proving that her decline is severe enough to warrant the activation of the policy. I ask Craig if he remembers what some of them are.

He thinks for a minute. "Things like, 'Difficulty using the restroom on her own'; as in requiring assistance," he replies. "Difficulty in getting dressed on her own, difficulty in getting up and down out of a chair, let's see…forgetting to take medication unless supervised…there's a bunch more."

"It's possible she could qualify, depending on what the other criteria are," I state. "Would they make that determination later, or right now?"

"They would do it once she gets back to Beecher," Craig explains. "One of Beecher's physicians would actually evaluate Mom; the DBM rep said that the staff at retirement homes know exactly what to look for, because they do it all the time, and then that doctor signs off on the eval and it's either 'yes, she meets the criteria' or 'no, she doesn't qualify yet'. But I'm thinking it would be easier to explain to her doctor at Holy Disciple what we're thinking and see if she'll give her the three days at Holy Disciple to automatically qualify her. It would benefit her anyway to be able to stay for that length of time and be so much easier than going through the mess of qualifying back at Beecher."

"If we've got the opportunity to do it, let's move on it," I say with conviction. "Craig, thank you for looking into all this today, and dealing with everything. I know it's been tense and stressful. You've been huge."

It's just a few phone calls," he responds, and I'll go ahead and talk to her doctor about it tomorrow. Mom deserves that, Bet. But here's the other big thing I found out today. I touched base with the staff at Beecher and any time one of their residents is hospitalized, no matter where they live on the campus, whether it's condo, cottage, assisted living, when they come back to Beecher, their portal of entry is through their skilled nursing facility over at Buckman. While they're at Buckman, their progress is monitored very closely, and they receive all kinds of assistance-physical therapy, occupational therapy, whatever kind of rehab they need. Then, when they are at a point where they can be discharged, the staff meets with the family for a Care Conference, and they make a recommendation about the level of care they feel Mom will need going forward."

I sit quietly for a minute. I've been twirling my hair ever since our conversation started, and I abruptly abandon the strand. "You realize this is probably the end of Mom being in her cottage, right?" I ask it as a rhetorical question, but it comes out as a statement.

"Yeah, it probably will be," Craig quietly agrees. "We've got some tough weeks ahead of us, Bet."

"This will break her heart," I say.

"All we can do is take it one day at a time," Craig reflects. "And, if there is a bright side, at least she's IN Beecher already if she does need a higher level of assistance. Think about it, Betsy. If she wasn't already there and something like this happened to her, they never would accept her as an entry level resident."

"That's true," I respond. "And that's a huge blessing in and of itself. Well, we've got a lot to process."

We talk a little more about our weekend plans. Craig plans to go back to the hospital tomorrow, returning there on Saturday when Mom's discharged, then will get her squared away at Buckman. I'll come up to Buckman on Sunday, stay overnight, and drive back on Monday morning. He gives me Mom's phone number for her room, and we leave it that he will call tomorrow after he gets her discharged from Holy Disciple. Our phone conversation spanned 70 minutes.

I call Mom as soon as I hang up with Craig, and she sounds decently chipper. "So I hear you have six beautiful stitches," I greet her. "I can't wait to see them."

"Oh, Betsy," Mom dives right in, "the trouble I've caused all of you! I feel so stupid. When I was walking over there, I just missed a small rise in the pavement, and didn't lift my foot high enough to clear it. What a dunce! Thank goodness Margie happened to be looking out her window. She came hurrying out and stayed with me until the nicest man from security got there."

I'm shocked that she can recount her fall in such a precise fashion. Frankly, I'm amazed she remembers much at all about it. This is also my opportunity to find out what she was doing walking outside.

"Why were you walking over by Margie's?" I ask.

"Well," Mom explains, "I wanted to be sure that I knew where I was going on Wednesday morning for my doctor's appointment and I kept putting off doing it all day Tuesday. Finally, about 5:00, I made myself put on a jacket and walk over to the office. It's not that far from my cottage. It was starting to get a little dark, and I think that rise in the concrete was in shadow and that's why I tripped."

Now all of this is making perfect sense…and I can't blame Mom at all for wanting to know where the doctor's office was. If only she'd asked somebody; one of the Knoll girls, or even Sandy. That's not Mom's style, though. She's always been Miss Independence, relying on no one. It probably never even occurred to her. We talk for a while, and she says she's going home tomorrow, that Craig was there all day with her, and that Rob and Col "have been very good to me." For some reason it really bothers me that she can say that about Rob and Col, but make no comment about Craig, who isn't even IN Cincinnati and who took the entire day off work to be with her as well. Almost like Craig is a given in the equation, but she's pleasantly surprised that Rob and Col are so involved. Gag me. That double standard can really do a slow burn on me sometimes.

I mention that I've talked with Craig, and make it a point to say how great it was that he was willing to take the whole day off to be with her and that it really helped me to get all of the updates I did from him. I deliberately refrain from asking any questions about Rob staying with Mom Tuesday night, or any of the subsequent flow of events, mainly because I don't want to activate any of my own negative emotions.

In addition, I don't want any discussion about their failure to let us know Mom had been hospitalized. I have a sick feeling Mom would somehow defend them, which would infuriate me. Far into this wicked game, I'm coming to realize that sometimes, what I don't bring up can't hurt me. I tell her I'll be up for a visit this weekend, and she begs me not to come.

"Honey, you were just here last weekend," she argues, and again, I'm amazed she remembers.

"You're such good company, I can't stay away, and you know you really want to see me," I answer. "Besides, you may want to take a field trip out of Buckman, and I can be your vehicle."

We talk a few more minutes, I tell her I love her, and that I'll call tomorrow, ("But I'll have a different phone number at Buckman. Will you know what it is?" I reassure her that the staff there will know and give it to me) and lastly, I inform her of the outcome of the pumpkin contest. (I ended up placing third; complete with a Target gift certificate and a third-place ribbon.)

"I'm not surprised," she replies. "At least one good thing happened this week." And we hang up. My hand is cramping from holding the phone so long.

Mike has deliberately stayed upstairs to watch TV, so that I could have a quiet conversation downstairs. I trudge upstairs and into the lair, walking slowly over to our old couch where he's watching an episode of 'Big Bang'. He looks at me, and immediately mutes the TV.

"Not so good?" he asks, but I think he already knows the answer.

"Not so good," I answer, sinking down on the carpet in front of the couch and leaning my head against his chest. "I think Mom's fall is a game changer."

I summarize everything Craig and I talked about, condensing it as much as I can and as calmly as possible. I just don't have the energy to get emotional. Mike is quiet when I finish.

"Do you want me to go up with you on Sunday?" he asks me. I know his intentions are the best, but I know he wouldn't want to spend the night. It would mean curtailing the visit more than I would choose to if it's just me alone.

"No...not yet...but I appreciate the offer," I say. "She's

probably not going to be able to be up and around and I think the visiting quarters are tight in Buckman. Let's wait a few weeks and see how things shake out-especially following the Care Conference. That's really where the rubber will meet the road."

We sit in silence for a while, my head on his chest, his hand stroking my hair. After about ten minutes, he asks me what sounds good for dinner and we decide on scrambled eggs and toast, one of our easy fixes when both of us are too tired to make anything else. Its 9:00 by the time we eat and finish the dishes, and after watching two 'Modern Family' re-runs and the news, I drag up to bed at 10:30. There just aren't enough hours in the day.

* * * * *

It's Sunday, early afternoon, and the beginning of a whole new month. Welcome, November. It feels like November, too. The temperatures have fallen into the upper 40's, and it's one of those days where it seems like it never gets completely light, remaining a semi grey gloom, and I love it. Our trick or treaters came in droves last night and it was a relaxing night just staying home with Mike and camping out on our front porch handing out candy. I put my pumpkin on display on the front porch, sticking a pillar candle inside it to light it up. I've also attached my third-place ribbon pin to the side of the pumpkin. This is my first experience ever in winning a contest of any kind other than my music competitions, and I feel the need to flaunt it.

True to Craig's word, he had discussed wanting to initiate Mom's long term care insurance with her doctor at Holy Disciple. Dr. Venkata had been very willing to make that happen by allowing Mom to stay an additional day. Moving forward, it will just be a matter of getting paperwork completed and documentation in order. Only Craig would have been thinking that far ahead, but this will be a financial godsend for Mom.

My drive up to Cincinnati is uneventful. I had stopped at Target on my way home from work Friday night and picked up two more packs of Depends for Mom to have in Buckman. I know she'll need a lot of items from her cottage in her temporary digs and I've been jotting things down as they occur to me. I'll be curious to see if I run into Rob and Colette. It would be so much easier if they weren't around, but I have a feeling there will be a strong showing today.

In talking to Craig yesterday, he had remarked that Col seemed extremely irritated with him when he showed up at the hospital to transport Mom back to Beecher. She told him that she was capable of handling Mom's discharge. Craig wouldn't hear of it. There's no desire on either of their parts for any kind of reconciliation, nor do I ever see that changing. As I've thought more and more about the situation with Rob and Col as time has passed, trying to make sense of it all, I have really come to believe that their communication as a couple is virtually nonexistent. I don't think Craig or I have any real idea of how little they talk to one another, let alone the lack of depth in terms of what doesn't get shared. Over time I've come to believe that Col has Rob on a need-to-know basis, and probably vice versa as well.

In terms of the situation involving all of us co-signing Beecher's financial responsibility document, I've really come to believe that Rob had no idea ahead of time that Col had met with Craig and I to discuss any part of Mom's move. To this day, I'd like to believe that Colette's intentions were the best, and that she was fully prepared to contribute, but without Rob knowing any of it. I think when she finally did tell him what we had agreed on, he blew a gasket, strongly feeling that they had already "done their share".

At that point, Col was backed into a corner she hadn't anticipated and had to tell Craig that all bets were off, which is when the words between them really started flying. All of this is total conjecture on my part, and there's probably no way I'll ever know what really took place, but I have a strong feeling that it played out this way.

So, regarding Mom's fall at Beecher and all the facts surrounding her hospitalization at Holy Disciple, Col may not even know all the real details. It's possible that she knows only what Rob chose to tell her, which could be little or nothing, some truth or no truth. And, in complete fairness to Colette, maybe she had just assumed that Rob HAD called us to let us know about Mom UNTIL she got to work and a co-worker had referenced Craig calling the nursing station on Wednesday night. Who knows? As much as I hate how events played out, I don't have the mental energy to assign blame and judgment.

So, today's set-up at Buckman could be awkward, but I've already made the decision not to let it bend me over. I'll certainly be civil to Rob and Col if they're there with Mom, but only for Mom's sake. In the past, conflict of this magnitude would have unnerved me and there would have been many sleepless nights…but no more. I'm not sure where the turning point occurred for me and I think it's come incrementally, but I'm grateful for it. Age has a lot to do with it; I also feel that my faith in God has changed how I view conflict completely; mainly because it's not always the 'I'm right and they're wrong' mentality, but more the practice of sharing an opinion or feelings in love, and then moving on, with the knowledge that not everyone has to share my feelings, nor I theirs. I've become much more comfortable 'agreeing to disagree' if the process of dialogue is handled well. Though that process was never strong to begin with in our family, it's broken down completely over past year.

I'm thinking a lot about this as I drive. Partly, there's resentment, but also surprise, on my part toward Rob and Col, because I feel like I've done nothing to deserve this kind of treatment from them, other than to try to be honest, yet loving, toward them. I'm making every effort to see things through their eyes, giving them the benefit of the doubt because I know everyone sees things through a different lens of perspective. That thought always helps me find some middle ground in relationships.

Ultimately, as the situation has worsened this past year, I've had to determine for myself how much angst I'm going to allow their behavior to cause me. These are the times God amazes me by imparting the ability to 'walk through the fire unscathed', so to speak. My reliance on Him in prayer is continual, and there's a daily strength flowing through me that clearly isn't mine. In all of this, I listen for the simple, quiet voice reminding me that I am solely responsible for the condition of my own heart, and I find peace in this as I'm driving to Cincinnati today.

Craig has left the keys to Mom's cottage under her doormat, and I haul my stuff inside her cottage before walking over to Buckman. The place smells stale inside, like food might be spoiling. I'm going to need to clean out the refrigerator completely, since Mom won't be back here for at least two to three weeks, possibly not at all. Walking briskly from her cottage over to Buckman, I take a deep breath as I enter the building, riding the elevator up to the second floor and her temporary room.

* * * * *

In retrospect, it isn't a bad weekend. Rob, Colette, and all three of their boys are at Buckman with Mom when I arrive, and I can't begrudge them that. John, Jack, and James are near and dear to her heart, and I know it delights her to have them here. I enjoy seeing them myself. We end up sitting in Buckman's family waiting area watching the Bengals game (as always, they lose), which is oddly relaxing in a sterile kind of way. We're all civil to each other, made easier by the fact that Craig isn't here; it's surface interaction at best, but benign enough.

Still, in reading Rob's body language, I can tell immediately by the set of his tight jaw that he's either angry, uncomfortable, or both. Possibly he's on call and stressed, or just irritated that he isn't doing something different with his afternoon. I wish he would leave. Col asks me if I'm just up for the day, and I make it clear that I'm spending the night and driving back tomorrow morning. They leave about 4:30, which gives me a good amount of time with just Mom.

Buckman is depressing and I'm sure Mom feels this as well. It has the distinct feel and smell of a nursing home, versus the cozy independence of her cottage. And, in reality, it IS far closer to a nursing home in many ways. In talking to the nurse, Rose, that will be supervising Mom's rehab program, Mom will receive physical and occupational therapy every day, including weekends, until her discharge. The physical therapy should build her back up strength-wise; the occupational strengthening her proficiency in performing simple 'life tasks'. She's working on lifting items, getting up and down out of a chair, and using a Claw. I've seen elderly people use these before and never knew that's what this gadget was called. Basically, it's an arm-like extension that has large pincers on the end that close around whatever object you need; preventing bending over or reaching down.

During the time I'm here, the therapist comes to get Mom for her occupational session, trundling her downstairs in a wheelchair that is collapsed and parked in a corner of her small room. She's sharing it with another lady, Carol, who has had back surgery and will be in Buckman for at least a month rehabbing. Carol seems nice enough, but I can tell Mom isn't happy about these close living quarters.

"I just wish she wouldn't talk to me," Mom remarks. "I really don't have anything to say to her and I'm tired of hearing about her kids."

This is classic Mom and I laugh out loud. "Tell her you need to meditate," I suggest.

Mom rolls her eyes. "That would go over like a lead balloon," she answers, but I can tell she's amused.

Her stitches are big and angry, extending down the

back, left side of her head from roughly the center to about mid-ear level, and they have shaved a big patch of her hair away where the stitches are. It looks pitiful and exposed. She's also using a walker now and I'm shocked by how weak she's become in just four days. Coordinating movement, especially getting up and down, is a huge challenge for her, especially if she's trying to get out of bed by using her walker.

I go to therapy with her, and once we're back from the hour-long session, I ask her what sounds good for dinner. She tells me she's not hungry, which I had anticipated. I'm starving and going to hit the coffee shop for soup and a sandwich, so I bring another sandwich and a milk shake back for Mom. Maybe that will tempt her appetite more than Buckman's dinner on a cafeteria tray. So we have some freedom from Carol, I set up our soup and sandwiches in the waiting area where we watched the Bengals game, wheeling Mom down in her chair, and we eat there instead of in her bedroom. She inhales the better part of the turkey sandwich I got for her, and all the chocolate milk shake, which delights me. She's such a sucker for milk shakes.

After we're back in her room, I run through a list I have compiled of things she might need from her cottage. Craig had already brought quite a few items on Friday when he settled her into Buckman initially, but I want to be sure she has everything she needs before I leave tomorrow morning. She mentions some more clothes, some other pajamas, her favorite pair of slippers, Depends and her makeup, so I headed over to retrieve these. I've stashed the Depends that I brought on the floor of her closet, where they are visible, and we joke about her using the Claw to pull them out. I've cut a huge seam down the middle of the bag so all of them are exposed, and Mom "practices" pulling them out of the bag with her Claw. At one point during our practice session, Mom has the Claw fully extended, and she has just closed the 'pincers' around the top pair of Depends in the stack. To complicate things, she's standing inside the steel perimeter of her walker, and the Claw has to be completely free of the walker. In a cramped space, this is no small feat. Mom slowly starts to bring the Claw back towards herself, with the Depends safely imprisoned between the pincers. Suddenly she loses her grip on the pincers, and they open, enough to let the pair of Depends slip sideways, then falling out of the pincers completely.

"Damn," Mom says, rather loudly. "I thought these Claws were more reliable."

For some reason, I think because she said it so matter of fact, I lose it laughing. I'm sitting on the bed watching this, and once I start, I can't stop. No one has ever accused me of having a quiet laugh, either. Mom, encased in the walker, can only pivot slightly to see me, because she can't let go of the sides, but I can tell she is highly amused as well, and that she's laughing too, by her profile. I fall back on the bed, guffawing.

"What? What is it? What's so funny?" comes Carol's voice from the other side of the curtain, which divides the room in half for privacy, and is currently drawn shut.

Mom draws herself up in the walker, using her arms for support. Turning her head as far as she can towards Carol's side of the room, and in her most imperious voice, she says loudly, "Nothing for you to worry about. Betsy has dropped something, that's all."

Now I am literally hysterical. The thought of Mom thinking fast enough to blame this on me is funny enough, but it's the entire situation. Mom just stands tall in the walker, staring into the closet, as if she thinks the dropped Depends will somehow leap into the grasp of the Claw and become cooperative.

Finally, I get myself under control and wiping my eyes, I slither off the bed and over to Mom's side, motioning to Carol and making the 'loony' sign with my hand at ear level. Mom is still grinning, shaking her head in mock disgust. I pick up the dropped Depends, put it in the Claw's pincers, and say to Mom, "Now bring it towards you." She does, and this time is able to get it all the way up to her walker, resting the Depends on the bar of the walker, and removing it from the grippers.

"That's a lot of work for one Depends," she states, and I start laughing again. There are still times when her sense of humor blindsides me. And again, for someone consumed with appearances for so many years, it's refreshing to be able to joke about the need for a Depends.

We watch some TV in the family area and take several walks (using her walker) around the square of hallway that makes up Mom's floor at Buckman. We talk about how important it will be to build up her physical strength, versus just lying in bed between therapy sessions.

"The more you push yourself to be up and around, the quicker you'll get your balance and sea legs back," I tell her, knowing how much she already wants to be out of here after just two days. She has asked me repeatedly when she'll get "to go home to my cottage", and each time I have patiently explained that they will build her back up with all of her therapy first, then evaluate how they think she's doing and decide if she's ready.

She has asked me very pointedly, "You mean I might be stuck here for good?" referring to Buckman.

As honestly as possible, I've explained that she wouldn't stay at Buckman permanently, but that assisted living might be a middle of the road option for her. Craig and I have decided that we'd better start mentioning the possibility to Mom and preparing her for what could lie ahead.

I help her change into a fresh undergarment, and a clean pair of pajamas around 9:00. Next comes washing her face, brushing her teeth, and running a brush through her hair, being careful to avoid contact with the stitches. All these simple rituals take well over half an hour due to Mom's slowness and seeming inability to initiate any activity on her own. I'm happy to have helped her with all of them, and I know she's clean and comfortable, but there is absolutely no way she could be doing this on her own, and I have a feeling that no amount of occupational therapy in the next several weeks is going to reverse that. Buckman will stabilize Mom, at best, but there will be no reversals, and certainly no miracles. I kiss her goodnight before I head over to the cottage and tell her I'll pop in before I head back to Louisville in the morning.

"Oh, Betsy, thank you for being here," she tells me, sighing heavily. "If I have to be here, at least it's better when you're with me. But you need to stop coming up every weekend. Mike needs you."

"Mike's fine on his own," I tell her. "Promise me you'll take good care of yourself and get as strong as you can."

"I'll do my best," she tells me. "My cottage is missing me."

I kiss her goodnight and head back to her cottage with some work ahead of me. I clean out the refrigerator completely, and then get a couple of bags of items together for Dan and Mary Claire. Knowing with almost 100% certainty that Mom won't be coming back here to live, I know that Craig and I will have to "pare down" yet another time to further accommodate the dwindling space Mom will have in assisted living. It's ironic to think that just about the time I was able to get her cottage organized completely, with only the items that Mom truly needed, she'll be making another move to half again the amount of space, minus even a garage.

* * * * *

I make it safely back to work Monday morning, with time to spare. I'm touched by the amount of concern expressed by numerous co-workers. They ask me about Mom's progress; how my drive back to Louisville was; Jeannie asks if Rob and Col were there on Sunday afternoon with me. Their interest always surprises me, and I'm very grateful for it. I can tell they're rooting for Mom, especially Linda, Jeannie, and

Patsy McKiernan. With many of us having aging parents, this hits close to home for everyone.

On Friday, November 5th, one of the nurses from Buckman calls Craig to let him know that they'd like to do Mom's Care Conference the following Friday, the 12th. Since the hospitalization mayhem with Mom, he has talked to the staff at Beecher and asked that they place him first in line of contact, which they have done and were very understanding about it. I go ahead and let Linda know I'll be off that day, and her response is to give me a big hug and tell me Mom is lucky to have me. I thank God for a supervisor as understanding as Linda.

Even as concerned as I am about the evaluation and its impact on Mom, I'm glad there's a definitive date set. This has been a stressful period for all of us. Mom's progress has been slow; minimal at best, nor has there been the rebound we'd all hoped for. It's as if the fall has popped the top off a whole can of degenerative issues, and they've all blown up on us since. In the back of my mind, I still wonder if Mom is having trouble with her stomach, and I hate it that she couldn't keep her appointment with her doctor at Beecher. There hasn't been any more vomiting since she's been at Buckman, which is encouraging, nor has she said anything to me about the abdominal pressure she had described to me, but I worry about everything else masking the issue. I've discussed it with Craig, and he felt that if it was bothering Mom, she would have mentioned it to one of the nurses, especially Rose, but I'm not so sure. The last thing Mom would want at this point is to be shipped out to Holy Disciple for more testing, only to return to Buckman a second time for re-entry and more rehab. I guess we just wait and see. Again, that grey area.

I've checked in every day, usually twice…I know Col and Rob have stepped up their game and Col's been there at least every other day, because often she's sitting with Mom in her room when I call in the evenings. Craig has also made numerous trips down, picking up food for her on the way, checking her mail at the cottage and bringing it over to Buckman. He's also taken care of any paperwork he can, including her bills. Again, I am so frustrated by my drive distance; my two hours from Cincinnati feels like a two-day flight right now. But, as much as I feel like my life is up for grabs, I strongly feel God's leading and loving presence in this situation, whatever the outcome is to be. And, being surrounded by Mike, Callie, Kerry, Craig, and Mary Claire is worth its weight in gold.

* * * * *

Friday morning, November 12th, and I'm heading to Cincinnati for what they term the 'Care Conference' at Beecher. Today will be the meeting of the minds to determine the best subsequent care for Mom. More like a sentencing, if you ask me. This will not be an easy day for any of us, but especially not for Mom. I've asked God for peace; (for all of us) for His will to be done, and to give me words of clarity, kindness, and love when it comes to selling this to Mom. I'm driving without any music on, feeling both the weight and the serenity of this late autumn morning. Crisp and clear, the predominant tree color is just the sere brown of November-bleak and oddly comforting in its uniformity.

I've allotted plenty of extra time, and the bridge traffic is moving well, so I pull into Buckman a good 35 minutes early. The first words out of mom's mouth are, "They better let me go back to my cottage," and my heart sinks.

I ask her if there's anything I can help her with, and again, her through-line: "Make them let me go back to my cottage." I have to laugh.

"Why don't you tell me how you really feel?" I tease her, as I bring her walker over to the chair she's sitting in, lining it up with her body so she can pull up directly into it. She's having trouble, so I half lift, half push her into the center of the walker, and she slowly moves her body to align with each side of it.

"Do you want to head on down to the conference room, or just go for a walk?" I'm asking her, when Colette appears. She's in her scrubs with a coat thrown over them, having come directly from Holy Disciple, I guess.

"Well, hello there," Mom greets Col. "You certainly didn't have to come to this." I know Mom doesn't mean this to sound dismissive, and I hope Col doesn't interpret it that way. Privately, I'm glad she's here. Regardless of everything that's happened, I appreciate the solidarity, especially with her nursing background. Secondly, she'll get to hear all the recommendations first-hand, which should eliminate any second guessing from Rob.

Colette smiles at Mom and me and steadies Mom's walker as she moves into the doorway. "I wanted to hear what they have to say, Joan," she answers simply, and mom moves off down the hall in front of us toward the conference room. I guess she knows where she's going. As we trail Mom down the hall, Col leans in to me, and apropos of nothing, whispers, "She smells like pee."

The timbre of her statement catches me off guard; it's out of character for Col, and I'm momentarily not sure how to respond.

"She probably needs to change her Depends," I surmise, wishing I had helped Mom get a fresh one on while we were back in her room. I hope my answer will make Col stop talking about it.

"They don't do a good job of monitoring that here," Col remarks, and again, I'm irritated, because I feel like she's judging the entire nursing staff at Buckman. This is where my anger can rise very quickly, because, with Col and Rob refusing to own any potential responsibility for Mom's financial future, criticizing protocol seems pretty petty. That's ridiculous on my part, I know, because she still has a right to her opinion, but it annoys me anyway. I remind myself that Colette has always had strong opinions; about everything. The two of us are just on a different playing field now when it comes to dealing with them.

In response to her comment I say only, "These nurses definitely have their hands full," and let it go. As we reach the conference room, Craig steps off the elevator and comes towards us, looking impassive, as always. Greeting us both, he gives Mom a kiss on the cheek.

"How are you, ace?" he asks her.

"I'll be better when I'm back in my cottage," she replies tersely, clink-clinking the walker into the conference room, with a 'let's get this over with' air.

He looks at me, throws his hands up, and makes a face, obviously acknowledging the challenge that awaits us during this Care Conference. Someone's going to need to care for me when it's over, I'm sure. We get Mom settled in a chair, and by this time the professional staff is gathering. Her occupational therapist is present, introducing herself all around as Anita. Rose is there as well, and the social worker they assigned to Mom when she was first admitted to Buckman. She'll be the one to discuss the results of the cognitive tests. Craig, Col and I introduce ourselves to each of them, and the meeting gets under way. I'm sitting closest to Mom, with her on my right. Col is to my left, Craig to her left, and the three staff members sit directly across from us on the other side of the table.

The social worker, Doreen, begins by talking about how many factors support their recommendations, and that they're based on a combination of tests, observations, and criteria to support their decision. She emphasizes the point that the resident's well-being is their first and foremost goal, and how any transition is hard, but that Beecher's staff is equipped to help make it as seamless as possible. I sit back in my chair and glance over at Mom, absolutely hating this for her. She's hunkered down in her wheelchair, her white hair askew every which way even though I brushed it back in her room. Her gnarled hands are folded neatly in her lap, right on top of left, and she's very still. Listening and waiting, her head pronates slightly forward.

Doreen begins to discuss the findings of the cognitive tests, and I find that she's looking more at me than at Col or Craig. Why, I'm not sure. Oh, probably because she knows I'm The Daughter, per my introduction. She's very honest, but in a gentle, caring manner, and I deeply appreciate that. She tells us (me) that Mom is showing marked cognitive deterioration, and in a series of tests, required extensive verbal prompting for any kind of task completion. I immediately recall helping her get ready for bed two weeks ago when I was up here, and I need no further clarification. Based on these findings, this totally rules out her returning to live in an unsupervised living situation.

She also cites the fact that Mom could not remember what day, month, or year it was, or name our current president. Poor Mom. It's like being at a parent teacher conference and being told your child is failing abysmally. Their unanimous recommendation is that Mom be placed in their assisted living facility (Breck) which, Doreen points out, is really the best of both worlds, because Mom will still have a large degree of independence, with the added resource of nurses checking in on her every two hours. The nursing staff assists residents with daily showers, administers daily meds, and are on hand to help with trips to the bathroom, if needed. Each assisted living apartment contains a bedroom, living area, tiny kitchen (no stove, just refrigerator and cabinets), and its own bathroom with a shower.

"But I can do all that on my own," Mom counters. "It's not a problem." It's literally as if she hasn't heard Doreen just speaking.

"You would certainly do your best, Mom," I respond, since no one else says anything. I turn to look right at her. One of the components of the meeting that has been difficult for me so far has been the fact that I feel like Mom has been 'talked over'. I understand some of it is unavoidable, because the staff has to pitch it to us, making sure Craig, Col and I understand the specifics, but there are points in the discussion where it feels like Mom is being unintentionally ignored. She needs her turn too, to say whatever she wants to, and whatever she feels necessary.

I continue, "But, Mom, if you were back in your cottage and you fell while you were inside, you probably wouldn't be able to get to the phone. We'd never forgive ourselves if that happened. You were so lucky Margie saw you fall this time, and that you were outside when it happened."

"Bet," Mom says plaintively, as if she's dealing with a five-year old, "that's the good part about living over there. (She motions vaguely with her right hand in the direction of her cottage.) Everybody knows everybody else, and we all look out for each other. If I did fall again, and I don't plan on it, all my friends would be there to help me."

I'm not going to point out the flaws in Mom's argument to her in front of everyone, but I can clearly see the level of her cognitive deterioration even in how basic her arguments are. If she fell inside her cottage, no one would know because she lives alone. Even if she fell outside, unless someone happened to see her go down, no one would know. Either way, it leaves her in an extremely vulnerable position.

"Mom," I begin again, I know how much you love your friends in the Knolls, but you'll still have them, and you can still do things with them. You'll just be a phone call away."

"It won't be the same," Mom says sadly, shaking her head. "I won't BE there anymore. They'll forget about me. Besides, what are we going to do with all of my furniture?"

Rose steps up to the plate on this. "You get to take it with you, Miss Joan," she reassures Mom. This strappin' young man here," and she leans down the table and winks at Craig, "will be making plans to get it into your new apartment for you. You just order him around and tell him exactly where you want it."

Craig laughs and says, "She orders me around already, Rose. I'm used to it."

Mom is just sitting in silence, seemingly not following this. I can't tell if she's mad, thinking, or both.

"I know this isn't easy for you, Mom," I continue, "and it isn't easy for us, either. You don't know how much I wish you COULD stay in your cottage. I feel like you just got settled there and started putting down some roots, and now you're being asked to make another huge change. It's so unfair. First, we tell you it's not safe for you to drive anymore, and now, on top of that, we're telling you that you can't live on your own. I know it probably feels like we're the ones making all the rules, and that you don't have a say in anything, but we're basing these decisions on the sound advice of people who know exactly what they're doing, and whose job it is to make these recommendations."

"And Mom, here's the other thing; the most important thing. We love you too much NOT to listen to their advice. As much as we know how much you want your independence, it just isn't the best, or the wisest option for you anymore. Our job now is to try to find you the best of both worlds, like Doreen said-to give you some independence, but also to make sure that you're safe. Moving to Breck will be the best of both worlds. Craig and Col and I all want to see you happy…always…but we also want you to be supervised, because that gives us peace of mind. Can you see that a little bit through our eyes, too?"

There's a long silence for several minutes, during which no one says anything. Col, especially, has said nothing through the entire Care Conference thus far. Then Mom quietly says, "I suppose so, Bet. I'm not happy about it, though."

Instinctively I put my arm around her. "And you know what?" I ask her. "You don't have to be. You can complain about it whenever you want to, Mom. You've been such a good sport about so much, especially all the change you've had to deal with recently. You're allowed to whine, and I promise we'll listen, but let's at least give it a try, okay? It's a big move, for sure, but all of us will be here for you, and we'll help you make it work."

She says nothing, but turns to look at me and nods slowly, and at that point I see a tear spill out of her left eye and roll down her cheek. This is more than I can bear. "It really will be okay," I say softly to her, with a lump in my throat. I gently wipe the tear away with my left thumb.

"I'm sad for you, too," I say quietly. "I'll miss being with you in your cottage. But, you know, Mom, Dad would be wanting this extra fall net for you, too. He would never have wanted you to be alone where you could possibly hurt yourself. I think he would have made the same decision."

"Probably," she answers quietly.

Rose speaks up, "Miss Joan, another thing we need to talk about is getting some meat back on your bones, and that's another big plus to being at Breck. You'll be eating three meals a day down in their dining room. And honey, their food is gooood. You won't have to worry about fixing your own meals anymore. It'll all be done for you, and you can have these folks (she gestures around to Col, Craig and me) eating with you whenever you want."

At this point, Col stands up and goes out into the hallway, pulling her phone out of her coat as she goes, presumably to take a call. I can hear her speaking to someone, and then she re-enters the room, puts her coat on, and says apologetically, "I'm sorry, I'm going to have to head back to work. They're getting really busy." She moves down the side of the table to give Mom a kiss goodbye, telling her she'll see her soon. I thank Colette for coming, and she heads out.

Rose resumes, "Miss Joan, you lost a lot of weight the eight months you were living in your cottage. When you first came to Beecher, you weighed 121 pounds, which is about right for you. When you came to Buckman three weeks ago, you were only 110 pounds. You lost 11 pounds in those eight months. Honey, something tells me you were forgetting to eat sometimes, which is no good. We need to beef you back up again. And here's the other thing, Miss

Joan…your blood iron is way low. Your lab work showed that you were 8.5 when you came to us at Buckman. Normal hemoglobin is 12 to 14 thousand. It's no wonder you're tired all the time. The staff at Breck will make sure you're eating well and getting your energy back."

The rest of the meeting deals with more specific issues. Since there are no available units in Breck, Mom will be moving into a temporary one in the building until a permanent one becomes available. In the meantime, we hang on to the cottage. I find myself thinking what a bonus that will be, allowing Mom to go back there periodically with one of us, as well as the fact that we won't need to make any hasty decisions about what to keep and what to get rid of. Mom will move into Breck on November 23rd, the Tuesday before Thanksgiving, remaining in Buckman until then and continuing her therapy.

Craig and I thank Doreen, Rose, and Mom's therapist at the close of the meeting for their kindness, understanding, and positive attitude. They've done a wonderful job putting a positive spin on what is anything but a positive situation. Craig needs to go back to work, and he kisses Mom goodbye, telling her what a trooper she is. He motions to me that he'll call me when I'm on my way back to Louisville, and now it's just Mom and me. I have a sudden idea, if the Buckman staff thinks Mom is strong enough and gives me the go ahead. I find Rose, pull her aside, and run my plan by her.

"Sure, honey, I think your Mom would love that," she agrees. "She's steady enough now on her feet as long as she's using that walker. You just keep a close eye on her getting up and down on the sidewalks."

Mom and I get back to her room, and I tell her I'm going to get us some lunch over at the grille.

"There's a surprise for you when I get back," I tell her.

"I think I've had enough surprises for one day, don't you?" she asks me pointedly.

On the way out, I make it a point to find Doreen. After

I've thanked her for her gentle way of explaining things to Mom, I ask, tentatively, "So this cognitive deterioration… and I know you see a lot of it…will it continue rapidly, or will it level off now that her body's stabilized following her fall? What can we expect going forward?"

Doreen looks me straight in the eyes, and responds soberly, "Based on what I'm seeing, I think your Mom is going to continue to decline rapidly. Be prepared and enjoy her as much as you can right now. I think you're seeing the tip of the iceberg, and it's only going to accelerate."

I nod wordlessly.

"They'll take good care of her in Breck," she reassures me. "And it seems like you have a very supportive family."

Again, I nod, and thank her. No need to divulge family dysfunction.

I head down out of the building, and over to the grille in a funk, re-processing the Care Conference. Once our lunch is ordered and paid for, I walk back to Buckman with it, and tell Mom she'd better put a coat on.

"Where are we going?" she asks me. "You've got our lunch already."

I give her the choice of the wheelchair or her walker, and she chooses the walker.

"Where are you ladies taking off to?" Carol queries from her side of the room. The curtain dividing the room is no longer drawn, and all our activity has been plainly visible to her.

"Betsy has a surprise for me," Mom answers Carol.

Carol claps her hands. "That sounds fun," she says. "Just be back before dark," and she and my mom both titter. I have no idea what this private joke is about, but I find it highly amusing. Even more surprising is Mom's comment to Carol as we leave the room.

"This'll be you before too much longer, as well as you're doing with your therapy."

I'm amazed to hear Mom offering such warm encouragement to someone who three weeks ago she wanted nothing to do with; especially after the morning Mom's had. Cognitive deterioration, yes…but her spirit is still enlarging.

"It feels good to be outside," Mom remarks as we move out and beyond Buckman's automated doors. She takes several steps out towards the parking lot, and then stops uncertainly and turns towards me. "Are we going to your car?" she asks.

"Nope," I answer. "To your cottage. Rose felt that you're strong enough to walk over there. We can eat lunch, check your mail, and hang out over there for the rest of the afternoon."

Mom looks utterly pleased. "That sounds divine," she says, and we head off. She knows exactly how to get there and does exceedingly well using the walker. Her only challenge is the slight incline from the parking lot up to where the sidewalk starts. Still, I'm thrilled she gets to be out for a while. I want her to feel empowered, and more normal… like a few things are back in her grasp.

We have a good time being back in her cottage. We devour lunch at the table, Mom eating her entire sandwich, all her chocolate shake, and half of an apple that I bought and sliced up for us. "You're probably at 115 right now," I joke.

She talks about how long it's been since she's had her hair done, and how badly she needs a permanent. "Easy remedy for that," I remark. "Let's do it the day I'm up here to help you move into Breck. I can call and schedule it right now."

She's fine with the idea, so we get it on the books. The 23rd will be an optimal day for Mike to come up with me, allowing Craig and him to do the necessary moving while Mom and I are at the beauty salon. Mom seems less tired now than she has in a long time, and I can't tell if it's just the adrenaline rush of being back in her cottage, or that she's just glad to be away from Buckman. She looks through her mail, opening several cards from friends at church who know about her fall. We watch an episode of 'Andy of Mayberry' and one of 'Let's Make A Deal', Mom counseling the contestant NOT to choose Door 3.

"Nothing good is ever behind that door," is her sage advice. Around 4:00, I tell Mom we'd better return her to prison.

"Only for a few more weeks," she retorts.

I smile, so glad that she remembers this. We take a few more pieces of clothes back with us, as well as her heavier winter jacket. "Mom," I tell her, "I'm so proud of the way you're handling this. You really could have made yourself and everybody else miserable about it…it's a lot to get used to all at once."

"Well, if it has to happen, and I guess it does, I might as well make the best of it," she answers. "It's not the end of the world."

"I think you're going to end up liking it more than you think," I comment.

"You're pushing it, Bet," she remarks drily.

As always, I hate leaving. This has been a buster of a day, and Mom gets the gold medal for being Most Accepting And Agreeable. As I make my I-275 connections, I'm lost in thought processing the day. In some ways, I feel like a month has gone by since I left to drive up this morning. One of the things I cannot help but be touched by is thinking back on Mom's comments about leaving her friends in The Knolls. How Mom, who hasn't made a new friend in 30 years, is so concerned about leaving a group of women behind that she's only known for eight months. Obviously, there has been a big emotional investment in these relationships in a short amount of time. Mom extended herself immediately upon moving into the Knolls, and she's done a lot socially with this group of four women that she didn't even know a year ago.

One of the saddest things for me is realizing how much she has enjoyed meeting these new people and doing things with them. If only she could have had this opportunity six or seven years ago when she had so much more time and health to invest. That's still hard to think about.

Another thing so apparent to me is how strong Mom's will to live still seems. Her digging her heels in on moving to assisted living, while unrealistic, tells me she's still got some spunk left, and is willing to put up a fight. To me, that speaks volumes. Still, it is incredibly painful to have heard what we did from Doreen and Rose today. I feel like I didn't see her decline in its entirety…I knew it was happening, but somehow, I failed to connect all the dots. Now I'm beating myself up for missing it. Were Craig and I in denial? As I look back over the last year of Mom's life now, I feel like what I did wasn't nearly enough. Our support wasn't aggressive or comprehensive enough, and there's a lot of guilt in that for me.

In fairness to the situation, and knowing Mom like I do, I wanted to give her every opportunity to maintain her independence, and I know the same holds for Craig. But maybe our desire for her independence, based on what we knew she would want, also worked to her detriment. I look back at her decline in hygiene, her weight loss, her anemia, and possibly even her fall, because if I had been going with her to the doctor's, she wouldn't have been walking to the building by herself, and I wish I would have monitored all these things so much more closely than I did. It's easy to second guess it all after the fact, but I think that subconsciously, maybe I was waiting for a "marker" to guide me forward. Her fall has been that wake-up call, and from here forward, I'll be taking a much more active role of advocacy for Mom.

All these thoughts take form, hovering and sinking as I process, until I feel peace, and my mind is still. I reach the beautiful stretch of I-275 that winds through the farmland and hills of Indiana and dig through my CD's for something to listen to. Latching onto a recording of last year's Christmas concert at church, I pop it into the player, and am filled with calm and a strong sense of God's presence as I drive south. The sunset is blazing and glorious, and as I hit I-71, I realize that God knew in advance how difficult today would be. None the less, He has been with me the entire day, giving me just the right words to strengthen and encourage Mom, and carrying both of us forward. Despite the emotional exhaustion I should feel, there is quiet endurance. And, as much as I wish I could be off tomorrow, I know He will bless my Saturday morning at work as well.

Thank you, Lord, for your faithfulness.

Joan, On Her Own

Chapter Ten

WE GATHER TOGETHER
(Thanksgiving – December 7th, 2010)

I love it when Callie and Kerry are home. They fill our home with an energy that Mike and I can't. It's their youth and their zest for life, and I draw heavily from this vibrancy. Kerry arrives home for Thanksgiving the Tuesday evening of the day Mike and I move Mom. Wednesday night brings Callie, driving up from Nashville after working all day. That's when I really feel complete; with them home and under roof. It's a reunion of joy, even though all of us are exhausted.

I work Wednesday after being off on Tuesday to help Mom move into Breck, Kerry doing a lot for me that day in the way of shopping and food prep to help with the Thanksgiving meal for Thursday. Our original plan had been to go to Dayton to spend Thanksgiving with Craig, Loire, and their girls. Craig had planned on picking Mom up on Wednesday, or possibly Thursday morning, depending on how she was feeling, and driving her to

Dayton, but Mom doesn't seem well enough to be away from Beecher that long.

It's as if any additional progress since the Care Conference has completely halted, and I find myself wondering if Mom has 'quit trying' once she realized there was no chance of returning to her cottage. She hasn't mentioned it in any of her phone conversations to Craig or me, but I suspect it's had an internal impact that would be hard to quantify. What also keeps surfacing in my thoughts is the comment Doreen made when I spoke with her privately at the end of the meeting, which was to expect the rate of decline both cognitively and physically to accelerate; that this was basically the tip of the iceberg. Mom is still very pleasant to all of us, seems to recognize us, know our names; nor does she seem angry, bitter, or even confused. Instead, we decided it would be easier for us to bring Thanksgiving to Mom, and we're going to do our big meal in her cottage. I'm hoping that the feeling of us being in "her" home will perk her up a little.

Her move into assisted living on Tuesday went well. Mike took the day off and drove up with me to help Craig, and they moved some of her smaller pieces of furniture over into her temporary room on the fourth floor of Breck. They also brought a lot of personal items to make the place feel more like home-lamps, her bedspread, afghan, some of her free-standing pictures, and whatever plants they could. While they lugged furniture, I took Mom to get her permanent. She had seemed tired and irritable on the way to the beauty shop, agitated about what pieces of furniture Mike and Craig were bringing over to Breck.

"I really should be over there supervising all of this," she remarked as we pulled out of Beecher.

I tried to reassure her, telling her that with it being a temporary room, they wouldn't be moving anything big, and that everything would remain untouched in her cottage until it was time to move into a permanent room. I also suggested her doing a personal inventory once we got back from the beauty shop, telling her that I could get anything else she wanted at that point. "I'm a good little pack mule," I assured her. It had occurred to me that if we could get as much as possible in the way of her small items over to her temporary room, it would make the final move out of her cottage much easier.

Her permanent took about two and a half hours, and once Pam, her beautician, got rolling, I slipped back to the break room in the back of the shop, made a pot of coffee, and did some journaling, walking up front periodically to check on Mom. She had obviously told Pam about her move into assisted living, because Pam was teasing her about being able to order people around for her every whim. Pam knows exactly how to play Mom, what tone to take with her, and still manage to treat her like a queen. Mom was smiling, but I could tell it was an effort for her. Once Pam had rolled all of Mom's hair, and applied the solution, she parked her under one of the hooded hair dryers.

When I came up to check on her, Mom motioned for me to lean down under the dryer hood, and proceeded to tell me, with the most vigor she had evidenced all day, "Bet, you really shouldn't be back there in their break room. That's where they go between appointments to relax, and they can't do that when you're back there."

A flash of irritation went through me, and I found myself thinking, *Only Mom would notice this and call me out on it*, but, maybe she had a point. Besides, I didn't want her concerned about my being back there, so I packed up my journal and came out to sit near her. Strange to be 53 and feel like I just got my hand slapped. Some parental dynamics never change.

Mom looked like a new person once Pam had completely combed out her perm, fluffed and sprayed it. She still has a beautiful, thick head of snowy white hair, and it looked soft and well-trimmed. I'm glad I carried through on doing this. Hopefully seeing how good it looks will lift Mom's spirits. As Pam rotated her around to face the mirror, Mom smiled a happy, genuine smile.

"Well, I can join the land of the living again," she stated.

Pam leaned down and hugged Mom's shoulders. "You were way overdue, Joan," she said. "It looks really good. Now you go behave yourself and start snapping your fingers at those nurses," she told her. "And listen…" she added, "You enjoy that new apartment."

She winked at me as she helped Mom out of the chair and into her walker. People like Pam remind me of how important kindness is in the world, and how something as small as a gesture or comment can make a huge difference.

We stopped to pick up lunch on the way back to Beecher and ordered a few extra sandwiches and fries for Mike and Craig. Now that Mom could focus completely on the task at hand, her preoccupation with the move was hurtling off the charts. Once we parked and got up to her room, Mike and Craig showed her what they had brought over already, telling her they could bring anything else she would like.

Instead of thanking them, or even looking around for what else she might need, she stated in no uncertain terms, "I need to get over there to look at everything, so I know exactly what I have."

I looked at both Craig and Mike and suppressed a smile. This is a flash of 'old mom', and I could tell Craig would have no patience with it. He tried to explain that with it being a temporary room, there wasn't a lot of room for any big pieces of furniture. This room is already furnished with the essentials; a couch, bed, desk, and a large recliner-like chair that has a remote on it to assist a resident in getting up from it.

"We brought over what would fit, but you don't want anything else in here, or you're not even going to have room to walk around, especially with your walker." He looked at Mike for support in this line of thought. Mike nodded like it was his job.

"Let's start a list of anything you want that isn't here, like we talked about," I suggested. "You probably want more of your clothes, and definitely more of your shoes."

"We brought your plants over," Mike said helpfully, as if this would be a game changer. Like Pam, he winked at me. So much winking around the elderly!

"It looks pretty home-y to me," I commented, really wanting to bust out laughing. Truth is, I felt badly for Mom, because I knew, even though it was semi-amusing to us, it wasn't at all humorous to her. Again, for the umpteenth time, everything was beyond her control. I also wondered if she fully grasped the idea that the apartment she's in was only temporary; that once she moved into her real room, everything would be moved over.

"You know, Mom," I started, "everything in your cottage stays exactly the way it is-untouched by anybody until you get into your real room in Breck. This is just your 'motel room' right now. Plus, you'll be over at your cottage for Thanksgiving in two more days. Anything you see then that you want to bring over, we'll do it. Craig and Mike are probably ready to call it a day for now."

I made a few more trips with Mike to carry more clothes and bathroom items over and felt like Mom had pretty much all she needed for the time being. Craig mentioned walking down to Breck's dining room with her, so she'd know exactly where she's going for her first meal that night. The elevator took us down to a big open waiting area that was the entrance to Breck. Replete with couches, comfy armchairs, end tables, and even a grand piano in a smaller alcove of the room, it gave the feeling of a huge, slightly dated living room. Via two big French doors, the dining room opened off the middle of the waiting area and ran the entire length of the back of the building. The entire back wall was continuous windows that looked out on the grounds, and it gave the dining room a sunny, airy feel. Visible outside were numerous birches and pines sloping up a gentle hill. Walking into the dining room, it struck me that this room was probably designed to be the type of dining room that most of the residents would have had as homeowners 25 to 30 years ago. It probably provides a strong visual of their family rearing, middle of life years, or the time frame they would have done the bulk of their entertaining. It had a very traditional, somewhat heavy feel, with lots of dark wood-a huge, heavy buffet off to one side of the room, and a monster of an antique china cabinet in a recessed portico off to my right. All the tables were round, with generous amounts of space between them for easy walker and wheelchair access.

"How will I know where to sit?" Mom asked anxiously, which, ironically, I also wondered.

"We'll check with one of the nurses," Craig replied. "One of them stopped in your room while you were at the beauty shop. I think they have information they want to go over with you, to get you familiar with everything."

"Well, I wish you would have let me know that earlier," Mom said, with obvious irritation in her voice.

Mike and Craig exchanged highly amused glances, and Craig shrugged and threw his hands up behind Mom's back.

"We'll catch one of the nurses when we go back up and find out everything," I told Mom, and after looking around a few more minutes, we headed back up to her room.

"I'll also need to know what time to be down there to eat," Mom remarked as we ascended in the elevator.

Upstairs, Craig found the nurse that had stopped in earlier looking for Mom, and she came down to Mom's room to chat, introducing herself as Crystal. She was very sweet, asking Mom a lot of questions about where she had lived before coming to Breck, if she had lived in this area of Cincinnati before coming to Beecher, and how many children she had. All three of us let Mom do the talking. A tad dismissive of Crystal at first, Mom gradually warmed up as she could tell Crystal was genuinely interested in what she had to say. I noticed that she didn't rush Mom and listened well. She nodded quietly as Mom spoke, watching her closely. I was suddenly very thankful she was a nurse on this floor.

After they talked a bit, Crystal said, "Well, Mrs. Bradshaw, we are really happy to have you with us. I know it can't be easy to leave your cottage. I know how nice those are, but I promise you we'll grow on you. Let me walk you through some of the things it's good to know, and then I'll answer any questions you might have. By the way, do you prefer being called by your first name, or your last name?"

"Joan is fine," Mom instructed her.

Crystal walked Mom through the dining times and gave Mom her seat assignment at Table 6.

"And Joan, if you're like me, and forget what I had for breakfast, if you get down there and can't remember your table number, they always have a list they can check for you. But you'll be fine after the first few times. And tonight, if it's okay with you, I'm going to take you down so that I can introduce you to the other ladies at your table. You've got some good table mates." I smiled inwardly at the use of the word 'mate', thinking of it emblazoned on the back of Mom's red shirt from Vacation Bible School. She smiled at Mom, and asked, "Is that okay by you?"

Again, I was grateful for Crystal. It's like she was doing this solely for Mom, even though they must go through this spiel for each new Breck resident. Still, it's so personal, and I could tell it was exactly what Mom needed. Crystal went on to explain how breakfast was up to each resident, and that the staff set it up each morning in the respective kitchen on each floor. Mom could visit the kitchen any time between 7:00-10:00, and either eat there in the sitting area, or bring a tray back to her room. She also covered daily showers, transitioning into the numerous entertainment events that Breck boasted, both in the afternoons and evenings, chronicling some of the more recent. This was another bonus that hadn't even occurred to me. Mom would be able to attend these events on a regular basis, without ever having to leave the building. What a great perk.

All of us thanked Crystal when she finished, even Mom ("That's a lot to remember to tell all of us old folks,"), and I could tell she was feeling much more at home. We stayed another half hour, talking and tidying up, and I went down to the nurses' station to double check on all of Mom's meds, wanting to be sure they'd all been transferred here from Buckman. I ended up talking to another nurse, Trish, who immediately stopped what she was doing and introduced herself. I told her I was Joan Bradshaw's daughter, Betsy; that Joan was new to Breck, and that I wanted to check on her meds before I headed back to Louisville. "So, you came up to help her get situated here?" she asked, smiling.

"My husband and brother and I all did," I told Trish. "It takes a village."

Trish nodded and said, "It's a tough transition. Most of our residents are coming from a situation where they had a lot more independence and are used to more space, and I think they feel like their wings are being clipped. I'll be sure to stop in and spend a little extra time with your Mom, especially since she's in our temporary room versus her own place." She verified that all of Mom's meds were there, and that her next doses would be administered after dinner.

"Could you do me one more favor?" I asked Trish. "Would you be willing to just remind her at 5 o'clock that dinner is at 5:30? I'm afraid she might lose track of time, and then, if she knows she'll be late, she won't want to go down, even with Crystal."

Trish giggled. "That's something I'd do," she remarked. "I hate being late, and walking into a crowd of people. I'll give your Mom a heads up."

Mike, Craig and I got on the road home shortly after that. It was nice to be able to say to Mom, 'See you Thursday', instead of knowing it would be another couple of weeks, or even a month. Having Mike for company on the way home was nice, too…it made the trip go much faster.

"That went as well as could be expected, I guess," I commented as we got onto the interstate. "I really hope a room opens up soon for Mom. I think she feels like she's in a dorm room."

"That might have some positive side effects," Mike said,

glancing at me sideways and smiling. "She really wanted to be over at her cottage directing everything, didn't she? I felt bad for her."

"Old habits die hard," I stated. "She was a good sport, for the thousandth time."

We got home around 6:30, called in a pizza, devoured it with Kerry, and my bed was calling.

* * * * *

Thanksgiving Day is cold and overcast. I'm glad it's at least chilly, because it feels more like Thanksgiving. All of us sleep in, and have a lazy, schleppy kind of morning with coffee, the Macy's Day Parade, and putting the finishing touches on the food I'm taking up. Loire is doing the lion's share of the preparation, but Craig assures me she "lives to organize stuff like this", so all I'm doing is two veggie dishes and dessert; a pecan and a pumpkin pie. I made the pies when I got home from work last night, and Kerry had assembled the Copper Carrot recipe while I was at work yesterday, sweetheart that she is.

This is an old recipe of Mom's, and a great 'make ahead', because everything can be assembled, marinated, and cooked ahead of time, leaving only the re-heating prior to serving. It's become a family favorite over the years, except for Callie, who hates carrots of any variety. You cut up carrot strips, combine them with chopped green peppers and onions, and then marinate them for several days or overnight in tomato soup, vinegar, Worchester, salad oil, mustard, and garlic salt. My other veggie offering is an asparagus casserole that Craig always used to request for his birthday dinner growing up; asparagus stalks covered with sliced hard-boiled eggs, sharp cheddar cheese, and cream of mushroom soup, then baked.

We roll out to Cincy around 2:00, settling in for a relaxing drive up. Both girls brought pillows and the "tie" fleece blankets Col made them for Christmas a few years ago, planning on a good nap. The drive has become a comfortable ritual, giving us time to talk, catch up on random events, and for Mike and me to savor being with Callie and Kerry. Kerry shares a lot about her classes. With this being her junior year, she's really in the thick of it, research papers and projects due over the course of the next two weeks, in tandem with finals. It seems like she is much more confirmed in remaining at UK for the duration, and I'm thankful for the resolution. She's not one to run from a challenge, and even though she could be the ultimate procrastinator in high school, I get the feeling she's grown in her time management skills. She's also one of those individuals who thrives under pressure, which probably serves her well in this crunch of finals.

Mike asks Cal about her recent trip out to LA, which is where the headquarters are for her parent company. Traveling out there roughly once a quarter, she's built some strong relationships with people she communicates with daily, albeit long distance. It's amazing to think she's been in the business for three, almost four, years already. I love listening to her talk about it now. She presents information so well, and her passion for the advertising industry is so evident.

In my heart, I know she is very, very good at what she does, because that has been the trajectory of her entire life. When Callie focuses on something that is important to her, it is always completed at a very high level of competency; both well thought out and well implemented. It's amazing to me to see the body of knowledge she has already amassed, not just in her specific area of advertising, which is social media and media buying strategy, but in terms of the digital and the creative aspects of it as well. We talk intermittently for the first 45 minutes of the drive and the girls drift off to sleep after that.

I smile as I look back at them in the rearview mirror, curled up under their blankets, thinking of how Cal has always said that she sleeps better in a car than anywhere else. This goes back to all our early travels north and south on this identical stretch of interstate, Callie snug in her car seat until she was big enough to be in just a seat belt. From the time she was two on, these trips were part of our lives. To this day, I can't remember a time when she ever cried when we were in the car. Like everything else in her life, she took it in stride and made the most of it.

The girls start stirring as we exit off I-75 onto Brampton Road, and are wide awake by the time we pull into Beecher. This is the first time either of them has seen the community firsthand, and they're enthused.

"This is sooo nice," Kerry comments as we drive back to the Knolls. "It's so calming."

We park in front of Mom's cottage, and I unlock the front door, allowing the girls to go in ahead of me.

Callie looks around, and up at the sky lights. "This is so spacious," she remarks, "and so open and light." She moves into the center of the living room and just stands still, continuing to look around. Suddenly she brings her hand up to her mouth, and our eyes lock. Her dark eyes are pooled with tears, and she motions with her free hand to the coffee table in front of the couch. "All the same stuff she had on it when we were growing up," she chokes out, "even the little games."

And Callie is right, everything is the same. The beautiful hand carved wooden whale on a delicate stand that Dad bought her when they were in Hawaii; the pristine white shell, and the Waterford glass dish with multi-colored glass orbs that look like wrapped candy. These are interspersed with a Rubik's cube and various puzzles of different varieties, one carved out of wood with inset marbles. Mom loves her puzzles.

Cal wipes her eyes. "It's so weird to see all of her furniture here, especially all of the same stuff we played with for so many years on Willowbend."

Kerry has been quiet for this exchange, soaking everything in. "I hate it that she doesn't get to stay here," she states quietly. "I can tell how much she likes it. You can just feel her presence here."

She walks back into the little hallway and peers into the bedrooms. "Is this where you stay?" she asks me, motioning to the bedroom on the right.

"That's my room," I nod. "Mine, all mine."

Kerry turns and walks over to me, hugging me hard. "I'm glad you had this time with Gramma here," she says, simply. "I know it means a lot to both of you."

We unload the food and the beer, refrigerating what we need to, and I hear Mike open the screen door and yell out into the parking lot, "Where have you been?"

Craig yells something unintelligible back and I can feel myself smiling. I'm happy that we're all together today. Loire has her arms full, and she's loading Viv down with a big Tupperware container of something. Emmy is carrying a bag, looking very serious about getting it inside safely.

She makes it to the door first, and I prop it open for her and say, "Put that bag down and let me give you a huge hug."

"Sure, Aunt Betsy," she answers in her sweet, unflappable way. No matter how much I see of her, it's not enough. She spots Kerry and lights up. The four of our girls are close, even though they don't see a lot of each other. Loire angles in through the door, guiding a huge platter of turkey and ham ahead of her, with a cheery "Hey, Bet, Happy Thanksgiving! How are you? You guys have had quite a week!"

Viv and Callie follow her in, laden with containers of food and bags, and we stash everything in the near-empty refrigerator and on the counters. Loire and I embrace.

"We've got a LOT to catch up on," I tell her, hugging her hard. She immediately asks about Mom's move to Breck and how I think she's doing. I launch into my recap of Tuesday.

"I'm so curious to see Breck and get a mental picture of it," Loire says.

"How about you and our girls going over to get Mom and bring her back here?" I ask her. "Mom would love showing you guys off to the nurses, and that way you can see it yourselves."

"Absolutely," Loire agrees. "Is there anything that needs to come over here with her, like her meds?"

"No, not really, unless there's something she wants to bring with her. Just remember to sign her out so they know we're over here with her," I mention to Loire. "But really talk up Breck, OK? This has been such a huge move for her, and I know it's killing her not to be able to stay here anymore."

Loire's face is beautifully expressive, and I see a look of deep concern fill her dark eyes. "I know it has, Bet. And, while we all acknowledge it's for her own good, it's so easy to put yourself in that position and feel the despair she must feel as her world keeps shrinking. Craig told me what an incredible job you did finding the middle ground for your Mom at the Care Conference. He said nobody else could have done it with the heart you did and how much easier it made it for your Mom."

I shake my head. "Loire, that's the stuff that comes easily to me. I felt so bad for her. Imagine listening to someone talk over you to your children telling them that you had no idea what day, month, or year it was, and that you couldn't remember how to brush your teeth anymore. I wanted her to feel like, in spite of everything, SHE still mattered. I think, no matter what, that deep down, she still feels like she's being a burden to us, and I can't stand her feeling that way. I'll run interference for her any day of the week. Craig does all the stuff I can't, Loire. He's always a step ahead, planning, anticipating, and asking questions...I could not be in this without him."

Loire smiles. "Thank goodness you two have each other, Bet. He feels the same way about you."

All four of the girls decide to go over to Breck to get Mom with Craig and Loire, and Mike and I set the table while they're gone. Loire has brought gold paper plates and matching silverware so that there will be minimal clean-up after dinner, and I open a bottle of wine for us. I piddle around in the kitchen, putting my carrots in a big kettle of Mom's, turning them on low heat, and arranging cheese, crackers, and prosciutto that Loire brought on a platter of Mom's.

They return with Mom in about 35 minutes. We're watching the Texas A&M game, and Mike goes to the door to hold it open. I'm surprised to see them pushing Mom in her wheelchair, rather than her using her walker. Immediately I think maybe Craig talked her into this so they could move more quickly. They stop on the porch, and I get a closer look at Mom. She looks terribly pale and completely out of it. It's hard to believe it was just two days ago we were with her. My eyes meet Craig's, and he shakes his head, which I know is his unspoken *This is not good.* Kerry and Cal are very subdued, and they both look horribly sad. I notice Emmy is holding Callie's hand tightly, almost as if to protect herself. I step out onto the porch and lean down to Mom.

"Happy Thanksgiving, Mom," I tell her, kissing her cheek. "Can I help you up out of your wheelchair and we can get you comfy on the couch?"

There's a pause as if she's gathering her thoughts, and she says in a small voice, "I think I just want to lie down in my bedroom, Bet. I'm so tired."

"Okay," I answer. "That's fine. You can take a big old nap. The good news is we all get to be with you."

She barely acknowledges this.

"I'm going to lift you out of the wheelchair," I tell her. "Are you strong enough to stand?"

I look around for her walker, and Kerry immediately realizes what I'm searching for.

"Oh, Mom, we forgot to bring it," she laments. "With the wheelchair, we weren't thinking about her needing it."

"No worries," I answer. "We've got Dad."

Mike comes and stands on one side of her, supporting her full weight as I straighten her up out of the wheelchair, and then I adjust my arm to support her left side. The two of us half walk, half carry her to her bedroom, getting her situated in bed, and removing her shoes. Mike gently pulls up the sheets and blanket to tuck her in, and I ask her if anything is hurting her. She shakes her head ever so slightly.

"I just need to rest," she whispers. I lean down to kiss her again.

"Do you want your door shut?" I ask her.

"No, leave it open," she answers, which I take as a somewhat good sign.

Back out in the living room, I look at Craig and Loire. "Wow," I exhale quietly, "What's happened between Tuesday and now?"

"She was asleep in that armchair in her room when we got there," Craig says.

"When she first opened her eyes, I'm not sure she even recognized the girls," Loire reflects. "I kind of primed the pump and said, 'Joan, all of your granddaughters want to see you and wish you a happy Thanksgiving.'"

I ask Craig and Loire if either of them had had any dialogue with the nurses.

"Trish checked on her while we were up there," Craig told me. "She said Mom had been doing a lot of sleeping from Tuesday on, but that she had made sure she was going to all her meals. Trish even brought her breakfast in her room yesterday and today. She said it's not really that unusual for an elderly person who's come through a big transition like this to be exhausted, and that it might take a while for her to catch up. Then, too, you add in Mom's head injury, and being anemic, and she's got a lot of ground to make up."

"I hope that's all it is," I answer. "She seems so completely out of it."

We relax for the rest of the afternoon, tiptoeing in to check on Mom periodically. The girls play cards for a while, and then their version of 'Beauty Shop', which largely involves Cal and Kerry French braiding Viv and Em's hair, and applying light makeup, at which point Loire, Craig, Mike and I pay compliments and provide faux beauty advice. Loire and I pour some wine and talk at length. She's been travelling a lot with her job and has a new boss, and I want to hear about all of it. She's full of questions about my take on what happened with Rob and Col in terms of the hospital incident.

One thing I try very hard not to do is to throw either of them under the bus when talking to Loire. I'm sure Craig does enough of that to override my more nuanced approach. I never want Loire to feel that she needs to take sides, although I know that based on what has already happened between Craig and Colette, the battle lines are well drawn. But even so, I don't have all the facts. I only possess the ones that have impacted my current perspective, which is far from a complete story.

"But why would they stoop that low?" Loire is asking me out in the kitchen, talking semi softly so that Viv and Emmy can't hear us.

Callie and Kerry know everything there is to know about the situation, but based on the age difference between my girls and Craig's, Loire tries to refrain from saying anything direct in front of Viv or Emmy.

"It's so underhanded, and it's so completely uncalled for."

I stir the carrots slowly, taking a long sip of my wine. "I don't know, Loire, unless they really thought they could get Mom in and out of Holy Dis and back home in her cottage before we ever knew about it," I posit. "But then you've got the staples in the back of her head, and they knew we'd be with Mom for Thanksgiving."

"That's ridiculous, Bet," Loire states. "They had to know you and Craig would call and not be able to reach her."

"You'd think," I retort. "But maybe it honestly never

occurred to them that Craig and I call Mom every day. You know, one of those situations where since they don't do it, they assume nobody else does, either."

"But look at the loss of face it probably caused for both of them at the hospital," Loire reflects. "They had to look pretty small in the eyes of their peers when word got out that the rest of your family had been completely in the dark."

Again, I shake my head, stirring the carrots and sipping. "Unless Col really thought that Rob had called Craig or me, or both of us, and then realized when Craig showed up that he hadn't."

"But," interjects Loire, "why didn't she tell Craig that immediately when they had their confrontation in the patient waiting room? That would have completely cleared her and helped Craig to understand the situation."

"Maybe she doesn't care that Rob didn't call," I answer, shrugging, continuing to stir and sip. "I can't ascribe motives. It angers me that it happened, for all of us, but especially for Mom's sake. I hate this ugliness, but I don't think it's going to go away. I just know I'm going to do my best not to add to it. For whatever reason, though, I do think Rob and Col have drawn their line in the sand."

Loire sets her glass down and sighs. "It makes me so sad for all of us, Bet."

We move on to other lighter topics, and once all our dinner preparations are fully under way, I have Viv and Emmy open their birthday gifts that I brought up with us. I'm rarely with them on their real birthdays, and I wanted to see them open their gifts in person. I've bought hats for each of them, as they've loved hats since they were little girls. Emmy's is more of a bowler style, with a broad brim, Viv's plaid with a visor. I also picked out sweater dresses for each of them. They like the dresses, but I can tell they're far more smitten with the hats, and they proceed to wear them for the rest of the day. Daylight is dwindling by 5:00 and the smell of turkey is wafting through the cottage.

"Let's eat soon," Kerry pleads. "I'm ready to consume mass quantities of food."

Callie goes in to wake Mom up and get her settled at the table while Loire and I get everything out of the oven and off the stove. As always, Loire has outdone herself. She is an incredible cook, and in addition to the turkey there is ham, mashed potatoes, and macaroni and cheese. She's also made one of my favorites, a cranberry orange mist molded salad, and her homemade dressing. Add in giblet gravy and yeast rolls, along with my paltry offering of veggies and dessert, and you have the perfect Thanksgiving feast.

"Woman, you have outdone yourself," Mike says to Loire. He possibly looks forward to this meal more than anyone. "This looks amazing."

Cal slowly walks Mom from her bedroom to our feasting table; I'm reminded again of how frail Mom is whenever I see her next to one of my girls. Callie is 5 foot 11 inches, and Mom literally looks like she's half of Cal's size. Settling Mom in one of the chairs, she pads her back with a pillow from the couch, and we all find seats around the table. It feels like Thanksgiving with all of us here together, and I'm thankful we could do this for Mom. I ask Callie if she'll pray for us before we eat, knowing she'll be comfortable doing it, and we all join hands around the table. Mom's hand is chilly in my left; Emmy's small and warm in my right. Cal's prayer is simple, to the point, and genuine:

"Dear Lord, we thank you for this day, and for this time to all be together, and for your faithfulness in the past year. You've blessed us in so many ways, and you've helped us to be there for each other. Be with Gramma, Lord; help her to settle into her new living situation and give her strength and health for each new day. Help all of us to be who you want us to be, and to be thankful in our lives, and for the gift of your Son that you've given us. We pray all this in your name. Amen."

"Nicely done, Cal," Craig says when she finishes.

"It would scare me to do that," Emmy says. "I couldn't make up all those words." We all start laughing.

"Cal makes stuff up all the time, Emmy," Kerry says, teasingly. "Not just prayers. Most of the time we just ignore her."

Now Vivie laughs. "Just like I do you, Emmy."

Dishes begin circling the table, hand to hand, serving spoon to plate, and with Mom next to me, I make sure to give her a little bit of everything, so she can nibble. I purposely cut her meat, a little ham and some turkey, into small, child size pieces that she can easily chew. My mouth is watering as I take a huge mouthful of giblet gravy, turkey, and stuffing all mixed together. Loire's dressing is killer.

Mom seems to be having trouble getting her food to stay on her fork, so I offer to help her, stabbing a piece of ham with her fork, and lifting it up to her mouth. Her lips close around the ham, and I see her jaw slowly begin to move. Suddenly, a horrible retching sound starts deep in her throat. I turn immediately, thinking she might be choking. I've never in my life heard her make a noise like this. She leans forward, her arms still slack at her sides, and without even consciously thinking, I grab my napkin and hold it directly under her chin, knowing she's going to vomit. She leans forward ever so slightly, and I cup the napkin as a pink colored fluid drips into it. Loire, thinking equally quickly, hands me Emmy's water glass that she has emptied into her own larger one. "Here, Bet," she says quietly, and I ball the napkin up onto my plate, replacing it with the glass. Another slow stream of vomit trails out of Mom's mouth into the glass, and then it's over. There's absolute silence around the table.

"Are you okay?" I ask her, as I dab another napkin into my own water glass and gently wipe Mom's mouth with it. What a totally ignorant question. Of course, she's not okay, and I can tell she's mortified.

"That ham just didn't want to go down," she croaks in that soft half-whisper.

"Joan, do you just want to sip on some Sprite or some chicken broth?" Loire asks. "That might be easier on your stomach."

"Oh, I don't know," Mom murmurs. "I just don't feel like eating anything. I feel terrible I've ruined your dinner."

"No, Joan, not at all," Loire jumps right in. "Sometimes when you don't feel well, the worst thing you can do is to be around food and all the smells."

"Would you feel better lying back down?" Mike asks her. "We'll miss you, but it might be more comfortable for you."

Mom nods slightly. "I think I would. But here…not over at…." She hesitates, and I know she's trying to remember the name of her assisted living facility.

"No, we're not taking you back to Breck yet," I finish for her.

Kerry stands up and moves around the table to Mom's side. "C'mon, Gramma, I'll help you."

I pull Mom's chair out, a bit of a challenge because of its drag on the carpeting, and then Kerry and I both gently pull her forward and up out of the chair, our hands under her arms, with Mike literally lifting the chair back and away from Mom so Kerry and I can each be on one side of her. We slowly walk her back to the bedroom, getting her comfortable for the second time.

"Do you want a basin or anything in case you get sick again?" I ask her.

"No," she croaks, "I'll be okay now."

"Mom, I'm worried about you," I say without thinking. "Have you been feeling sick all day?"

"I'm not sick," she whispers, "just tired."

Kerry leans down and kisses her on the forehead. "I love you, Gramma," she tells her, and strokes her hair. "We'll be right out here if you need anything."

"Thanks, honey," Mom murmurs, and we return to the table.

Craig, Cal, Loire and Mike are talking quietly. "What do you think?" Craig asks me as I sit back down. I shake my head.

"This brings the whole stomach thing back into play," I respond. "It's been a long time since it's happened. The weird thing is that Trish told you Mom's been going to all her meals over there. But how is that even possible? She was too weak to even pick up her own fork here with us. Even if they are taking her down to meals, is she eating anything? Does anyone monitor that in the dining room?"

Mike volunteers, "It almost seemed like a gag reflex kicked in the minute that food hit her mouth, and then she vomited."

"Could she have possibly picked up some kind of stomach bug?" Callie asked. "Maybe even just from being around everyone in the dining room? It's been awhile since she's been around large groups of people, and her immune system is probably pretty compromised."

We discuss the situation in more detail, agreeing that we need to let the nurses at Breck know, and to get as much feedback from them as possible. They need to be completely aware of everything going on. Attempting to lighten the meal, we turn the conversation to other things, but there is a marked dampening of spirit, Mom's empty chair a sad reminder. This is the first Thanksgiving dinner where neither of my parents are present with us at the table, and it's a very unsettling feeling. All of us try to make the best of it, everyone making an effort to keep the conversation going, but it's just not the same.

When we're ready for dessert, we cut the pie, everybody taking their piece and going to sit on either the couch or the floor, almost as if no one wants to remain at the table. We let Mom rest for a good hour and a half, during which time we eat dessert, talk, and clean up, then decide we probably ought to get her back to Breck and talk to the nurses. Craig and Loire get her up; we wrap one of her heavier winter coats around her and gather up some extra toiletries and pajamas she might want. Mom's cooperative, but still visibly exhausted, and Craig, Mike, Cal and I take her over to Breck. Once up in Mom's room, I offer to help her change into her pajamas so she's ready for bed.

"Oh, I'm fine in my clothes," she answers, obviously not wanting to bother.

I convince her she'll feel better in her PJ's, helping her undress and slip on a nightgown, no small feat. Once I'm done with that, I have Mike help me get her from the wheelchair into the bed. Her strength and body awareness seem completely gone, which is very concerning to me. I'm wondering if the nurses are questioning Mom's ability to remain even in an assisted living setting, given the amount of care she's requiring since her arrival at Breck.

One of the night nurses, Vicki, comes in with Mom's evening meds right as we're getting her into bed. I step out into Mom's living area, where Mom can't hear me, and explain the evening's events to Vicki.

"I'm not even sure she'd be able to keep the pills down right now," I tell her. "We can try…what do you think?"

Vicki asks about the amount that Mom vomited up, and whether there was any blood with it. (There wasn't.) "You know, I think we'll hold off on the pills until tomorrow," she says. "I don't want any of this upsetting her belly further. But I do want to monitor her fluid intake to make sure she's getting enough. I'm going to go grab a Sprite for her and see if I can get her to drink it. Poor thing."

Craig asks Vicki outright if they monitor the residents' eating in the dining room. He explains that Mom has gone down to the dining hall for each meal so far but seems so weak and out of it that we're questioning her being able to eat at all. Vicki reassures him that there is always staff present in the dining room, as well as the fact that the servers communicate with the staff and watch for 'untouched plates.'

"It's possible your mom may be nibbling, or pushing food around her plate, and I'll pay close attention, as well as giving the day staff a heads-up," she assures us. "The other thing is we have a stomach bug going around Breck. I think six residents missed dinner tonight because of it."

I go on record with Vicki and communicate my concerns regarding Mom's previous stomach complaints, telling her that Mom hasn't mentioned it since she fell, but that I worry the fall, her hospitalization, and subsequent decline may have masked the problem. Vicki listens intently, assuring me this will be noted in Mom's chart as soon as she gets back to the nurses' office.

"So, she was to have seen one of our doctors, but because of her fall, it didn't happen? When was that appointment scheduled?" she asks me, wanting to note it in detail.

I think back, telling Vicki it would have been the last week of October, and how mom had fallen as she was executing a trial walk over to the office the day prior to her appointment.

"We definitely want to follow up on that and have one of our docs stop in and see her," Vicki suggests. "I'll be keeping a close eye on this. I'm glad you shared all of this with me."

She also encourages us to check in with the nurses' station each day regarding what kind of a day Mom is having.

"That's why we're here," she states.

She tells us to ask for any nurse we're comfortable with, pointing out that Crystal and Trish are always there during the day except on alternate weekends, and she's always available from 7 PM to 7 AM. All of this is valuable information to have. Hopefully we can follow it through to a logical conclusion. I'm thankful that a doctor will be double checking Mom tomorrow, and that we've covered all the bases with Vicki.

Mom is already sound asleep when we tiptoe back into

her room to kiss her goodbye. Vicki's going to have one dickens of a time waking her up to drink any Sprite. The four of us are somber as we return to the cottage. This certainly hasn't been the kind of Thanksgiving we'd envisioned with Mom, and there's a cloud of deep concern blanketing all of us.

"It's going down fast," Craig says, running his hands over his face. "It's like she's totally given up."

We stay at her cottage awhile longer, as if huddling there together will somehow give us more strength before we leave, and all head out around 8:30. As if Mother Nature is responding to our mood, it has started to rain…a cold, sheeting downpour that is going to make it a miserable ride home to Dayton and Louisville. Hugs go all around as we pack up. It's been so good to be with Craig's family today, even though it felt incomplete without Rob, Col, their boys, Donny's family, and, of course, Mom. *The beginning of our new normal*, I think to myself. It pours the entire way home, and I don't talk much, nor does Kerry or Callie. Mike concentrates on his driving. I pray for our safety, thanking God that our two families were so willing to do this for Mom. My heart is hurting.

The rest of the weekend bustles by. Both Kerry and Callie get together with friends at various points, and I work a half day on both Friday and Saturday. Saturday evening, we're able to make it to our 5:00 service as a family, which both the girls enjoy. Kerry is thrilled when she realizes Jim Kennan is doing the message this weekend. It centers on the idea of how, even in the midst of the 'not good' times, being thankful is important, and how cultivating thankfulness often opens the door to further blessing. Hearing that, and the accompanying Scripture, Philippians 4:6-9, is a huge encouragement to me. We have a fun family dinner out afterwards, and I draw a lot of comfort from having had this time with the girls.

I've called Mom each day, as well as checking in with the nursing station at Breck daily. Mom hasn't gone down for any of her meals Friday, Saturday, or Sunday and they've got her on a liquid diet. They also had the doctor come over on Saturday to check everything, and they've done some extensive blood work. Each time I've talked to her she's sounded worse. Her voice is wispy and weak, and it's difficult to even understand her over the phone. On Sunday afternoon, Craig calls me, asking if I've talked to Mom this weekend. My answer is yes, once every day.

"Did she say anything to you about Rob coming to get her to take her for additional tests?" he asks me.

"You mean, as in more blood work?" I ask, thinking that, at this point, anything is possible, especially if it involves Rob.

"Well, I guess," he says, somewhat ambiguously. "Because she told me that Rob came and picked her up yesterday and drove her up to Greenwood, Indiana, to have more tests run. Is that possible?"

"Greenwood, Indiana?" I repeat blankly. "What's up there? That's totally random. Is there some state-of-the-art laboratory there? Why wouldn't he just take her in to Holy Dis and do it there?"

"I have no idea," Craig answers. "Maybe it didn't even happen. Mom could be delirious."

"Well, let me call the nurses' station and find out," I offer. "They'll know. Rob would have had to sign her out." I call, and get Crystal, since it's before the evening shift change. I ask her very specifically about Rob having been there at all over the weekend, or Mom being taken out for testing at any point.

Crystal's answer is clear and immediate: "No, no one has been here since you and your husband and your brother's family were here on Thanksgiving."

I explain to Crystal what Craig had shared with me.

"You know," Crystal muses, "It's possible she got that mixed up with the fact that Dr. Hasbrow was coming to see her yesterday. He did order complete blood work, but no, other than that, no one's been in except you."

I thank her and relay this back to Craig. "No Greenwood, and no Rob," I report.

"Boy, she's slipping," Craig muses. "Each day it's noticeably worse."

"It's scary, and so sad," I agree. "Doreen said it would only accelerate from here on out, but it's been a stampede these last three weeks. I guess an injury to an elderly person, no matter how good their relative health is going in, can really make everything go south."

I tell him how glad we were that all of us could be together Thursday, and how much we love Vivie and Emmy.

"You know, Bet, this could have been Mom's last Thanksgiving," he remarks. "Especially at the rate she's going. At least we were there. The saddest part of all is that her two sons that live in the same city can't even be bothered to stop by for a visit over the course of the entire holiday weekend. Those two make me sick."

Callie leaves for Nashville around 4:00 on Sunday afternoon, the best part being able to say, and "See you in three weeks."

It's much easier on the heart. Cal's agency closes completely for the week between Christmas and New Year's, so we'll have her home for that stretch, in addition to the days she usually takes off preceding Christmas. I hug her hard before she gets in the car and tell her I love her.

"Keep me posted on Gramma," she tells me. "I'm so glad we went up, Mom."

Kerry departs for Lexington and the last three weeks of her semester early Monday morning, as I'm leaving for work. "Kick it to the curb these next three weeks," I tell her. "Dad and I are pulling hard for you."

"Oh, Mommy," Kerry sighs. "It's going to be brutal. Pray for me; especially for my oral presentation. It's not even finals I dread as much as it's everything else that's due before then."

I hate seeing her go back to this pressure, but I also know she'll do exactly what she needs to. Kerry is one of the most tenacious people I know, and she inspires me. I need that inspiration.

I drive into work feeling like we've turned another sharp corner onto a whole new avenue of losing Mom.

Joan, On Her Own

Author

Jillian Calder has lived in Louisville, Kentucky for over 30 years with her husband. The decline of her mother's cognitive and physical health and subsequent move to a retirement community began an entirely new chapter of their relationship. This is the narrative of the final three years they shared, involving numerous trips from Louisville to Cincinnati.

An avid reader since childhood, Ms. Calder has always loved writing, and this is her first book. Another love is music, and she is strongly committed to her church's adult and youth music programs. She has two daughters and enjoys visiting them on the east and west coast.

Please visit www.jilliancalder.com

Joan's story continues with "'Where I Am Going" due out in Spring of 2020.

...Craig calls me the Tuesday night following Thanksgiving, letting me know that after Dr. Hasbrow saw Mom today and reviewed the results of her bloodwork, he wants her to have a transfusion. She's dropped even farther into the 'high 7's', as he puts it, and wants to try to get her red count up. I ask Craig if it's to be done immediately, and if he wants me to come up to take Mom.

"No, you stay put," he tells me. "You were up here twice last week, and who knows what's going to happen from here on out. Loire says she'll handle this one. She's in town, doesn't travel this week, and can stay with Mom while they do it."

I feel guilty for feeling relieved, but that does take a load off, and gives me a full week to bear down at work. Still, I'm worried, and I feel bad that I won't be there with Mom.

"Will Loire take her to Holy Dis for the transfusion?" I ask.

"No way," Craig responds. "Dr. Hasbrow wrote the orders, and then we can take them wherever. Loire's going to take her to Emmaus."

Emmaus is where Dad used to be on staff, and there are still a lot of doctors and nurses there that remember him. Hopefully that will give Mom some additional comfort. She's continued to sound weak and exhausted when I call, and in the days since Thanksgiving I've taken to calling the nurses' station at least once a day to get updates from them. They're pushing liquids with Mom and bringing meals to her room, but she's eating very little, even though there's been no more vomiting.

Loire takes Mom to Emmaus the following day to get the transfusion, and I catch up with them that night after my rehearsal. Apparently, it was an all-day procedure, and a very slow, tedious process. Loire tells me Mom was very uncomfortable, finding it difficult to lay in one position very long, and needing to use the restroom frequently, which wasn't much of an option once she was hooked up to the machine. Add in Mom having an accident in Loire's SUV on the way back to Beecher, and it's pretty evident my sister-in-law had more on her hands than she'd bargained on.

"Girl, you've earned some big old diamond chips in your tiara today," I tell her.

"Bet, I just felt so sorry for her. I think the whole procedure exhausted her," Loire states. "I really hope this will give her some energy back."

Over the course of Thursday and Friday, it does seem to perk Mom up a bit, and she's able to return to Breck's dining room for meals. We all hold our breath and life moves forward.

* * * * *

Rob comes in and we've deliberately left the seat he sat in vacant so there's no re-shuffling. My heart plummets when I look at him. I can tell he's been crying. Ever since he was a little boy, he's cried easily, and I'm sure that's difficult for him on some fronts. Moving swiftly to the empty chair, he sits down and reaches for Mom's hand nearest him. "Mom," he says quietly, and Mom turns to look at him fully, "We've got some decisions to make. Your ultrasound shows a mass in your lower abdomen that has perforated your colon…that's why it's been hard to control your bowels. We won't know until we get in there whether it's cancerous, but the odds are pretty good that it is, based on its location. With your bowel perforated, they'll have to remove a section of it along with the tumor, and it will mean that you'll have a colostomy bag after the surgery is over." He exhales quietly. "I know this is a lot to take in."

"What happens if I don't do anything?" Mom asks Rob, looking full into his face.

His eyes brim with tears and he pats Mom's hand. "We could lose you," he starts, and then breaks down completely. Instinctively, I reach across the bed from where I'm sitting on Mom's left side to squeeze Rob's arm in support, but as my hand touches his arm, he jerks it away vehemently, as if he's just been burned by a hot iron.

I'm momentarily stunned that he reacted the way he did…I know Mike and Craig witnessed it, as well as Mom, and I simply withdraw my hand from across the bed and sit quietly, waiting for Rob to continue. Mom needs to concentrate on what he's telling her. He hastily wipes his eyes, sniffs, and gets himself under control, then continues.

"We need to get that mass out of you," he starts again, "because, with your bowel ruptured, a lot of your waste is seeping into your abdominal cavity, and there's probably infection. That'll only get worse if we don't do surgery, Mom. Dr. Hemmer, the surgeon who'll remove it, feels like it needs to happen pretty quickly. You're already in a compromised state, and that will only get worse if we wait. You weren't in good shape at all when you got here today."

There are a few seconds of complete silence, and I can tell Mom is digesting everything.

"Well," she says, as if she's telling us what she wants for breakfast, "I say we do it. It's the only option I really have besides doing nothing."

Rob tears up again, and nods slightly. "I'll let Dr. Hemmer know what you've decided, Mom, and then they're going to work you into his schedule, okay? He'll be down to talk to you in a little while, and he'll walk you through everything. He's the best, and he'll get you through this, Mom." He stands up, and tears are pouring freely down his cheeks.

Mom reaches up and lays her hand on his left cheek. "Rob," she says gently, "Don't be so upset. I'm going to be okay. Thank you for everything you've done."

I know it kills Mom to see him like this, and it breaks my heart for all of us.

"I love you, Mom," he chokes out, which I'm glad he gets to hear from her, and he leaves.